The Jersey Surf Diaries

A TEN-YEAR LOGBOOK OF FISHING ADVENTURES, CATCHES, AND TIPS

Nick Honachefsky

HeadWater Books

STACKPOLE BOOKS

Published by
STACKPOLE BOOKS
5067 Ritter Road
Mechanicsburg, PA 17055
www.stackpolebooks.com

10 9 8 7 6 5 4 3 2 1

First edition

Cover design by Caroline M. Stover
Cover photo by Nick Honachefsky

Library of Congress Cataloging-in-Publication Data

Honachefsky, Nick.
    The Jersey surf diaries : a ten-year logbook of fishing adventures, catches, and tips / Nick Honachefsky. — First edition.
        pages cm
    ISBN 978-0-8117-1249-1 (paperback) — ISBN 0-8117-1249-4 (paperback)
    1. Honachefsky, Nick—Diaries. 2. Surf fishing—New Jersey—Atlantic Coast.
    3. Fishers—New Jersey—Atlantic Coast—Diaries. 4. Seasons—New Jersey—
    Atlantic Coast. 5. Atlantic Coast (N.J.)—Social life and customs. I. Title.

SH457.2.H66 2014
799.1097—dc23
                                                                    2013017878

Contents

Dedication

This book is dedicated to God's wondrous ways for graciously giving us the surf as our playground, along with the knowledge and respect that come with it. To my mother, for her everlasting support and encouragement, and for packing grilled cheese sandwiches and allowing me to skip a day of school here and there as a kid, so I could head down to Island Beach State Park to catch stripers with my father. To my brother, for always being a shining beacon of inspiration. To my Babchi (Polish for grandmother), for always picking me up in my younger years when I wandered too far away from home to walk back from a fishing trip. To all my cousins, uncles, and friends who are always willing to share their love and laughter to fish. And last, but not least, to my father Bill, the ultimate outdoorsman, who placed the spark in my soul to immerse myself in the woods and water and who offers eternal encouragement to always have my eyes forward, walk straight into the sunrise, and revel in the beauty, the message, and the love of the wonderful outdoors.

Acknowledgments

I would like to thank every single outdoor writer who has kept my passion going since the day I was born, as well as outdoor writers yet to come, who will keep the fishing and hunting lifestyle of paramount importance to future generations. I thank Jay Nichols and his trusted editors at Stackpole for having faith in this publication, and mentors such as Al Ristori of the *Star-Ledger*, the late John Geiser of Asbury Park Press, Pete Barrett and Fred Golofaro of the *Fisherman*, John Brownlee of *Salt Water Sportsman*, Doug Olander and Andy Hahn of *Sport Fishing Magazine*, Tom McGurk of the *Daily Journal* and the *Courier-Post*, and all their editorial staffs, as well as many unbelievably talented writers in the outdoor industry whom I have worked with for the last 15 years. We are all one soul in motion, and we are all here to promote the hallowed lifestyle of spending time outdoors with a fishing rod in hand.

Cast of Characters
and Dubious References

The following terms are an introduction to some of the characters, local establishments, and slang that have made ten years of surf fishing the most enjoyable passion known to man.

Abby. My beautiful, but mouthy, black Labrador retriever.

Amos. Local drinking buddy. Doesn't fish. He drinks.

Austin/Au Dog. Brooklyn's finest. He's always up for a surf outing, so long as there is prosciutto around.

Bennies. Term for summertime tourists or any non-locals.

Blackberry. Leroux blackberry flavored Polish brandy. The drink of champions, and only for the most hardcore of surf fishermen.

Brick 1, 2, 3. Public beaches of Brick Township. Three separate beaches about a mile apart.

Broadway/B'way. Saltiest fisherman's drinking establishment on the East Coast. A place of tall tales of the high seas and suspect individuals. Happy hour, dollar drafts, lands from 5 to 8 a.m. Yes, a.m.

Brother Billy. My big brother Billy. Always there for encouragement or keeping me in my place.

Bugsy. Local drinking buddy. He fishes. And drinks.

Cali/Johnny Singles. Bearded and slightly overweight, a craft beer connoisseur with dubious knowledge.

Crab's Claw. Restaurant/bar in Lavallette. Only bar open through the winter along my stretch of coast, and thus, well-patronized.

Dad. Well, my dad. The consummate outdoorsman. At home whether stalking whitetail deer with a bow or clamming a striper.

Dog Beach. Inside cove on the north side of the Manasquan Inlet, where everybody walks their dogs. A virtual doggy minefield.

Glen and Mark. A package deal: my cousins-in-law who always come together to visit and fish when fleeing their wives.

Heckel. Puts the party in surf-fishing trips.

IBSP and A10. Island Beach State Park, and respective areas of the park, i.e., A10, A21, etc.

Irish/Big Irish. My buddy Kelly. Always smiling, always big and Irish.

Jackson/Guy. Big, burly prison guard who becomes a kid when he fishes

Jimmer's Hole. The only fishing hole that my neighbor, Jimmer, fishes. He doesn't move left or right from it. It's right up from his road, and that's where you'll find Jimmer if he's fishing.

Joe O. Local surfer endlessly dedicated to the beach and beach sharking.

Joey. City kid. Skinny as a rail, always seasick on a boat, but can deal with the surf.

Lido. The most hardcore, ragged fisherman in the crew, bar none.

McD/Architeuthis/Teuthis. The Giant Squid. A six-foot-seven towering Irish lad with arms that stretch as long as Architeuthis tentacles.

Mickey. Twenty-four-hour, 'round-the-clock fisherman. Angler of rock star status.

My Beach. The sands that I walk every single day, about 100 yards south of the Thunderbird Hotel in Normandy Beach, NJ.

Nite/Knightlius. Nemesis of Architeuthis, also known as the Kraken, only angler big enough to scrap with Teuthis.

Peck/Fancypants. The best-dressed angler on the beach, J. Crew corduroys and all. He's very fancy.

Piper. Sandpiper, gentlemen's club. Now defunct, but once a place of incredible glory. (Thanks Sr. and Jr.!)

Seany. The tog dog. Consummate angler, Always up for a fishing outing, even if he has to drive 24 hours to fish.

Sledgehammer. Big Irish's counterpart, same size; they always travel together. Very witty.

T-Bird. The old Thunderbird Hotel, now called the Ocean Club.

UB's. Used to be Be's. Summertime bar up the road where predrinking usually occurs before a summer surf outing.

Uncle Greg. Flat out, the finest chef that can make even roadkill taste sweet.

WaWa. Twenty-four-hour grocery store in Chadwick Beach, open year-round. The lifeblood of the community during the off-season.

Introduction

THE SUN ALWAYS SHINES

I can never wake up for work feeling refreshed. Not even if I slept for a solid 12 hours in a big, comfy bed with lots of soft pillows and some buxom blonde Swedish supermodel gently massaging my feet. I can, however, get two hours of tossing and turning, writhing, unconscious half-sleep on a solid wooden floor, hungover as all heck, and comfortably rise at 4:00 a.m. with a smile on my face to surf-fish, feeling as lively and invigorated as a kid on Christmas morning. That's just the way it is. Pain and hardship be damned. The spirit knows when it's doing something good for itself. Surf fishing is that constant gift to be unwrapped and learned from.

There are defining times in one's life that absolutely validate and justify the business of life itself. Every person will at some point in their life look in the mirror and consider whether all the choices he or she has made add up to a dignified, worthwhile existence, whether one has been exercising time well spent. Some people search their entire lives for that particular moment of revelation, to find that certain time of enlightenment. To some, it comes easy; others need a bit more searching. Then there are the wise few who avoid the spiritual conundrum altogether, cut out all the bullcrap, and surf-fish. It's that simple. Surf fishing equals enlightenment, spirit, and love all rolled into one sweet package. The following passages are a compilation of ten years of detailed journals in the life of a Jersey surfcaster—some raw, some unrefined, but all true. This is a journal showcasing a gut-check feeling that runs the gamut of all glory, disappointments, good times, and—above everything—the love and experience of living life plying the sands as a surf fisherman.

GARDEN STATE PLAYGROUND

New Jersey's 128 miles of wondrous coastline stretch from the industrious Raritan Bayshore and protruding Sandy Hook, down through the rocky seawalls and

1

jetties of Asbury Park and Long Branch, past the natural soft sands of Island Beach State Park, winding in and out of the flat, pristine sod bank expanses of Brigantine and Ocean City to where the sand juts out off the Victorian peninsula of Cape May's bed-and-breakfast hotels. Jersey beaches are eclectic. The inherent makeup of the Garden State coastline is magical. Every 10-mile stretch of New Jersey's coast is a completely new playground, offering a never-ending fresh set of conditions to test your merit and mettle to ply a fish from the sands. Jetties, sea walls, inlets with concrete jacks and dolosse (pier structures), canals, piers, docks, sod banks, soft sands, pebbles, bricks, and pilings all comprise the surfcaster's playground, and you can never get tired of finding new spots to fish.

If the bass aren't biting off Island Beach, head to the canal and find blackfish from the banks. Tired of catching bluefish in the inlet? Hit the docks for some fluke or flounder. Want to battle with monster sharks? Find the deeper water. Every little piece of salty real estate holds secrets; it just takes a heart full of passion, a soul filled with wonder, and a will of motivated dedication to put in the time to unlock them.

That's what makes Jersey tops compared to other surfcasting locations. Sure, Montauk has its mecca designation with its boulders, fields, and exquisite bass environments, and rightfully so. Cuttyhunk has its storied history and grandiose designation of exclusiveness. The Outer Banks have their churny surf and long, flat outer sandbars. But Jersey . . . well, Jersey has something special.

I've fished these beaches most of my 37 years of life, and every single experience is different from the next in its own unique way. From the cold, blustery months of December and January, when I'm tightened up with thermal underwear, six layers of fleece, and balaclavas wrapped tightly on my head chasing stripers, to the swimsuit dog days of summer, with nothing but bare feet and maybe a cold beer, looking for a fluke, the seasons of the Garden State surf beckon. The following passages encompass a 10-year relationship with the surf; a face-to-face, word-for-word account of what great, soulful times can be had in a chronological year's time surfcasting in Jersey. The entries show both victorious results and dogged defeat through 10 years of surf outings. Some journal entries may be raw and unrefined, others inspirational and detailed, but all show the truth and unbridled passion of what it is to put in your time as a true surfcaster, and maybe you can learn something from it. Pick up this book, choose a date or turn to any page, and just start reading. Plan your surf outings around the information within. Put yourself in the pages of the book when you read it, and then make your own memories, because we are all brothers of the surf.

HOME BASE—THE SHACK

Every surfcaster needs a beach shack to call home base. It's your wildest dream to have one as a kid, and even more so when you become an adult. I've been lucky enough to purchase a homely little bungalow in Normandy Beach, NJ, set back only 100 yards from the crashing surf. It has two small bedrooms, a kitchen, a tiny bathroom and sink, living room, a front porch, one parking spot, and not enough property to squeeze around the outside. It isn't much of a house to raise a family in, or to entertain friends, but it's my slice of heaven, because I know my real playground lies only steps away.

Over the years, the house has stretched its confines to entertain over 20 wader-clad fishermen in and out at one time, but it can comfortably handle three people tops. The bathroom is a claustrophobic stall and shower, with only enough room to wash the salt off the rods and reels. The front porch is dedicated entirely to surf fishing: dozens of rods and reels hang from the ceiling rack; plugs, poppers, hooks hang precariously from the blinds, and there's surely some old forgotten dead bait strewn about under the buckets and sand spikes in the corner. A pair of 3 mm neoprene waders hangs from a boot rack next to the front screen door, the bedroom closet is the fully stocked tackle box, and, save for some frying pans and cutting boards, there's not much room for the house to effectively contain anything more than all things involved in the pursuit of surfcasting.

A '99 cherry-red Jeep Wrangler sits outside the front door, equipped with an army shovel, sand spikes, tow rope, fire extinguisher, and—the last time I looked—an old, mummified blackfish fillet that escaped my sight, but not my smell, for a good month. That's the way I like it. Needless to say, with a setup like that, I am not married yet, at least to a woman. I am, however, married to my passion. In this modest house is where all things start and end, surf-wise. A good surf outing must start from somewhere worthy, and this little house sets a righteous mood.

The walls of my surf shack have stories. Good times, bad days fishing, tall tales, colorful characters, tides, times—and all of that is included within the following passages, broken down in chronological order by month and day, but not by year; this presentation will better allow the study of seasonal times, tides, and temperatures that may repeat. My hope is that you, as a reader, may get a good sense of patterning and a general sense of wherewithal to figure out when the Jersey surf will present some true magic to you. You'll also get a good dose of general debauchery, achievements, and failures from some of the colorful characters who make up the soul of surf fishing.

Not every day is a winner; there are plenty of days when there is nary a fish to put up on the board. But the simple, solemn fact that you are out there, even for just a few hours, as a witness to the ocean's oftentimes mysterious and mad—but always beautiful and splendid—ways is enough to grant a lifetime of joy, even in one simple surf session. There are trials and tribulations of joyous, action-packed days; there are days with nothing to show but a sunburn and sand in your shorts for the time you put in. It's all good. What this book will hopefully get across is that no matter when you go, what you do, or whom you're with, it's *always* time to be out surf fishing.

Two weeks before October 29, 2012, I submitted this manuscript to Jay Nichols at Stackpole, and for that moment in time, I consider myself lucky. On that date, Superstorm Sandy hit my area at Normandy Beach—ground zero for the most destructive storm/hurricane ever to hit the Northeast in recorded history. I had to evacuate the barrier island the night before as a mandatory order from the state, but not before choosing to run to the beach with a fifth of Captain Morgan rum in my hand in order to avoid the police as they went knocking door to door to check that everybody evacuated, or if you were to stay, then to write your social security number in black permanent marker on your wrist to help identify your body. I planned to stay and ride it out. After seeing that the surf was already breaching the 20-foot dunes of my beach, and with the eye of the storm still 48 hours away, I decided it was in my best interest to leave. I eventually pulled anchor and left about 9 p.m., after the bridges were officially shut down, and drove my Jeep through a breach in Bay Head to luckily make it out alive before the real stuff hit on the high tide.

I hunkered down in the town of Brielle with my friend Shannon and her son Kyle, about 10 minutes north and a mile inland, eyes glued to the local news and ears listening to the local police scanner as the eye of Sandy hit us directly—that is, until the power went out. Hours turned into sleepless days and nights. Two days, four days, six days passed. My island was quarantined, smoking, burning, seething from raging fires, and flooded from newly formed inlets. I did not know if I had a home or not anymore. Turns out, I didn't. After trying to access the island and being turned back dozens of times by National Guard and police checkpoints, roadblocks, and soldiers with fully loaded and aimed M-16s standing the island down, on the fifth day I finally managed to sneak in with a compassionate police officer who couldn't stand seeing my tearing, sleepless, black eyes and all the anxiety I must've exhibited. The officer told me to hop in the cruiser and we navigated a labyrinth of destruction to see my house, or where it was, along with 94 others in my neighborhood, just . . . gone. No sign left of any of them, not even a foundation, a rooftop, a car, nothing. Thirty-foot-high, free-flowing natural gas fires spouted out of the sand and raged like a scene from the Kuwait initiative. The hissing of gas was omnipresent, bubbling up from the toxic sludge all around. It smelled like war. Charred, mangled remains of homes littered the scene as far as your eyes could see. Before the 8-foot tsunami surge came sweeping across the island on its five-hour rampage, a transformer explosion on the beach ignited a firestorm fueled by 90-knot winds that wiped my home off the map, along with everything I've ever owned. One neighbor who stayed through the storm told me he was in his attic cutting a hole into the roof to escape the rising waters, when he looked out and swore he saw my home floating down Route 35, on fire, when it connected with a floating car and exploded in one God-forsaken hellstorm. For the last 15 years, I have been a full-time professional writer and photographer in the sportfishing industry. In Sandy, I lost twenty-five thousand photos for work and memories, 15 years of writing on my hard drives, and four separate backup drives; all my fishing rods, reels, gear; and every single last thing I've ever owned.

All right, enough of the harrowing story. I just needed to tell you this before you begin to read the book. I thank God that I was able to get away with my life intact and to shoot this book off to Jay two weeks before the storm. This book, the journal entries in it, and all the passion, love, and experiences written, are all I actually have left of my previous life, and I give that to you.

So when you read these words, be jubilant and joyful as they are, full of memories, good times, and bonding friendships and family. Read these experiences with an acknowledgment that your beautiful life and memories can be taken from you at any moment, and truly—truly from the bottom reaches of your soul—be thankful for what you've got when you've got it.

Like they say—Jersey Strong. Mark my words: I will be back on my own beach, in my own home again, to continue the story that has yet to be written. Love and live life as passionate and soulful every single day that you have been given, and never look back on things you could have done. Get out and do the things you can and want to do now. And that means, well, go hit the surf.

Sandy has nothing on me.

1 March

THE WAKE-UP CALL

I suppose it's fitting to start a surf-fishing book with March—specifically, March 1, an "opening day" of sorts. In Jersey, no other surf fish is pursued with as much passion and intensity as the striped bass, a fish with as many pet names as it has pursuers—Linesider, Rockfish, Cow, Squid Hound, Ol' Pajamas, or, as intellectuals know it, Morone Saxitilis. New Jersey law dictates that striped bass season closes for fishing in the backwaters and bays from January 1 through the end of February, and opens on March 1, and though the beachfront is always available to fish, any resident bass hanging around will undoubtedly be hanging in the backwaters.

Opening Day is a call of reckoning. For any Garden State surfcaster, all the pent-up wintertime anxiety comes to a head, from being locked inside, a slave to only eight hours of daylight, freezing and snow-blind through blizzards and massive nor'easter snowdrifts covering the house. The scraping of ice and hardened salt off the car windshield, and the need to fix broken, frozen water pipes in the sand all seem to come to an end, and we are refreshed by the promise that the hallowed and revered striped bass can again be targeted without a hitch. March 1 is about rekindling the fire inside to pursue the passion, about simply getting outside to make a few casts with the promise of something hitting your plugs, about pulling yourself out of the wintertime funk and bringing you back to where your blood flows and you feel alive.

There are some back-pocket spots that striper hounds look to put their first bass of the official year on the boards, and just saying the names elicits that opening day adrenaline rush: Graveling Point, a sod bank jut that pierces the waters of Great Bay in Mystic Island; and the hard sedge compound of Cliffwood Beach in Raritan Bay. You can always check online; click on Scott Albertson of Scott's Bait and Tackle in Mystic Island at www.scottsbt.com (check out the history here), and see the madness of the first of the year reports unfold. Most every fisherman in the state who is at work on March 1 is glued to that computer screen, clicking refresh every hour to see who put the first bass of the state on the boards. Albertson's shop prides itself on the prospect of claiming the first official keeper (currently 28 inches and over) from Graveling Point to be weighed in Jersey waters. Over the years, since he has been keeping track, Albertson has weighed in fish on March 1, though sometimes the first keeper doesn't hit the scales until late March.

Water temperature is crucial to getting the early-season resident bass to open their mouths, and usually the magic mark for temperature is 48 degrees F. Graveling Point is a little jut of a sod bank isthmus that greets the waters of Great Bay, dipping in depth from a foot to 12 feet in the channel, and you can reach it with a long cast. The shallower waters bring in the resident bass to feed, and early-season anglers come out in droves to hit Graveling Point with sandworms, bloodworms, and clams in anticipation of bending a rod.

The other big-time early-season spot for northern Jersey anglers lies within the confines of Raritan Bay. Striped bass spawn in three major estuarial locations: the Chesapeake Bay, the Delaware River, and the Hudson River. The Hudson River strain of striped bass inevitably has to enter through the mouth of Raritan Bay and migrate upward in the Hudson River, way up past Tarrytown, and into the headwaters. The major saltwater compound bass stick to is Raritan Bay, which separates Staten Island, New Jersey, and Manhattan. The shores of Raritan Bay are as varied and eclectic as the cities that line them. On the Jersey side, a few spots are well known to hold the early-season bass: Cliffwood Beach, Union Beach, and Pebble Beach. Raritan Bay is usually where you'll find the most hardcore of dedicated bass hounds searching to break the mark for first striper of the year. Short bass usually find the baits first, and provide for a well-needed tussle to "get the skunk off the back" for the year. Right now, it's all about the resident stripers that winter over, and the back-bay marshes and sod set the stage for a beautiful and promising time to get out of the house and target hungry linesiders. Wherever you may roam, pick your place; in the early season, stripers abound.

R-BAY

Richie Swisstack goes by the name Swiss; a well-respected, burly, six-foot-four striper aficionado, a guy who you want on your side in a barfight as well as a guy you can count on to watch your dog when you are away, he's just about as dedicated as any angler when it comes to putting the first bass of the year on the boards. Swiss plies his home water of Raritan Bay with the enthusiasm of a wide-eyed kid. I had a call come in from Swiss; it was a short but sweet conversation that went something like:

Swiss latches on to an early season Cliffwood Beach linesider. RICHIE SWISSTACK.

"Hey Nick, it's Swiss. You've got to meet me tonight up here. The bite is on! Gotta run, fish on." *Click.*

This was the journal entry from that particular night.

March 16

Hit the Leonardo Flats with Richie Swiss and Dave Torrick. Started at 6:15 p.m.—sundown, nightfall at about 7:15 p.m., wading out far casting out clams on fishfinder rigs. I went 6 for 9 on bass to 29 inches, Dave had about 4, Swiss claimed both of us going 16 for 18—awesome fishing! Swiss had them to 32 inches and already bagged a 17.5-pounder three days ago. Dead-low tide at 6:00, fished all the incoming until midnight—with some blackberry brandy of course to warm us up in the 20-knot bone-chilling northeast winds, cold out about 32 degrees, water temps about 43. Dirty water, but fish were biting so long as you casted out and waded out far. Total bass—31 caught. Cliffwood beach doing very well!

It was a good start to the year, and yes, the blackberry brandy was most definitely needed to keep us warm and fueled to withstand the biting, cold wind. The Raritan Bay bite generally kicks off the year for dedicated bass hounds, as clamming tactics will put the first back-bay bass on the boards. You'll always find Swiss and his crew on the Cliffwood Beach flats in March, though to actually see him, you'll have to traverse the craggy sod banks at some odd hours and squint to the horizon for a big outline of a shadow against the moonlit sky.

BLACKBACKS

Bassing is just gaining momentum in March, but for one second, there are certain species out there in March nobody cares to target, but should. Other quarry besides bass abounds to divide attentions for surfcasting and bankcasting. Promise comes in the form of a simple, humble flatfish: the winter flounder. Historically, winter flounder were the staple that got bank fishermen through the blustery winter months when bass fishing was closed, but in recent times, the winter flounder has fallen on hard luck from the constant pressure of fyke nets and trawlers, both in the back bays and offshore, making for a tough fight for an angler before you even wet a line.

Jersey's winter flounder season is a short one, spanning only 58 days from March 23 to May 21. But with the newfound energy from pent-up winter doldrums, there are enough of the blackbacks staging in the backwaters to make just a one-fish day feel like it's worth the time. Winter flounder pounders hit the docks and bulkheads even though flounder fishing can be very fickle, many times tossing worms and sitting through 6-hour differential tides to wait out the bite when they finally turn on.

You can usually hit your local tackle shop to pick up bloodworms or sandworms by the dozen or half-dozen, those nasty little creatures waving and snapping their alien-like protruding pincers and puking out their inner guts in agitation. Man, I hate those things. But the cabin fever from January and February has a way of making you get a little proactive. I had never done it before, but thought I would go about heading to some local sod banks to procure some sandworms, tapeworms, and bloodworms for myself.

When you go out and pitchfork the sedge muck for these mud-dwelling nasty aliens for your own baits, it's an ethereal feeling to pull one out of the carton, lance it on your hook, and send it down to a cold-bodied flounder. The whole process of unearthing and collecting these minute wormy beasts for baits certainly puts you on an elevation above regular fishing. It makes you feel like you have a one-up on everybody else, if only for the fact that you're the lone nut out there with a pitchfork, standing knee-deep in tidal muck and neoprene waders, pulling worms out of their holes.

March 19, 2003

Well, the war with Iraq just began minutes ago around 9 p.m. Flounder are being caught at Oyster Creek outflow for the last two weeks on bloods and sands, and the upper

Barnegat Bay at Dale's Point and Gunners Ditch have apparently been producing flatties. Some stripers to about 23 inches have been caught at Oyster Creek, but I have not seen them personally. The water temps are still around 37 degrees in the Atlantic, waiting for them to rise with the warmer weather. All the old salts are predicting a great flounder season due to the influx of fresh water from all the snow sitting on top of the ice. We'll see. I think we're hitting it up on the *Miss Point Pleasant* on Saturday for flatties. Cross your fingers, and pray for a quick, painless war, and more fish than ever this year. High tide in the surf is at roughly 8:00 again and with the full moon of course, every time every month around the 18th on a full moon, high tide will be at around 8.

March 20

Full moon tide. Went to train tracks to dig sandworms and bloodworms. Brought a shovel, def need a pitchfork instead. Dug up about 18 keepable sands, two bloods, and a tapeworm about 3 feet long. A ton of small sands, gotta find larger ones. Seemed to hang more by the sedges just off them. Also hit Glimmer Glass and dug up a few sands and a lot of weird mussel-like clams. These plump, feisty worms make prime time bait for hungry flatfish, though I'm not so sure I wouldn't rather spend the $9 for a dozen instead of putting in hard labor to dig worms when I'd just like to be out fishing. Point duly noted.

In late March, if water temperatures are colder than average, in the low 40s, the winter flounder tend to stay rooted in the mud to spawn out, but if the sun shines for a few days straight and water temperatures rise above the 50-degree mark, then they go on the move to make their exodus out the inlets and into the ocean. I always hit my local spots, a certain little off-avenue in Bay Head, where you can cast a worm when all else seems to fail, and you can sit at a bulkhead knowing you can hook up with a tasty winter flounder for the dinner table. My little "Ditch" (and local boys know it) is a brilliant place to be in springtime, where mallard ducks can be shot in deftly hidden gunblinds on the sedges, amid the million-dollar mansions of summertime Bennies. Winds whip in cold, freezing streams of sleet, and you are there.

March 21

First day of spring today. Northeast wind blew the past two days, so today hit the beach at low at around 4:00 to collect three dozen clams on the beach. It is best to have an east/nor'east wind to churn it up, then a nice west wind to blow the water out and expose the clams at low tide. Going to try flounder fishing tomorrow on the *Miss Point Pleasant*. Flatties being caught when it is nice out by Pelican Island, BB/BI Buoys, and Dale's Point. After shucking those clams, kept all the ribbons and scallops for fresh flounder bait tomorrow.

March 21

Surf temps at 44 degrees or so, flounder being taken at usual upper Barnegat Bay spots, Dale's Point, Hospital, and now in the Manasquan, also BB and BI Buoy in Barnegat Bay. Flounder have mud on their bellies, and seem to be spawned out according to local reports.

With cabin fever still running through my veins from the excessively long winter, certifiable lunatic actions most assuredly ensue, though they can offer up some unexpected observations.

March 23

Amazing how much goes through your mind in the course of a day. And what you learn. Went to Sedge Island to open up the state house today, and what I couldn't give to live on that island in the middle of Barnegat Bay for some solitude. After done with "work," as a seasonal employee with the Dept. of Fish and Game, which consisted of replacing one fire alarm, I hit up the Bay Head bayside with the remainder of the worms from Saturday's exploits for flounder. Casted out and had two solid hits at the Ditch, but only had on small size 8 gold hooks, the flounder were biting the tails off to the eye almost and not getting hooked. Switched to Chesterfield hooks but the tide switched and the bite seemed to go off. I had my hits at the end of the incoming. Anyway, came home and grabbed two strip steaks from A&P. No propane in the grill, so I tried the ancient charcoal I had sitting around in the shed, put it in the grill and lit it, and everything lit but the charcoal. I decided to grab the steel grate, my steaks, my potato, and my ketchup and go to the beach. It was blowing about 10 to 15 out of the south, grabbed all the Blizzard of '03 driftwood still lying around and made a fire. Cooked that damn steak until I was satisfied and ate it. More importantly, I noticed that it might be easier to find cuts in the bars and holes when you search at nighttime. You can see on a clear night, with stars in the sky, the whitewater breaking on the shoals and bars, and the empty blackness where the hole lies. I noticed this up and down the coast, since it was low tide. Could be an interesting way to determine fishing holes.

March 25

Not enough people for afternoon trip on *Norma K II* so hit up Lyman Ave with some leftover sands. Had one hit on the beginning of the incoming tide around 2:30 p.m., then sea snot (the dead marine undergrowth that the new stuff grows under and pushes up and out when it gets warm enough) and current got too strong to fish.

March 31

Surf temps at 44 degrees or so, flounder being taken at usual upper Barnegat Bay spots, Dale's, Gunners, Hospital, and now in the Manasquan, also BB and BI Buoy. Graveling

Point usually goes off first for schoolie bass. Flounder have mud on their bellies, and seem to be spawned out according to local reports. Cliffwood, Union, and Pebble Beaches start their striper producing now on clams and bunker on the sedge banks.

Flounder pounding and chasing schoolie stripers certainly have their place, especially in March, but March is like the little brother who keeps nagging at you to go outside and play. It's not too serious, but it's not to be taken lightly, as you have a responsibility to get out there and play. March offers up just the littlest taste of what's to come for striper fishing. It lights the fuse, but the powder keg begins to burn in April, setting up for a May explosion. Once April hits, surfcasting for dinner-sized stripers begins to get serious.

2 April

A NOR'EASTER'S BLESSING

No other month can be defined as the awakening of the Atlantic's soul like April. The air seems to be injected with the sounds and smells of a thousand different seafaring sensations joining in a symphonic melody of Earth's oceanic heartbeat. Easterly winds waft with a kelpy sort of scent that tells of purgation—a long winter's wait for the ocean to get busy and let life live. A sea-borne smell permeates like none other I have ever experienced. Crushed clam-laden breezes, hints of oily menhaden schools, and a clean, salty tang bring promise to the surfcaster and saturate the human soul with freshness.

Errant kelp leaves float on frothy, whitecapped, incoming tides. Black-backed seagulls begin to set up shop again and flap their wings in unison over the crashing waves in an attempt to feast on crushed clamshells and sea worm bits. April is a time of rebirth, a moment to recharge the soul. Maybe it's because I've been locked up in a cramped house for so long over the winter, or maybe it's simply the excitement I feel as the Earth wants to purge itself and bring back its glory— I am not too sure, but whatever it is, it energizes my senses and keeps me flowing full and strong, not only to fish, but to work, thrive, and enjoy life to its fullest once again. April is truly the month of redemption.

April is marked by the presence of the nor'easter. It is Jersey's recurring little brother of the hurricane, and it always comes with a sibling's "trying to prove itself" fury—spitting out 5- to 8-foot surf on the first day of its arrival, short, swift, and soft, but then it hits like dynamite, a three-day menace barreling out haymakers at 8- to 20-foot seas, destroying beaches with a vicious swell that devours and swallows them into the belly of the beast, leaving wrecked waterfront mansions, destroyed dunes, and all sorts of flotsam and jetsam behind. The little nor'easter that did.

When the maelstrom subsides, a good week of westerly offshore winds passes before the seas simmer down and water clarity returns to normal. The offshore winds in this "clean up" session expose the tiny, clean, and clear yellow quartz pebbles that litter the shorelines, and then, like clockwork, some serious early-season bassing begins to take form. Thousands of seagulls seem to come out of nowhere, cackling, screeching, and diving, stretching their wings from their wintering over, picking up the bits and pieces of naturally killed worms, baitfish, and crustaceans left from the disaster. There is life in the air, and the sea is downright electric. The pounding, churning, and mixing of the rough surf unearths zillions of surf clams, smashing and cracking them up to unleash a virtual smorgasbord for newly migrating bass. Fresh clams on the hook reign supreme here and now. When it's all said and done, surfsters hit the beaches hard for stripers. That's what April is about.

DEADSTICKING

Clamming isn't rocket science. Tie up a hi-lo rig set with 4/0 baitholder hooks and a 3- to 5-ounce pyramid weight, bait with a clam, cast it out into the surf, and deadstick it in a sand spike. Simple, right? But there is a little bit of strategy. The cuts, sloughs, and bowls that form from the nor'easter ruckus create feeding avenues of all sorts for bass. Walk up at low tide and try to define the structure through visual cues. Look for whitewater breaking; that's where the sandbars are. Where the wave breaks, then reforms again in a rolling, constantly breaking, white-topped push of wave is where the deep water slough, hole, or cut is. That's the place to launch a clam.

When setting up the PVC sand spikes for clam rods, it's hard to overlook the natural debris field that the wave action has spilled onto the beach. It's a beachcomber's paradise. Everything washes up. Busted-up clam shells and sand fleas, mostly scavenged by black-backed gulls and picked at by sanderlings; fully bolted pieces of docks from northern Jersey oceanfront mansions that couldn't handle the storm surge; neon-green plastic kid sandcastle rakes and hi-top sneakers; balloons and Hi-Fliers from lobster pots that come numbered with red flagging, white Styrofoam blocks, and bright orange wreck buoys. April nor'easters take everything from the sea and bring it to shore and take everything from the shore and bring it back out to sea. It's a virtual minefield of destruction.

In the midst of the mess, April sounds the siren for the primordial horseshoe crabs to spawn out and sink their clinchers on each other to mate. You'll see a bunch of horseshoe crabs washing up on the high tide, sometimes marooned and flipped over on the high sands, incapacitated like a turtle. As a steward of the ocean, if you see them stuck on a high tide, delicately grab the male's tail, clamped on top of the female, and gently push them back into the ocean. Natural selection be damned; help these creatures to get back to what they've done best for 250 million years before the gulls get them.

Now get back to your clamming rod in the sand spike, kick back with an adult beverage of your choice, and watch the west winds push down the surf under blue, sunny skies. This is when bass hit hard. April linesiders are mostly in the 20- to 28-inch range, not large by any means, but they are the first real surf bass of the season, and they kickstart the passion for the year. Every season is a little bit different depending on the timing of the nor'easters that come rumbling through, usually within the second and third weeks of the month.

Bluefish then move into the waters. Racer bluefish, the ones that are skinny from wintering over in the Carolinas, are big-headed and ugly, with rail thin bodies, looking to fatten up and gorge themselves on anything that passes in front of them that might be edible—or not edible for that matter—anything that fills the stomach. These feisty bluefish, smaller stripers, and lowly springtime skates, all of which hold a dear place in my heart, get April moving along in the right direction. Here's the kickoff to April surf fishing.

April 3

Went down to the beach with fresh-shucked clams to hit the 15- to 20-knot east-northeast wind, high tide 8:30 a.m. Nothing. Water hovering around 44 degrees, still cold, but scattered reports of a few stragglers being taken.

April 7

Me and Mickey fished with James at IBSP. Nighttime tide at 7 p.m. Mickey got hit at 7:15 p.m. by a 23-inch bass! Dark at 7:30 p.m. It ate a clam bait.

April 8

Fished my beach in the morning with Mickey 7:30 a.m. to 10 a.m. No hits, one skate, they are moving in now, had 5 skates yesterday. Gillnetter S——— Tours is out and had killed 27 bass in the 15- to 20-pound class I saw, what an ass.

Mickey hoists a night shift spring striper.

Gillnetting stripers—the method of setting out a long net into which bass run and get stuck by their gills—is illegal in NJ, but this guy puts them out supposedly for the minute amount of weakfish and bluefish around, simply in order to spite the commercial bass regulations. He kills bass to make a convoluted point. Every year. What an idiot.

April 9

Mickey, his son Mikey, and Ellen fished IBSP, saw a seagull scarfing down a small fluke in the wash. Only fished an hour and half. South winds, no hits, one skate.

April 9

High tide 5:30 a.m., set out my beach, lots of bowls and point breaks, water around 50 degrees, light southwest winds, water off-color. Overcast. Cast clams out and landed first surf bass of year! 26 inches, beautiful purple sheen on him, too. Also had two skates and another bass hit. Fished from 2 p.m. to 5 p.m. Bass at 4 p.m. And so it begins. By the way, last two days were 86 and 89 degrees, today 60.

The April spring tide moons have astronomical pull over the water levels, and when April gets its planetary pull on, the spring tides can really swing heavily. Full and new moon April surf makes low tide hours tough to fish as there is barely any water in the cuts, almost like a tsunami dragging the water out on the low tides. But mid tide hours can really offer up prime water flow for bass to stage and gorge themselves on the funneling flow of crabs, clam bits, and seaworms.

April 14

New Moon, seas flat to 1 foot, west winds, clear with west wind, light just like summer. Fished 7:30 a.m. to 10:30 a.m. with clams, got a skate bump right away and at 8 a.m. got a whackdown that looked like a 20-pound classer, but hook did not set. Slow morning, but coolest thing ever, a live seahorse washed up at my feet! And I revived and released him in the surf! High tide at 8:30 a.m. Also later in day, noticed a big black bait ball caught in a low tide slough—probably sand eels or bunker, and bass have stormed into the local waters with 15- to 20-pounders for boaters, much earlier than usual, very excellent presence around. S————Tours has his nets out again though. They stretch right from the breakers out a couple hundred yards and he sets 8 to 10 of them along the stretch from Lavallette to Manasquan. Killing bass for no purpose.

April 14

START OF THE 3-DAY NOR'EASTER

April 16

Tried the T-Bird with clams on an incoming tide, to no avail for an hour. Little sick today, so came in early. Bass starting to get caught at Island Beach and Seaside to about 17 pounds, no heated action just yet. Raritan Bay still giving up plenty of schoolie and slot bass but no big un's just yet.

April 18

Hit the Thunderbird with Sean, he came up to screw around. We cast out clam sticks in a northwest blow, incoming tide almost high tide. Water is cut and holed nicely after big nor'easter of last week. Didn't even get a hit, but bass are beginning to be caught at Brick through Seaside. Flounder bite has been real slow especially in Raritan, but is just now picking up at Mantoloking Bridge and Barnegat with the 82- to 88-degree temps of the last few days and this week.

April 19

Uncle Greg came up at 6 a.m. to fish, we set up on my beach and fished from 6:30 to 11:30 a.m., only one freakin' skate! Bass apparently all over IBSP and everywhere but not today. Northwest winds 10 to 15 knots. High tide at 11:15. What's up with that?! Some bluefish now being caught at IBSP.

April 24

Hit T-Bird with Bugsy for first surf expo and clammed up a 22-inch striper. High tide around 5:30 p.m., hit evening hour around 6 p.m.

April 27

Hit Jimmer's Hole with clams, high tide 1:45 p.m., got there at 2:20 p.m. Rainy, overcast, north winds 10 knots. Cali joined me chucking clams for the first surf episode. Hi-lo rigs, 4 ounces holding. There's a nice sandbar that extends out and almost hooks around. I kept casting on the point of the inner hook and getting hits. The early-season bass tap-tap-taps lightning quick, you need to be holding the rod in your hands to connect. I connected. With a 23-inch striper. We had about 7 hits combined after that but no stripes to show. They are fast-hitting, and you need to scale down the baits to strips. One skate as well.

Since I mentioned Jimmer here, I might as well tell you that Jimmer is one of my local neighbors, in about his early fifties, and when you mention Jimmer, you think clamming. Jimmer loves to clam for bass. He's up at the beach nearly every single morning and evening when the season runs strong, cup of coffee in one hand, bag of clams in the other. Thing is, he only fishes directly in front of the end of his beach path, and thus, whether a hole is actually there or not

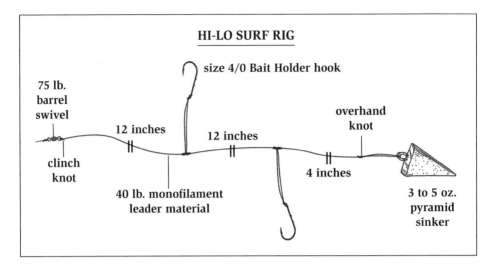

during any given time, any hole within 25 yards of the area is considered Jimmer's Hole.

April 28

Jimmer's Hole. Hit it at 2:00 p.m. with the freakin' stinkiest, most rank clams I ever used from Ernie's. I mean bad. I couldn't even put them on the hook without gagging, literally.

Let me interject here on that note. There are days when the clams you get from a tackle shop stink. Literally. They are old, rotten, bad clams, the ones that have been sitting around, marinating in the tub a few days longer than they should have been. There are days you talk to the tackle shop guy and he says something along the lines of, "I threw another 3 or 4 in there for ya. They're a little old." They say those things so not only do you not feel slighted, but in fact, you feel pretty good that you are getting something for free, more clams to cast for bass. In the mind of the tackle shop proprietor, though, he just unloaded his troubles on you: stink clams that have no place in his fridge. Clams so potent that he wraps them tightly in the heavy plastic bag and practically vacuum seals it before you can actually get a whiff of the misfortune you just got for free. I've had some rank clams over the years, enough to water my eyes and make my stomach feel uneasy, with one particular time, upon opening the bag, the stench that hit me was so foul that my throat gagged, and I actually threw up in my mouth. That was no joke. I wouldn't wish that evil upon my worst enemy, and I was done fishing for the day right then and there. Couldn't even pack up the gear right as it was downwind of the mess. People on the beach walking hundreds of yards away told me they could smell it all the way down the beach. Dogs that walked by wouldn't even attempt to take a nibble. For the most part, you get good decent clams from tackle shops, but be suspicious if your local bait store gives you more than one for free. But you know what? Sometimes they work, if you can muster the internal fortitude to put one on the hook, like this . . .

I cast out, Jimmer already mentioned he'd been there for about 15 minutes and had a shorty. About 20 minutes later I saw my line go slack and limp, no telltale hit though on the tip. I reeled it up and found weight on the end. Striper. Battled the little brute and he came in at 24 inches. Hi-lo rig. Other rod went off with a fishfinder and two-hook rig on it. I set up and reeled in an 18-incher. Incoming and dead-high seemed to produce today, 10-knot west winds, sunny as summer. 4 to 5 ounces holding, incoming tide weight holds better, outgoing tide may need to bump up an ounce to prevent current drift. Flounder now at the Cedars in Raritan and bass are hitting clams, and bunker have begun to move in the Bay. Weakies are just starting to show in the back of Barnegat. Reports of lots of marks back there and a few confirmed 9- to 12-pounders caught backside IBSP.

April 20

Took the rest of the clams and bunker and fished from 9 a.m. to 11 a.m., not a tap. Though when I did get up to the spot, a pair of blinking eyes and bald head with whiskered face was staring at me—a seal! He was checking me out, wondering what I was all about. Summer-like surf conditions, even blue-green water, but about 68 degrees.

SPRING TRASH FISH

Trash Fish. It's a term of endearment, really. Any fish you don't want to have on your line when you are clamming for stripers fall under the trash fish blanket. All sorts of surf beasties begin to get the hunger in April, as sea robins, smooth dogfish, and blowfish start to awaken and nibble, peck and hijack baits intended for bass. Baitstealers they are. But far and away, there is one fish that deserves disdain and earns the moniker of trash fish more than any other.

SKATES

Skates. The lowliest fish of the surfcaster. In the Garden State, we've got clearnose skates with tiger stripes and an ornery attitude, and common skates that are lumpy and near catatonic in their fight, like a wet sock filled with sand. Neither is glamorous or pursued with intent. Skates alone hold the dubious distinction of trash fish kings, and no surfcaster wants them on a hook. Plain and simple, they are pretty much the object of all the hate a surfcaster can hold.

Doubleheader skates—a trash fisherman's trophy.

But that doesn't mean we shouldn't hold them in high respect. On the first casts of a surf-fishing year, many times those little skate taps on the end of the line are the first action you get to relieve the yearning to reel something in. Those first skate hits singlehandedly lock winter away for good, and inspire you for the year ahead. They bring the initial spirit of the spring surf, and should not be thrown up on the dry sand, killed without remorse, and left on the beach to be picked apart by seagulls, but should be given respect as any other creature of the ocean.

Here's something I wrote for a fishing column, in an attempt to beautify these lowly creatures.

As printed in the *Daily Journal*, Vineland, New Jersey:

"It's a funny thing, but the beginning of the surf season does something magical for me. I honestly don't know what makes it sink in; if it's the cabin fever of the wintertime, the boredom of having to stay inside when it's cold out, or the longing to cast out into the sunrise at the crack of dawn. Whatever it is, there's something special about the first cast of the year.

"As I check my fishing logs and records from years past, the first cast into the suds usually revolves around hucking a few gobs of clams, bunker strips, and even a sandworm or two into the cuts and sloughs carved by winter's fury, sometime at the end of March or beginning of April. I stumble down to the undertow in my neoprene waders, throw two rods out into the water, walk back up the sandy slope, and stick the rods into the sand spikes, spaced 10 feet apart with my lawn chair precariously placed equidistant between them. Then I sit. And wait.

"The kelpy smell of the Atlantic wafts off the ocean and into my nose, my hands carry a slimous, clammy essence, the gulls stand at the water's edge occasionally emitting halfhearted screams, and my brain is absolutely tickled with the anticipation of seeing that first rod twitch and then pump two or three times signaling the virgin strike of the season. Which brings me all to my point.

"If you're lucky, the first fish of the year will have stripes on its sides. But more often than not, it's probably not going to be so pretty. In fact, if you're an early-season fisherman, hitting the beaches in March and early April, chances are your initial surf-caught denizen is going to be a flat, lethargic, and kinda ugly denizen—a skate. As much disdain as they garner from surf anglers, I am going to volley for the beauty and excitement of catching such a creature.

"The skate's purpose is important. The spiny creature represents the ushering in of the surf season. For all the badmouthing they get, you have to look at them for what they bring to the table. They, my friends, are the culmination of all our pent-up anticipation which wintertime so grudgingly suppresses. They singlehandedly relieve us from our prison. With that first twitch of the rod tip, all our boredom and winter blues are whisked away in an instant and we once again enter the realm of our inner surf soul. We rush to the rod, pick it out of the spike, and set back to feel the first weight on the end of the line pulling back at us. Our heart pumps, blood races, and we begin to reel in, feeling tiny pumps on the end of the line. Our excitement is at a fever pitch, crank after crank, reel after reel, and in a short fight, a small, flat, spiny thing is sitting at our feet, its mouth protruding and sucking, its spiky tail slowly swinging to and fro, a small representative of the Atlantic lying at our feet.

"Unhook him and let him be free. For he brings with him all our dreams for a new year in the surf. And before you begin to badmouth that homely-looking creature, take a second and thank him for the first fight of the year, and respect his mission. The skate, he ain't pretty, but he, quite simply in his own right, is what it's all about. Skate on!"

Still, I get it, skates suck. But treat them with respect nonetheless!

THE CLEAN UP SURF

Nor'easters rumble through in April, and like clockwork, you can expect at least one and maybe two of the beasts to hit the shores in the second to third week of April, no doubt. At the end of their three-day rampage, offshore westerly winds swing around to push down the remaining swell and clean up the waters from brown to blue. That clean up time is when resident stripers are on the prowl to feed and fatten up as the zillions of uprooted clams litter the coastal surf, and bass are looking at a smorgasbord. The two days leading up to a nor'easter push the barometric pressure down while the two days after make it rise, with plenty of crushed and cracked up forage to make stripers go wild.

April 23

Mick and I went to IBSP A11 at 2:30 p.m. Clear skies, beautiful bluebird-blue high tide 6:30. Couple of skates, then at 5:45 p.m. had a keeper bass at 28 inches, fat, about 9 pounds on a hi-lo rig with clam. West winds after nor'easter blowing 20 knots, little brown water. Then this weekend had the 85-degree weather that is usually associated with mid-April but it's here now and late. Mickey just had a nice 11-pounder in Holgate on the 26th. First reports of blues and a 20-inch weakfish in Bonnet Island backwaters. Blues not there yet. Water temp 50 degrees.

Spring bluefish are usually skinny in stature, "racers" in local terminology, as they aren't the full-shouldered brutes of the fall, but skinny specimens with lob-heads and slender bodies that have slimmed down during the winter in North Carolina and now maraud up the Jersey coast filling their guts with anything and everything available to them. In 2008 to 2010, the spring blues were fat and furious, thick-bodied beasts that gorged on healthy bunker schools, now prevalent since political legislation demanded that ominous commercial bunker reduction boats leave our waters. When you stop mass netting all the bunker, bass and bluefish populations rebound. Not so hard an equation to comprehend, right?

April 25

Solid nor'easter, first day of it coming thru, 6- to 11-foot seas, should last three days or so. Hit morning tide high around 6:45 a.m., and had two bass of 20 and 24 inches on clams, light west wind. Air temp in the high 60s. Water temps around 54. Big blues moved in last few days from 8 to 15 pounds solid, no racer slinky ones, though haven't fished for them yet.

Bluefish begin to make their spring journey up the Eastern Seaboard in late March and early April, and they enter the back bays like Great Bay and Barnegat Bay en masse. When the blues run in the spring, it's an all-out surf circus. If you have four rods out baited with bunker chunks, four rods will go down at a time with arm-wrenching bluefish on the end of each line. When the southeast wind turns on, ripping the April Atlantic waters into a gray, white-capped frenzy, early-season blues go ballistic, chasing down any baitfish in the waters, but they also will not turn a nose up at scavenging anything and everything stinky and blood-ridden on the bottom, like a freshly cut bunker chunk. The southeast winds and gray, sloppy waters in April always bring the bluefish in.

Chopper bluefish singlehandedly keep the tackle shops in business in the early season, as they make a job out of busting lines, tackle, and rigs. You go into any one of the shops, like Grumpy's Bait and Tackle or Betty and Nick's in Seaside Park, and the laundry list of catches is long and dirty, with the walls full of Polaroid photos of 6- to 12-pound bluefish. One thing to mention about

Grumpy's: you can't get in and out of there without taking some down-home Jersey Coast abuse as Grumpy, the old bastard with the long, smoke-stained white beard and caustic wit, will regale you with impressive surf stories about himself, and jokes, mainly about you. Flat out, it's an experience just going in to buy clams at the shop, and you will leave with a smile on your face—along with a thicker skin!

April 26

All out bananas fishing on IBSP! Me and Mick, 3- to 5-foot east blow, full moon tomorrow, set up at 1 p.m. dead-low and had bluefish all through the incoming tide to 3:30 p.m., when we ran out of bait! Mick got a hammer-down from a 34-inch striper on a chunk, then we landed another 27 bluefish to 14 pounds! INSANE! Oh, by the way, one bluefish had these type of feathers or quills coming out of its mouth, thought it was squid tentacles at first, then saw it was feathers, must've eaten a small bird too! And that one same blue inhaled my hi-hook chunk, low-hook chunk, and the 6-ounce Hatteras sinker in its mouth! Couldn't get the sinker back, so that blue will be 6 ounces heavier forever.

Bluefish choking up spearing, always biting off more than they can chew.

Springtime chopper blues rumble through the surfline, crashing poppers and devouring chunk baits.

April 27

Hit my beach to clam and chunk bunks for all the blues that have been in town. East winds 15 knots, 3- to 5-foot seas. Fished noon till 1:45 p.m., so much salad in the wash couldn't fish effectively. The shorts are there along with lots of 3- to 8-pound blues, but didn't get whacked.

When the stars align, the bluedogs really invade in full force, and those days, it's as hard to manage as controlling a whirling tornado: rigs snapping off; running around hooking, fighting, and beaching fish after fish; chasing knock-down rods into the surf; and unhooking one bluefish after another. It's nuts.

BLUEFISH CHART

Jersey's generally accepted key to bluefish and their respective names/sizes:

Snapper:	3 to 5 inches long
Tailer:	half pound to 1 pound
Cocktail:	2 to 3 pounds
Chopper:	4 to 9 pounds
Slammer:	10 to 14 pounds
Alligator:	14 to 20 pounds
Gorilla:	20 pounds plus

April 28

>   Dead full moon. 8 p.m. high tide, Mick and Marc came down to shoot film. Got to IBSP again in a burnt log hole about A12, and this was one of the finest days of action I've EVER seen! From the first moment our chunks got struck by 7- to 9-pound bluefish, enough so we took the rods out at 11 a.m., dead-low about 3 p.m. Around 1:30 p.m. low tide bar out enough with full moon tide, northwest winds 25 to 30 knots, seas 1- to 2-foot, windy as all heck. Topwater popped so many bluefish I can't even imagine to tell how many, about 53 bluefish. Other blues were following the hooked bluefish in on the poppers, swimming by my feet! Bluebird white-cloud skies, it felt like the fall! Water temps about 53 degrees now, and air last night was 39 degrees. Bunker schools getting worked over, gannets diving. We also clammed up two bass of 28 and 26 inches, probably could have had more if we didn't decide to stop as Mick's truck got stuck in the very soft sands that haven't settled from the storms yet. Tried to freakin' dig out for an hour with a snow shovel, a guy tried to tow us out, then had to call Lukoil Mobil Tow to tow us out. Dave was his name. Thanks, Dave! For the $200 charge that is. Ouch! Bass had old bunker chunk and sand flea in his gut. Blues to 14 pounds again! Seriously unreal!

April 29

>   You know the drill. Me and Mick went to IBSP same spot around A10, A11, or so with the World Fishing Network guys to film. Blues began to hit a few chunks, bluebird skies, west winds 20 knots, water looked like Florida Keys, flats clear with sandbar extending out. Beached about 4 blues when I started seeing blues on the lower tides cruising on the outer bar. I jumped down with poppers, they swiped a few times but were lazy, then switched to a Hopkins and bang! Fish on! Then off, as he took my metal. Switched to Deadly Dick and realized they were hitting lazy, so I slowed up the retrieve and dragged it on bottom, a bunch of bumps before the hook set. Back to back about 12 bluefish in a row, the crazy thing was seeing them cruising through in black pack. I helped the guy next to me, who didn't have polarized glasses on, telling him where to cast— 11 o'clock! 1 o'clock! and to switch to metal. Nobody else really hooking up except for a few chunkers. Ended day with about 43 total between all of us, but so strange that the blues were fickle on the bite. Fished 10:30 a.m. to 2:30 p.m. Dead-low at 4 p.m. or so.

Bluefish bombing that way in late April? What a day that was! And it made for great filming. Check out www.nickymagnummedia.com and click on "Bite Club TV" to see all that insane footage over those two days. My arms still hurt from landing triple digits of blues.

FLOUNDA POUNDIN'

In April, probably the most joyful happening is the simple fact that the month ushers in longer days in the blessing that is daylight saving time, sparking motivation in most anglers to get out from under the grind of the winter months.

Though the late April days are filled with the new joys of bass and bluefish in the mix, there is still a faction of dedicated winter flounder pounders who take days off work to pluck flatfish off the warming bay bottoms from various bayside docks. The relatively diminutive flatfish tend to fatten up quickly in the spring; equipped with small peanut-sized mouths, they definitely have a penchant for sucking down worms and clams, and give quite a nice fight on light tackle. Putting together a good catch of flounder for the frying pan is definitely a belly warmer. Mmmm, succulent, flaky flounder meat!

April 2

Hit Lyman Ave bayside with Bugsy. Low tide at 1:57 p.m., hit spot at 2 p.m., still outgoing tide back there. Held with 3 ounces, cast out into Gunners Ditch with yellow twisty tails, sandworms, and Gulp sand fleas, let it sit and felt some little taps and pulls, left it out then reeled in a nice 16-inch blackback that swallowed the whole deal! Not too shabby. That was the only action for 2 hours or so, but had some excellent dinner. Bass starting in R-Bay, lots of shorts, few keepers. Flounder on and off in Oyster Creek.

April 4

Hit Mantoloking Bridge again with mussels and clams to no avail, then went to Bayside Park to make a cast, and got snagged on some large debris out there. Put the clump of mussels I took from the river by the pilings at this dock to see if they hold. First day of trout season tomorrow!

April 17

Hit Lyman Avenue with sandworms and clam strips off the bulkhead for flounder. Lots of brown snot in the water. Saw a few guys pull a few over (about six) at around 11 a.m. The tide switch is approximately 4½ hours difference from tide chart of ocean back there.

That "brown snot" is like a death knell and can make flounder fishing absolutely impossible. If the snot is really around, moving tides will be complicated to fish, as the snot collects on your line like a string of bad laundry, weighing you down, sticking to the line like cement. Slack tides will be your best bet to hook a flattie then. I hate even talking about it. Frustrating!

April 18

More info. Hit Lyman at 9:30 a.m. with sands and clam pieces at parking lot. 80 degrees out. Wind south at 15 knots on beach, not bayside though. I figured out that you need to hit the end of the incoming tide, the bite is the best then, and the beginning of the outgoing, to avoid all the early-season snot, and to be able to hold bottom with a 2- to

3-ounce bank sinker. One guy was anchored right in the hole, hard to cast around when the tide was moving, but when he left I cast where he was at and had the winter flatties mouth my bait every time—you feel a tap-tap-tap, then nothing. I scaled down to size 8 to 10 baitholder hooks and put on half-inch sections of clams. They were all over it. I managed to connect with one flounder about 14 inches long, that released itself at the bulkhead, but here's the gig—small hooks, 2 to 3 ounces, clam baits, top of tide, even slack tide is hot, you avoid the snot moving around, and you can reel in little by little to cover some ground. Reports of bass coming in from the IBSP surf, 10 to 12 pounds on clams. Still slamming cold flatties in Raritan Bay, moving out toward Romer Shoal now. Party boats catching in the hundreds.

April 24

Keating told me about the Bayside Park, how he has been at netting bunker in the 30-foot hole off the bulkhead and livelining bass to keeper bass in the hole! Bluefish too! Went out at 1 a.m. to 3:30 a.m. Raining, miserable conditions, with mackerel chunks sprayed with the Bioedge smell. Nonstop flounder hits, but had too big 5/0 hooks so couldn't hook into them! Seriously? Flounder bites at night?! Also reeled in two crabs that hung on the baits. Freezing, shivering, certifiably insane to be out there, holding two rods in hand—*I* even thought I was nuts.

A winter flounder caught off the bulkhead in upper Barnegat Bay.

April 25

Hit Dog Beach. Watched *Miss Norma K* in the channel bailing flounder day before, waded out amongst about a dozen boats to trump their slicks, cast out and got whacked by a 13-inch flundie that made the bucket. Then had 7 other nice quality hits, though couldn't get them to stay on the hook. Some blues moving through the inlet, fished from 9 a.m. till 1. Dead-high noon, sandworms and Gulp sands worked for the fish. *Reel Class* and *Angela Rose* out there. Told a guy to move out of my casting range!

Dog Beach in the Manasquan River is a cool, under-the-radar place to fish. If you can avoid all the dog stink bombs and make it to the water, cast out from the banks and steal the slicks from the flotilla of flounder fishermen in boats. Hey, free chum!

3 May

MIXED MAYHEM

May kicks off Memorial Day weekend and the tourist season, and in the Garden State, local surfcasters look forward to Memorial Day weekend like a hot stick in the eye, as beaches close down from 9 a.m. to 5 p.m. to accommodate the tourists, a.k.a. Bennies, who flock to the Jersey Shore, all acting like goons trying out for some Guido-based MTV show. The serenity of the daytime beaches is lost until Labor Day, but the days are nonetheless filled with uncompromising promise and adrenaline-infused surf outings, because May equals monsters.

Clam rods are put aside in favor of heavy-duty chunking and casting rods, as clams are replaced by bunker chunks, homemade wooden plugs, and snag rigs to snake live bloody bunker to send out back into the surf, awaiting cow bass that push scales past the 50-pound mark. This is the arena where dreams are realized with a trophy surf bass of a lifetime, or at the very worst, legendary stories are told of the one that got away.

It's a dedicated game, fit for night owls willing to give up their jobs, relationships, and responsibilities to venture out under the cloak of darkness under a moonlit, starry sky, when all others are tucked away warmly under their sheets. There's no breakfast here; the diners aren't open at this hour, and the only fuel is a hot cup of WaWa coffee—or a continuation of beer and whiskey from the night before. Late in the month, it gets to be a bit more sensible, as bunker schools push up onto the beaches in the daytime under the high noon sunshine. Surfsters equipped with weighted bunker snags can deftly launch as far as their strength and gear will let them to snag one lone bunker out of the school to drop back in anticipation of a bone-jarring strike. If there's anything that May teaches a surfcaster, it's that the month itself is too short at only 31 days long.

The first week of May is transitional, as anglers aren't sure if it's warm enough yet for bass to actively chase down plugs and shads, or whether clam baits will still get the job done with more effectiveness as the linesiders may still be too sluggish to chase down a meal. Deadsticking bunker heads or chunks always brings results either way in the first week, with bluefish getting thicker by the hour, prompting many to go exclusively to clam baits until big bass show up in earnest to minimize lost bait and tackle. Shortie bass of 20 to 27 inches all cover up clam baits on the lower tides when the waters are at their skinniest, allowing the late spring sun to warm it up. Add the fact that world-class weakfish begin to sneak around, and flat out, May is grand.

BLUEFISH CARNAGE
Nothing gets the blood flowing like when those first late spring bluefish really push on in. The early racers are hungry and motivated to whack at anything thrown in front of them. When water temps move up into that mid- to high-50s range, the choppers come alive to shred up the bunker schools. May's not a good time to be a bunker.

May 4
Bluefish!!! Low tide at 3:30 p.m., light easterly winds, water semi-clear with a lot of branches, logs, debris, and stuff in it. Fished Brick III at 4 and saw some terns dropping, but they scattered. Cast there anyway and pulled in 43 bluefish in just over an hour! All 5- to 12-pounders, had one short bass on the white teaser on the first cast. Blues busted off all my tackle hit on plugs, teasers, and metals poppers. Every single cast had a fish on, and 4 or 5 blues would follow the hooked one all the way to my feet. Saw them cruising in the waves following my metals. Seas 1-foot. Unbelievable! Big blue had an adult bunker in it, along with maybe a weakfish fillet. Herring around.

May 5
Hit my beach at 2 p.m. and see some terns diving though casts did not produce yet. Southeast winds, water clear 1-foot, fished till 3 with no hits yet, sunny day. Did see what looked like big herring swimming in the clear wash, strange looking fish, not sure what they were, maybe small blues, but were very wavy in their swim pattern.

May 6
Me and Mick hit IBSP at the Foxhole A11, started at 2:00 p.m., high tide at 5:30 p.m. Had 7 bluefish all 10 to 13 pounds on bunker chunks and one short 22-inch bass, all tagged and released!

May 6
Singles and I hit my beach. Nothing to talk about but did see a weird school of something in the gin-clear water at low tide, looked like a pack of skates, or rays, but couldn't

really determine what they were. Surf still slow. Black drum bite in Grassy Channel and D-Bay, early for this year.

May 8

Hit B'way with Amos at 5:30 p.m., left at 8:30 p.m. Got to my beach with stink-ass clams leftover from Wednesday sitting in the sun. Had two skates on a rippin' south wind current. Full moon tomorrow.

WORLD-CLASS WEAKFISH

Though the weakfish fishery in the last 14 years has been cyclical and about as reliable as the weatherman's forecast, weakfish do enter the big bay waters of Raritan and Delaware Bays in early May to spawn out, and historically, this is the time of year to land a true tide-runner weakie, one over 10 pounds, and even up to 15 pounds, with some freaks every year hitting the 16- to 17-pound mark. Most of that fishing is done from a boat, but bayshore anglers

Mickey wearing the "mad bomber" hat and hoisting a slammer spring bluefish.

up in Raritan Bay and off the banks of Barnegat Bay toss bunker chunks in hopes of bass, though one year in particular, Richie Swisstack was up off a Great Kills beach one night guiding a charter when this happened:

May 11

World-record weakfish: 19 pounds, 12 ounces, caught by Swisstack off Great Kills! Other 16- to 18-pounders there too!!

That year, 2008, those monster weakfish were inundating the big bays, and true to their silent and secretive ways, they have been ghosts in the years since. If the scientists can one day figure out where the weakfish go and what they do, it will be a monumental accomplishment, both for regulatory purposes, and to finally solve the gnawing mystery of their whereabouts and patterns that keeps anglers like me awake at night.

SECOND WEEK EXPLOSION

You can set your clocks to it. The second week of May somehow, some way, always ushers in the first round of 20-pound-plus class bass, as they relentlessly start the business of hound-dogging bunker schools. Most of the big bass are taken from the boats, but with the right luck, schools move in close to feed on the inside of the sandbars during the night hours. While shorties are pouncing all over clam baits during the sunup hours, bunker chunkers attach headlamps to their foreheads and set the clocks for ungodly hours to connect with larger linesiders.

May 12

Bugsy and I hit the surf. Bugsy had his first 21-inch striper fishing the Thunderbird with his buddy yesterday. We hit the hole about 6:45 a.m., low tide around 5:30 a.m., didn't have a hit until 8:30 a.m., no wind. I caught a 17-inch striper on clams, then Bugsy had about 4 to 5 hits that were obviously smaller size bass. Water temp 52, way behind schedule. Bugsy landed a 23-inch bass that had a severe lesion on its tail and sea lice all over it, it was pretty ranked up. We had fun until 9 when we left, the incoming tide seemed to produce best. Bluefish apparently moving in all over, hopefully get some blues when Joey and Phil come down on Monday.

Then, like a switch has flipped, bigger bass begin to shack up in the local waters. Surf days are now not all about schoolie fish; there are some fish with shoulders on the move in mid-May.

May 13

Hit my beach at 6 a.m. Sun already up, light east winds, low tide at 6 a.m. IBSP gave up a load of 20- to 25-pound class bass yesterday on poppers and clams. Popped up my beach for 45 minutes, nothing doing. Got Grumpy clams and bunker and hit Princeton Avenue, guy to my left had three bass already, guy came down on my right, cast outside the sandbar and he bailed a 29-inch bass, at 10:30 a.m. High tide 11:15 a.m. He then had two more bass. Another guy came down to my right in between us and he had two bass, so I casted out to the right on the edge of that sandbar. I then had a quality bass at around 11:30 a.m., but lost him right in the undertow, about a 32-incher. Then about 12 noon I beached a 26-incher. All on clams and fishfinder rigs. 5 to 10 knot southeast began kicking in around 11:30.

May 13

Fished the 6:30 a.m. high tide casting black Mambo and AVA 17 with Fin-S on back. Saw little ripples in the undertow directly in front of me and birds were kind of picking here and there. West winds at 20 knots or so, and finally, on one retrieve, a schoolie rat bass whacked my AVA jig, almost directly in the undertow, he put up quite a scrap for a mini model! Then I noticed some more little ripples splashing here and there in the tow, must have been some littler bass on spearing that moved in. Had one follow it right onto the beach and then it boiled back into the ocean. Funny thing here is I saw a big white balloon floating out in the surf when I walked down first light. Birds were trying to pick at it, I thought it was a wounded bass because it moved with fins and splashed a tiny bit. Eventually it righted itself and went under before it got picked apart. Then later in the eve, I walked up to the beach and found two huge, inflated blowfish sitting upside down on the high tide line! They seem to have been stranded, feeding right in the wash and getting washed up with the waves! They were spunky little critters, mean looking all right, with red eyes, and bird beaks, spiny skin and tiger lily colors, they were sweet! I threw them both back and they deflated, spurting water out, then moved enough water and swam away. Looks like blowfish have invaded, if they are feeding in that close, close enough to get beached. Muddier water from steady 20- to 30-knot west winds last three days.

There's something to be said about blowfish. Back in the 50s and 60s, the locals called 'em "chicken of the sea" for their succulent strips of meat, and bay trippers could catch well over a hundred on a boat trip in the bay. Nowadays, blowfish seem to be an anomaly, but every few years or so, they kind of come back with some force, enough to stage in the spring surf some years in May, and if you actually scaled down all your tackle and baits during the right times and tides, you could probably load up a bucket of them from the sands. If you notice your clam baits being pecked at with triangular missing cuts out of them, you've found your culprit.

_____

May 14

Singles came over at 2:30 p.m. to fish my beach. We chucked out hickory shad chunks and bunker chunks and clams in surf with high tide at 5:30 p.m. Northeast winds 10 to 15 knots. One hit then no action for a bit. Then all of a sudden, terns, gulls, and gannets working the inside bars. Cali cast out a Hopkins and immediately hooked up. 3- to 12-pound bluefish, Cali beached four, then they were gone for about 15 minutes. All three hi-lo rig rods were going off, but I kept getting to them too late. Then Cali left to go get something notarized, and soon as he left terns got real nervous real quick, started picking the surface, then all hell broke loose. I had bluefish for one hour straight from 4:20 p.m. on! They were hammering the Hopkins 1-ounce metal, on the surface, down below, anywhere, right in the wash to outside the bar. Was insane! I managed a total of 18 beached fish and missed or dropped another 20 or so, no joke. Biggest was 10 pounds, real slammers. All the rods went off again, but couldn't get to them, just let the blues break off the rigs or unhook themselves, too much pandemonium going on at once. Cali came back, managed a few for himself, some guy Don from Michigan came down, lent him a rod and reel and AVA jig, and he caught a short bass, Cali had another short bass dragging the Hopkins. The blues didn't like the AVAs nearly as much as the flat, broad-sided Hopkins. On one of my last casts on Cali's 700 Calcutta, a wind knot loop wrapped around my thumb while I casted a 3-ounce Hopkins and decapitated the

Chopper bluefish are a worthy opponent in the May suds.

tip of my thumb in a split instant, almost to the bone! Looks real interesting. Hello, blitz! Blues were coughing up 7- to 8-inch herring and spearing. BTW, a 60-pound bass was caught yesterday at the Shark River jetty on a live bunker.

May 15

Spann came down and we fished IBSP with clams at Area 21 and 22 at IBSP. Hit morning tide with hi-lo rigs for bass. So many blowfish and crabs out there they kept picking bait off. So we switched to fishfinder rigs to allow a drift, which kept our bait on a little longer. We had no luck there so we hit my beach up. At the beginning of the incoming tide around 1:30 we had our first bass hit, dragged my pole halfway to the water, because I was making a cast with a Bomber at the time! Ended up being a 24-inch slot, which we kept for Spann to take home for dinner. Matt caught a 15-inch rat bass on his line, it was funny to see how small the thing was. We packed it in around 3:30 p.m. then I had to get ready to drive to Hyannis for cod fishing.

For the last 14 years, mainly in late October or November, I hold a Fall Fish-N-Fiesta party, and it's nothing but camping and surf fishing on my beach for 72 hours straight. I'll get into more detail about that later in the book, but for a year or two, after some inquiries from the local boys, I dabbled in hosting a Spring Fling Fiesta, to try and target the lunker bass of May. The experiment was a failure in terms of fishing action, but a stunning success in terms of getting the boys to hang out away from their wives for a night.

May 15—Spring Fiesta!

What a sham! Crappy south winds and thick sandbar across Mantoloking Beach. Set up at 4:30 p.m., high tide at 1:30 p.m., extreme low water, it sucked. Coolest thing were finback whales about 200 yards offshore, breaching and blowing water 50 yards into the air with their blowholes for a good two hours! Two of them, male and female I think. Seas 4- to 5-foot, light south, brownish water. Fished all through the night, total about 20 hours, only one skate fished till 7:30 a.m. Had to pack it in, due to a bone-dry sandbar. Uncle Greg, Nite, Big Irish, Kevin, and Heckel all in attendance. We all ate elk burger, kielbasa. Had a red fox come sneak up on me and Kevin about 3:30 a.m. We fed it bunker heads and it kept edging closer to us to about 6 feet away to eat. Pretty cool. Tough fishing.

It really is all about friends and family. Even if you aren't catching jack, the camaraderie and adventures that come with surf fishing keep you fed with enough laughter and suspect stories to last a lifetime. That's the real catch.

May 16

Joey and Phil from Newark came down to fish. Hit T-Bird hole at around 10 a.m., high tide around 2:30 p.m. North wind 5 to 10 knots. Had three bass on frozen clams of 17, 23, and 26 inches, the latter of which Phil kept to bring home to eat. Phil also reeled in a whopper 13-pound bluefish that was kind of shaded yellow in the top and bottom of his body. Had a blast! The city boys loved it!

Some days, you go to wet a line and need to bring a fish home to prove to your significant other what you're actually doing when you say you are waking up at 4 a.m. to go fish, or have to stay out until 2 a.m. to cast a line. Women get suspect real quick that you may be drinkin' or doing some general foolin' around, and there's no better way to ease their minds than to take them out with you to see the surf firsthand. And maybe get them out in the suds to bait their own hooks.

May 16

Hit my beach with Shannon for her first time out in the suds. At T-Bird hole, low tide at 2 p.m. We went at 2, light south winds, 2- to 3-foot. Clammed up for two hours and had five bass from 20 to 27 inches. I let her reel in the first one though she thought she hooked it as I had it on the line when she came back from calling Kyle (her 10 year old son)! Then she cut her own clams, baited her own hooks, and made her own casts and had two fish all on her own. Nice! Quote: "Now I know why you like fishing so much, it makes you feel like a kid!"

When the first heat wave of early summer air hits the cool ocean waters, you get fogged out. Dewdrops bead on your brow and soak you to the bone without you ever going in the water. Fishing in thick fog is like being wrapped in a big, warm, soggy blanket, and it is quite solemn. You get kind of an ethereal feeling of silence and complete solitude, with potential unseen beasties creeping into your thoughts, especially at night. Maybe it's the basic instinct of fear of the unknown and diminishing of your visual senses that fog brings, even when you have your feet planted on the shore.

May 17/18

Fished my beach three days through rain, 50-mile-deep fogbanks, and sunshine. Caught nothing. Saw ospreys hunting the surface and saw bluefish splashing around, one osprey dove down and pulled out what looked like a big bunker or maybe small bluefish?

May 17

Hit Princeton again to prove the crappy conditions wrong, high tide at 2:11 p.m. Hit it at 1 at dead-high tide, had a 28-incher on a fresh clam leftover from the fiesta. Lots of water in now, north winds about 15 knots. Guy to my right had a shorty too. Black drum being caught on clams in IBSP surf.

On that note, I haven't caught a black drum from the surf yet, but the ones that are caught seem to localize around the IBSP and Brigantine area beaches in the late spring and at this time of year, I am usually too fired up for bass and blues to target them. But make no mistake, the "Boomers," some up to 90 pounds, have been beached on sloppy gobs of "surf turkey" clam baits during the month of May. I still have yet to claim one from the sands, and I plan on making that a reality in the near future, if only to feel the weight of a fish built like a Clydesdale pulling drag off into the sunrise.

Abby inspecting a freshly caught striper, nose to nose.

SHORTY CIRCUS

Looking into these next entries, it seems that May 21 to 23 always seem to offer up prime fishing opportunity for shorty bass. This is what's cool about keeping a log: you check for patterns. Whether it's the tides, time of day, winds, or water temps—there's always a way to find repeated patterns that allow you to plan out a surf strategy.

May 19

Me and Bugsy hit the T-bird with clams at 4 p.m., high tide around 6 p.m. Southeast winds 15 to 20 knots, seas 2- to 3-foot, chilly around low 60s air. Two- to three-pound bluefish were working schools of rainfish right in the undertow and I had two on an AVA 17 and Hopkins, one took off my teaser. No bass on the clams though.

May 20

Hit my beach with clams, 15 knot west wind, 3- to 4-foot, water temp about 56, just dropped 6 degrees lately, high tide 2:45 p.m. Was out at 1 p.m., had three bass of 27, 24, and 15 inches, and left at dead-high because of lack of clams. Probably would've had more bass, four skates too, and think blowfish are back as baits were getting nipped up. Spann and friend Eric came down; they hit IBSP during the day for tourney. They had 3 bass on the day, all small. We hit my hole again later around 6 p.m. but nothing doing. Bite seemed to be on the incoming in the afternoon.

SPOT BURN

A spot burn is defined as the systematic release of information to the masses through a public forum, mainly pertaining to specifically where a bite is going down and usually associated with Internet forums. It causes immediate over-crowding at a spot and is very much frowned upon.

All fishermen have their sneaky little secrets. Like the one spot they can always go to any time of day, any time of year, and pull out a bass. Or, it could be a certain ritual they perform with their baits before they fish that outcatches everybody else three-to-one. My own little secret will only get a quick mention in this book, so that my local boys won't hang me from the Lovelandtown Bridge for a spot burn. Blackfish. There, I said it. No big deal, right? From the banks, feet planted on earth. Got your attention, right? How about limits of 2- to 5-pounders in a half-hour's time? Unheard of, but true. There's a walk-up sweet spot in Jersey that always holds blackfish, and in the spring and fall months, it goes off, so long as you know when to fish it, tide-wise. I know many people are going to know where I speak of, but before the Internet boards went and got loose with sloppy mouths and bragging, this spot was quiet and productive, though now, it's a bit more pressured. The place in the immediate passages is no

Sean Reilly grabs one of many tog taken from the banks.

longer a secret, but there are other surf-based spots for blackfish, Triple Dog Secret, that I won't mention by name.

May 20

Brought Lido back down and we hit the spot for blackies. Had tons of bergall hits and small blackies, then using clams, Lido set up finally on a nice 14-inch tog. We fished from about 5:30 p.m. thru till 8:30 p.m. and the tog bite got great at sundown, defying conventional logic. Irish met us there and had three tog for himself, Lido had four, I had one. Fished incoming to high.

May 21

Hit my beach again around 1 p.m. to get incoming, fished till 2, southeast winds 20 to 25 knots, too heavy to effectively fish, so packed it in. Sunny day though. Noticed some spearing being picked at by the terns.

May 21

Lido, Irish, Jerry, and I hit IBSP at Pavillion from 6:30 a.m. on, high tide around then, hard northeast 10 to 15 knots, surf 4- to 6-foot. We held with 6 ounces at high tide and pulled in four bass to 31 inches, two of which were 24- and 26-inch slots, and Jerry tail-hooked the 31-incher. 10 bluefish to 6 or 7 pounds on fresh-cut bunker chunks. I had one early, broke the tension with a black Bomber, and had the first bass on a clam. Some black drum were caught to 30 pounds by other people for the tournament, a 27.5-pound bass won it. We had a blast, fished till 3 p.m. and had our last hits around 1 p.m. Dead-low was hard to fish with a strong littoral current from the north.

May 21

Hit the beach with clams again, it was high tide 2:30 p.m. or so. Had no luck in the rain, but it looked good. Eventually had a hit when my bait was lying on the sandbar in the breakers. I reeled it in and it was a sand fluke, which is a kind of hybrid looking thing between a fluke and a sundial. It had yellow and light brown sandy colorings on it, but had darker brown patches and spots all over it. It was interesting.

May 22

Me and Bugsy hit T-bird Beach with a nice hole. 9:55 p.m. high tide, set out at 9 p.m. Had 5 skates with fresh clams, which Abby helped me find, but Bugsy landed a 2-pound porcupine fish from the surf! Wild looking thing! West winds 15 knots, 2-foot. Where are all the big bass??? Fished till 12:30 a.m. Spectacular bright red hunter moon rose off the ocean at 11 p.m. and a rainbow at sunset with the passing showers, phenomenal time to be alive!

May 23

Hit the T-bird with Bugsy at 6:30 a.m., high tide around 8 a.m. Light west winds, 2- to 3-foot glassy. Set rods out with clams, and cast a black Bomber when I saw my rod go down, reeled in a 5-pound blue immediately. At about 8, I scored a 23-inch bass, and at 9 Bugsy's rod went down and started to drag into the surf, Bugs reeled in a 23-inch bass as well. Seems like blowfish have moved in, because my clam was nibbled by a beak-like creature extensively. Guy to the left had two nicer bass in the teardrop slot size (24 to 28 inches long, a slot limit of the previous year that was eliminated this year) and also had a hit that stripped my clam off. Stayed till 9:30 a.m.

They say bluefish will eat anything thrown at them, and they will, but every now and then, you hear hard-to-believe stories of how the blues, no matter what you cast out, won't touch a thing. This was one of those bizarre days:

May 23

Hit my beach at 2:15 p.m. after I went up to the beach and saw a 2-pound bluefish that beached itself, and a gull was sucking down another beached blue. Then in the surf saw blues tailing like permit! Right in the undertow and up on the thin wash, no bait around, they were just kinda fooling around in and out with the waves. Grabbed my little rod and reel and went back. Saw some bunker getting played and toyed with on the surface, a lone bunker and the big gator blues of 12 to 15 pounds were just toying with it like a cat does with a mouse! Then saw gators moving in and out at my feet with the south winds 15 to 20 knots, 2- to 3-foot. Water around 55 degrees. Couldn't believe it, the blues had lockjaw and would nip at the plugs and not hit them even with super slow retrieve, even with shads that just hung on the ends of the tails, not ripping them off, just mouthing them! What a weird experience! Finally hooked into three 10- to 15-pound blues that hit the shad, and Mambo plug, but even they fought lackadaisical and only made runs near the end of the fight. Saw some herring move in with the waves too, and possibly even a weakfish. I think I might've had a weakie on as I reeled in one for half the time then lost it on a shad, tail intact. What a weird day of experience!

MEMORIAL DAY MADNESS

Memorial Day weekend is, bar none, always nuts. Between tourist traffic jams, spilled-over garbage cans from the kooks, hootin' and hollerin' into the wee hours of night, and all sorts of Bennies-Gone-Wild type of action, it's no wonder bass fishing is an endeavor regulated only to midnight and predawn hours. But it's a funny thing. The exact moment the work bell rings on Friday afternoon of Memorial Day weekend, bluefish and bass blitzes seem to cooperate and trigger on cue, sparking immediate insanity all up and down the coast. The dam breaks, and the floodgates can't handle the massive migration of tourists to the waters. It's usually when I lock the doors for the weekend, only to come out at night to make a few casts and possibly see some naked chicks running around skinny-dipping in the water. Actually, it's not that bad. At all.

May 25

Day after Memorial Day Massacre! Absolutely bonkers last four days, new moon on 24th, hundreds of 20- to 50-pound class bass hitting poppers and bunker off IBSP, "Best ever" apparently is the word going on! Hit it with Mickey at 8 p.m. for dead-high tide, fished till 12:30 a.m. without a bite, one skate. Bass stopped biting early this afternoon. Seas 2- to 3-foot, hit A13 then A7 IBSP, unbelievable we missed it today, it just shut down in 12 hours' time, but the cows are all over the place.

James Amore knuckling down on an alligator bluefish.

May 26

Hit Mantoloking hole with bunker chunks, high tide midnight. Guy there already had 5 blues of 7 to 12 pounds, I landed 3 blues to 8 pounds, got bit off by more. Fished till 2 a.m., no bass, but lots of blues. South winds 15 knots.

May 27

Hit Mantoloking again, this time at 7:30 p.m., saw Spiro there, set up and had a 7-pound blue right away, then three more hits. Lightning storm came in, had to pack up at 8 p.m. Bugsy met me at my house, we went to Crab's Claw to wait it out, set up at 10:30 p.m. again. Bugsy had a short 7-pound bass that had a Sabiki rig fly in its mouth. No blues tonight, though did see a bright red hunter moon come up on the horizon at about 1 a.m., fished till 2:30 a.m. South winds 15 knots.

Dad does battle with a squawking sea robin in Bay Head.

May 28

Lido came down, met him on my beach. He had about 8 blues already to 13 pounds on bunker chunks, at T-Bird we moved in front of my path. First toss out with clam in the cut he had a 7-pound bass, then we pulled on about 5 more bluefish, had 12 skates. High tide 2 a.m. but packed it in around 1:15 a.m. Southwest winds 10 to 15 knots.

May 29

Hit Mantoloking. Been blowing northeast last three days, seas 3- to 5-foot, gray and full of seaweed, garbage bags, and all crazy twigs and stuff from east blow, including a dead baby dolphin and some tropical rhinoceros beetle! Cast out bunker chunks on fishfinder rigs, wouldn't hold, so switched to a three-way rig with chunks, couldn't keep line in water for over two minutes before it was up on beach clotheslined with weed. Then one cast into the cut, saw rod tip twitch a few times, reeled up heavy weed on the line but felt some resistance, it surfaced out in the cut and reeled it in on the surface– bass 34 inches and fat! 13 or so pounds tagged it and had two hot surfer girls come over to check it out, had them hold it up for a pic, 12 noon.

Then, as usual for Memorial Day, we got drunk. That seems to be a recurring happening when night fishing, now that I ponder it.

Night

Got smashed with Lin, Popp, and Heckel on my beach. Midnight cast out bunker chunks, had two 3-pound bluefish, Heckel almost got taken out with the high tide he was so drunk and stumbling!

May 30

In the morning, Mikey Tornado and I cast out some fresh bunker chunks on my beach with fishfinder rigs, and we kept getting hits every ten minutes or so. The bites would rip off the chunk right below the hook. Must be smaller bluefish in the 3- to 4-pound range that have been present lately. Smaller blues around, but a lot of them. We packed it in around 12 noon and went surfing for a bit.

May 30

High tide 11:15 p.m. Hit Princeton with Bugsy with fresh bunker and clams for the big bass again, nothing too large yet, 10 to 20-plus being taken, but big girls should be coming soon. New moon tides, went up at 9:30 p.m., left at 1 a.m., and only had one hit. There were hundreds of spider crabs out there picking away at the baits as soon as they hit the water. New moon passed three days ago, water temp around 60, light east winds. Fog rolled in and it was thick as cement.

May 31

Fished Mantoloking with Cali with clams and fresh hickory shad for bass. High tide 5:30 a.m., light NE wind. Got to Princeton Ave at 5 and Cali met me there a bit later. Set up near Albertson. Some bunker flipping or shad? In the sloughs. Had one bass fooling with a hickory shad chunk, took it for a second and dropped it, and the Meat Stick had a nice hit on the clam, most likely a 28- to 33-inch fish. Cali had a tap on his shad chunk, but no dice. Big bass starting to move through IBSP, a bunch of 30-plus bass taken there over the weekend.

May 31

Me and Bugsy fished Princeton, high at 3:30 a.m., got there around 5:15 a.m. with turquoise water and 1- to 2-foot seas, light west wind. Cast out right at bottom of the ramp and saw fish breaking surface outside sandbar. Cast clams out and my rod went down, Bugs grabbed it and reeled in something that kept getting slack, then heavy, then slack. Eventually in the undertow a bluefish of 6 pounds surfaced and I grabbed it. It wasn't hooked. It had a hi-lo circle rig with bunker chunks still hooked into its mouth with a 4-ounce pyramid sinker and a bunch of braided line, another hi-lo rig snagged into that, and our rig in the mess with our 4-ounce weight! The thing was dragging two rigs around with weight and chunks until it ran into our lines and we saved it! I cast a black Bomber and hooked into two mating horseshoe crabs that are coming up every-

Bugsy's 29-pound clam-caught surf bass, his first trophy.

where now for the mating season, thought I had the fabled 50-pounder . . . Bluefish and bass were swirling and working what may be sand eels and big bunker schools. Bugs' rod had a 16-inch bass attack his clam. Big bass starting to get caught off our coast now, a 58-pounder and 51-pounder taken off Asbury this weekend and D-Bay gave up 57-, 54-, and 45-pounders.

And that ushers in June. The time of world-class bassing.

4 June

THE MONTH OF MONSTERS

Full moons, midnight runs, fresh bunker, and sultry, sweaty nights set the stage for fantastical tales from the June surf. Backyard dogfish trippin', world-class surf stripers, night prowlers, and untold jagged-toothed monsters in the midnight sea—they all entrench themselves into June's surfline. Morning winds become predictable with the start of the summertime; lazy offshore westerlies that gently lay down the surf and bring clear, clean water to the shores, while past 2 p.m., the south blow kicks in and takes over for the rest of the day. Moon jellyfish bloom, like translucent Egg McMuffins, jamming up the undertow on low tides. Ospreys begin to leave their nests and hunt the nearshore waters, calling out diminutive *peep-peep-peep* sounds as they ride the updrafting breezes, hovering above an unwary bunker that has forgotten its instinct and falls victim to gripping talons.

The air is warmer now, with 65-degree nights and 85-degree days, and the sweet, succulent smells of the Atlantic seem to stick to the breezes wafting from the surf. The scent of bunker schools on an easterly blow divulges when they are close to the beach. When that telltale smell wafts on the breeze, it brings the promise of a good day's fishing ahead. The last remaining pig stripers in the area are on a nocturnal schedule now, and this is your best chance of the year to go trophy hunting and beat your personal best surf striper. This is the time to break the 20-, 30-, 40- or even 50-pound mark from the sands.

And as night shift surf chunkers get spooled or snapped off on the full and new moon tides, more menacing creatures begin to fill in—brown, dusky, and thresher sharks that push the 60- to 80-pound and 500-pound marks. The thrill alone of potentially landing surf sharks keeps me in a state of insomnia all through June, but I know that only the full and new moon high tides bring in sufficient water for the predators to move in and feed.

Kyle O'Rourke and I grab onto a toothy night prowler.

The human element really shows on the beach now. Families begin to fill up the sands with multicolored umbrellas and cargos full of coolers, with tiny toddlers trailing behind. Before sunrise, the bulldozing surf rake machines drone on, breaking the morning silence as they comb the beaches to a flat, featureless oasis, devoid of any footprints. Day-trippers set up sand spikes with a clam bait and the rod gets left out for three hours, without a second check.

On low tide and mid tide hours, the surf is littered with early morning treats in the shape of flat, spotted, wonder-fluke. It's simple pickin's to catch them if you know how. Strange-looking sea robins with their brownish-reddish fan wings glide in and out with the tides. My bed has noticeably more sand in the sheets now, as waders are unnecessary for surf outings, just a plain pair of boardshorts with big pockets, pliers, some sunscreen, and a 5-gallon bucket of rigs and lures does the trick. You know what? June just rules. Summer is really here.

June 1

Hit Princeton again. Overcast. Hard northeast about 15 knots, and 3- to 4-foot, salad (kelp) all over the place. 5 ounces held. Got there at 5 a.m., high at 6:30 a.m., water a bit dirty. Had fresh clams and fresh bunker chunks from Betty and Nick's. At 5:45, had a nice hit on the 9-foot Loomis, now spooled with 50-pound PowerPro and 25-pound leader, immediately grabbed the rod and set, fought a bass, came up to the surface, then dogged me south on the beach for about 40 yards, running with the current. Got him in on one of the waves, a 33-inch bass, nice form! Other than that, no real hits, some maybes, a guy right at bottom of Princeton had two bass, a slot and a 28-incher. Used bunker heads for bait, I know these bass will be in again like last year and I am ready for them. Cali's got the newly dubbed frog suit! Silly-looking green Orvis waders . . . And we saw what looked like a pirate's chest floating in the turbulent waters, turned out to be a hunk of wood, but nonetheless carried a warning curse, I'm sure! Oh, two lucky mallard ducks stood next to us and kept us company, weathering out the winds and sea spray.

Sometimes, in the spring and early summer, those northeast winds howl at night, battering the windows with spraying sheets of rain, like they have something personal against you. On those nights, I feel alone. The same feelings of aloneness take over when roaring blizzards roll through in the dead of winter, shutting all roadways and businesses down as there is no plow seen on the barrier island for three days straight. Its every man for himself, and all the locals always pool together to help dig each other out as we wait for the town to come save us with a plow, or leave us to our own devices. Living in a virtual ghost beach town for 9 months of the year, it's always nice to have a neighbor.

My neighbor was Frankie. When I first moved down to Normandy Beach, Frankie was there. He was about 65 then, and was a wild ladies' man, taking Viagra every day. He had no natural teeth left, with partial dentures giving up a Cheshire Cat smile. Frankie had operated various bars in the Sinatra Days of Hoboken. He was a big-time drinker who hit the early-bird American Legion happy hour from 6 a.m. to 2 p.m. every day. He did jail time with Vinnie "The Chin" Gigante, played the lottery and horses with all his welfare money, smoked two packs of Lucky Strikes a day, lied about his age to serve in the Korean War, and could tell you a dirty joke that would make you have to take a shower when you got home.

Frankie was my neighbor, my only one. He was family, my long-lost granddad of sorts. And I loved him. Without going into the many beauties of Frankie, I'll just tell you that he loved to fish, though his arthritic legs wouldn't let him get to the beach anymore, only to hobble to the car to drive to the bar. But Frankie and I were always there for each other, during blizzards, hurricanes, nor'easters, and the brightest, sunniest days of life, to just hang out, crack a beer, and have some laughs.

Anyway, Frankie and I were family for 14 years, and the day the cancer closed its final grip on him was a rough one, but he went down in style, as he lay in the hospital bed the day before he died, with a fifth of Cutty Sark in one hand and lottery tickets in the other, and his loving family by his side. He had a smile on his face in the final moments of his life, and he went out on his own terms. I only say all this to tell who Frankie is in the next journal entry, to embellish the one-word mention of his name. The ol' bastard wouldn't have let me live it down if I didn't introduce him.

June 1

Couldn't sleep all night, found out my good friend Frankie died last night, I know he loves me. Woke up at 4 a.m., left Shannon's and hit my beach at 5:30 a.m. Bunker schools all over the place. High tide at 2:30. Fleet was off Lavallette, I snagged a big bunker and livelined it but it got off, tried 3-oz poppers, no hits. Walked down to 2nd Avenue and saw a thresher shark roostertail in a small, compact bunker school, then saw four or five big bass busting on the school up and down in ten seconds, then saw something wild inside the breakers when a huge V-wake was traveling parallel to the beach, either a big bass or small thresher! Water temp about 59 degrees, flat water with 2- to 3-foot surf. Waded out on the sandbars to cast out to the bunker schools, but no takers today.

June 2

Woke up at 4:30 a.m. and hit Princeton with the fresh bunker again. Dead-low at 7:30 a.m., high at 1:30 p.m. No hits, runs, or errors, some porpoises moving through, fished till about 6:45 a.m. Some green lettuce on the lines, but other than that, was kind of silent. The beaches at Princeton are shallow now from the storms over the winter and spring, and have yet to regain the depth they are famous for. Fog rolled in around 6. Southwest winds 5 knots.

June 7

Northeast blow moving through. Hit Princeton at roughly 6:45 a.m. with clams, high tide was at 1:30 p.m. so I hit the end of the outgoing. Had one nice hit which missed, and a sand shark. Fished until 8:30 a.m. soaking wet, and held with 4 ounces. Noticed that when casting fishfinder rigs, it's not a good idea to use them when the wind is east; no matter what weight you use, the bait will get caught in the wind and tangle up the rig as the sinker flies out. The only way to combat it is to reel in the bait once it is cast in hopes the line passes through and actually reels the bait out where the sinker is.

June 4, 5, 9, 11

Hit Mantoloking Beach, Downer, Princeton, my beach with bunker chunks both morning and night shifts, with no success but skates, no bass but bunker schools thick outside. Guys livelining up 25- to 40-pounders, but not close enough inside yet. This morning was a rough one, as I had some pretty bad coffee from WaWa and had nowhere to go, if you know what I mean. Yeah, we've all been there.

MONSTER BASH

From 2006 to 2010, during the second and third weeks of June, some mind-blowing occurrences were going on in our waters, the likes of which had never been seen in the surf before in Jersey. Rods were ripped out of their spikes, literally launched like they were shot from a cannon, into the surf, never to be seen again. I found out about it early one morning while I was chunking for bass, and when I realized what the culprits were, well, my mind-set changed and I evolved. I saw that my lines were being chopped off, and 20 yards of braided line were being chafed like sandpaper rubbed against them, hard and rough. Bunker schools were being pinned into the beach, and like some cheap horror movie, wildly flailing roostertailed whitewater streaks were slashing through the schools. It was only when I could get a clear, solid look at a tail only 50 yards off the beach that I knew decisively what was terrorizing surf anglers: thresher sharks! You want to talk about adrenaline pumping through your veins when you see your rod bend like it shouldn't be! Oh man! And to top it off, big, menacing brown sharks, and dusky and spinner sharks all joined the shark circus, not to mention the cattle line of cow bass of 30 to 50 pounds every single night. What a time!

Monster sharks put a hurtin' on the rods and reels.

June 8

Let's not even bulls%$@ here. A surfer got attacked by a shark and got 50 stitches in his leg today. The only species that are around in the 57- to 61-degree temps are, let's see, browns, duskies, and great whites. The media is portraying a great white—the first NJ attack in 30 years. New Moon was on the 6th. Now, high tide 9:30 p.m., light south winds, clear skies, 90 degrees daytime today, bunker schools along the beachfront. I went after the great white. Went to Crab's Claw to get a drink on, at about 6 p.m., left at 7:30 p.m. Couldn't take the suspense anymore, flew down to Betty and Nick's and bought fresh bunker and 105-pound cable wire with size 6/0 treble hooks. Set up at Princeton at 9:30 p.m., and Cali joined me. Before we even got the second rod out, first rod went down and Cali reeled in a 4-foot sand shark. That was followed by three others of huge caliber on chunks and a hi-lo rig. At about 10:00 p.m. the other rod, rigged with a treble haywire twist and 4 feet of cable fishfinder slide and a bunker head, went off hard. I grabbed it and it went to the horizon peeling off drag with 14-pound test on. I fought the beast into the suds, Cali manned the light and gaff, and I beached and released a 44-inch 32- or 33-pound bass! We also missed a few hits from smaller bass. But here's the scoop, Cali left at about 11, and my rod with the wire went down hard again. I grabbed the rod and set back to absolutely no weight at all, upon reeling in, no rig, weight, or anything left, just a 5-foot section of my running line all chafed up. Now mind you, I had a 4-foot cable leader on; what could have chafed the line that far back and gotten away???? Most likely a small thresher? or great white! Immediately re-rigged and cast out again within two minutes, and the same exact thing happened. I was astounded and out of barrel swivel. That rig was on a fishfinder rig and a bunker head. Methinks the bunker heads on fishfinder rigs specifically target big bass, period. The fishfinder makes the bunker head look alive as it rolls in the surf, whereas a hi-lo stays put. No, I'm not going out tomorrow night, am I?

June 9

Me and Au hit up Princeton Ave again at 5:00 a.m. to chuck clams for bass. We set up four rods. I got whacked at about 5:45 a.m. by a massive bass that bent the 9-footer— painful, right at the butt. I set back and fought the fish for about two minutes, saw it surface and boil in the 3-foot east 10-knot seas in the fog, then no weight anymore, the hook must have pulled. Broken dreams. It was a single bottom rig. It must have been a 30-plus-pound fish. Austin then nabbed three bass to 26 inches, and we caught three bluefish to boot. Au had a bluefish on that snapped his 60-pound Fluoro leader in two, it had to be a 15-plus-pound gator. Au used bunker fillets and heads for the blues, in hopes for a big bass, they were marinated in bunker oil. I had another solid hit on the fishfinder rig, but by the time I set back on the rod, he was gone. Seemed like another 15- to 25-pound class fish. Hitting it tomorrow for that big boy. Water a bit muddy still from the east wind, lots of trash in the water, bags, etc.

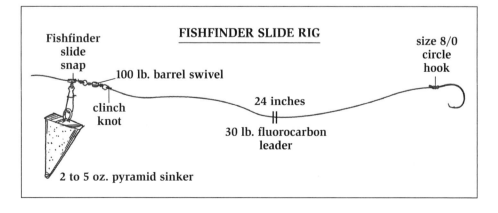

FISHFINDER SLIDE RIG

Fishfinder slide snap

size 8/0 circle hook

100 lb. barrel swivel

clinch knot

24 inches

30 lb. fluorocarbon leader

2 to 5 oz. pyramid sinker

A well-earned June nightshift pig, taken on a full moon high on a bunker head.

June 10

I haven't slept in 25 hours. I have bass fever. I tried to sleep around 11 p.m. so I could wake up at 4 a.m. and go fish Princeton Ave. Tried. Couldn't sleep. Got out of bed at 1:30 a.m., started tying rigs, left the house at 2:15 a.m. Set up on Princeton at 2:30 a.m. with Cyalume sticks on the rods. No hits until just before sunrise at about 5. High tide 4:37 a.m., west winds 10 knots. Only had a dozen clams thru the night, and realized I was probably casting them off. Soft, stinky clams. After 5 a.m., I had a 30-inch bass, then a bluefish, then a skate, then a dogfish, then a humongous horseshoe crab, then a striper about 23 inches with each of its sides rubbed off from the middle back to the tail, his red flesh was actually exposed near the tail, then one huge-ass dogfish about 3 feet in length. About 6 other guys came down after 5:30 a.m. The guy who fished just to the left of the walkway nailed a 25-pound bass right as I ran out of bait. I can't sleep. I wanted to hit my beach but Ernie's not open, Brackman's not open, it's 6:15 in the morning and I need clams. I can't try to sleep, I'm not tired. I want a cow.

Yeah, bass fever can be downright debilitating.

June 7, 9, 10

Fished with Cali and once with Bugsy surfstyle, didn't get much but a bluefish runoff and a skate, but the fleet of boats was literally 50 yards off the beach at the low tide in the bunkers, 28 boats snagging and livelining bunker to pull up 40-pound bass. Gene Quigley boated a 58½-pound bass right in front of us, 200 yards from the surf. No matter what we did, we couldn't cast far enough out, though we cast about 20 yards from the boats. Bunker heads and clams. Oh, by the way. There are thresher sharks in the surf. Frank from Betty and Nick's tied up to one, others are getting spooled daily, and a 40-pound bass came up bitten in half, a half mile off Manasquan. People are seeing tails rip through the bunker schools and crashing and thrashing them. Frank said the one he had hooked up to was 8 feet long and it broke his line—60-pound braid. I want to target these from the surf.

June 10

Full moon on the 7th. Morning hit Albertson in a hole and had a monster bass whack my Big Ed popper clean out of the water 6 feet! Came back three other times and tail whacked it into the air 6 feet each time, missed the hit! Had another swirl on it, fished from noon to about 2. Then came back . . .

Albertson Avenue 10 p.m. to 12:30 a.m., one 3-pound blue, some dogfish, two knockdowns, then the beast bass of my life! Light east winds. 2- to 3-foot high tide at 10, I missed two major knockdowns with the j-hooks and fishfinder rigs, so set out with a three-way rig and a leftover 5/0 circle hook, bunker chunks, weren't touching heads. She didn't know she was hooked! Made seven long runs with braided line, battled her into the undertow, grabbed her 45 inches 23 inch girth! Oh my god! If fat she would've easily been a 40-plus! I had to keep her because the circle hook and braided line pressure ripped a hole in her lower jaw, said my prayers and had dogfish move in on the dropping tide. Went to Reel Life to weigh her; she went 28 pounds on that scale, empty stomach, totally spawned out. Sand fleas, not mole crabs all over the beach. As soon as moon broke from the overcast clouds, got all the bites.

Another monster cow bass hooked in Mantoloking on a full-moon summer high tide.

HICKORY SHAD INTERLUDE

Bassing is incredible during June, but there are some magical little wonders in the form of hickory shad, a.k.a. Jersey Tarpon, and cocktail 1- to 2-pound blues that are fun as all heck to tangle with using light tackle or a fly rod from the banks of the Manasquan River. Hickory shad make for a fun time, as they vault out of the water, shaking their heads like little tarpon, and will run fast on you, changing directions with every turn. They are a blast! Scrappy little battlers. Check it out.

June 10—Evening

Hit the canal, hospital side, down the bulkhead to catch hickory shad for strip baits for the JCAA fluke tourney Saturday. Was unbelievable, just at sunset around 8:10 p.m. Splashes everywhere, then hundreds and thousands of hickory shad exploding the water chasing little spearing. I cast a 007 with a yellow-and-white teaser and had hits or hooked fish on every cast. Kept a dozen with some small blues and dropped another 3 dozen. These shad are incredible fighters! They vault out of the water at the last moment opening their mouths trying to ambush and Pearl Harbor the teaser from below, four or five at a time would do it! I didn't expect to catch so many shad so I put seven shad in my canyon bag, looked around and shoved another 6 with a bluefish down my pants, tails hanging out all around my bathing suit. What a sight! flopping around in my pants! Then I felt a mouth slide down onto my Jimmy and freaked out, shaking myself silly in case it was the bluefish! What a night. Got plenty of strip baits for tomorrow's fluking.

BACK TO BASSIN'

The following entries detail some fine surf-bassing episodes. I may never see the size of bass that I did from the surf with such consistency in the Junes from 2005 to 2010 again, but I hope it comes around. I'll let these journal entries speak for themselves.

June 11

The year of the big sticks. The red zone. I can't believe it. I fished Princeton this morn, light east wind, high at 5:37 a.m. Had two sand sharks then moved to Albertson. Cast out, incredible hit again, peeled line and drag, then snapped my 20-pound line above the barrel. I can't believe it. Had another wallop on the Meat Stick, but got to it and it was gone. Sea robins started to move in. This is too much to have to be at Gullotta's wedding the next four days. Huge bass are here. I must've dropped another 30-pound-plus fish. You need at least 30-pound fluorocarbon leader, 8/0 Gamakatsu hooks, and at least 20–25-pound line spooled. At the last cast, ready to pack in, got hit, reeled in, my Daiwa reel busted its gears, and a 23-inch striper came up. It was the same exact striper I caught yesterday with the abrasions on each side! He must've moved down to the next hole from Princeton to Albertson. Food for thought. I can't believe I can't fish the next four days. These bass are the generation of brutes that come around every 10 years or so. You need serious tackle, reels greased, new line—everything—to land one.

June 11

Cast yellow wooden popper on my beach with reports of cow bass around still, had one 15-pound class blue tarpon bite on it and jump and shake wildly until he shook me off in undertow. Seas 2- to 3-foot, east winds, new moon tide tomorrow.

June 12

Awesome! Hit Princeton Avenue at 9:30 a.m., guy already had a 48-pounder on beach, another guy had a 45-pounder. Followed bunker schools all the way up to Lyman Avenue through rain, sun, clouds, east winds 5 knots, seas 3- to 4-foot greenish-blue beauty water. Bunker in close enough to snag, sometimes snagged and dropped, but no takers, popped, still no takers, fished to 1 p.m., then took clothes off for a swim with sun out and 80 degrees now. Saw bunker flipping, grabbed rod and snagged one, then it busted wide open! Bass were pushing bunker right outside the breakers, I got picked up and it ran like a wild boar! Set on her battled for 15 minutes, had to run down to undertow to grab the jaw, 44 inches with a 27-inch girth, which means a calculation of 40.095 pounds! The Forty Club! Oh man, released her beautifully back into the surf, then bad clouds, wind shift came in and I left to my beach where bunker schools flipping but snagged one to no avail. What an awesome day, worn out and spent!

June 12

Surf with Dad and Uncle Greg, came down after they hit the boating course at IBSP. Set up on high tide 6:30 p.m. with fresh bunker chunks and clams on Princeton. Had two whacks right off the bat but no hookups, then Dad had a big hit and reeled in a 15-pound bluefish on a chunk! Then rod went over again right when I casted and dad reeled in a 35-inch striper! We also had a sea robin and had tons of fun on the beach, fished till about 8:30 p.m., when a storm was coming in. Uncle Greg cooked up the fish with all the extra stuff like barbeque sauce, Captain Crunch, and mayonnaise I had in my fridge and we ate like kings! UG slept over.

Uncle Greg is the flat-out, hands-down, finest wildlife chef ever to grace the Planet Earth. He's Jack Kerouac and Top Chef combined, and has created culinary masterpieces as a head chef in NYC, Alaska, and Colorado, living out of dumpsters and cooking for celebrities and politicians. He made me deer heart on an open flame when I was 10 years old. Give him a worn-out shoe and pepper, and he'll make it tasty. He's our resident surf chef when the boys get together.

The bass just keep on coming.

June 13

Shanks came down, and on the way to UB's for happy hour, we saw Bugsy walking down the path at about 3:30 p.m. smiling large and holding a 27-pound striper he caught off T-Bird on clams. He was jumpin' for joy! We weighed it in at Ernie's, and then cruised around in my Jeep to show it off along the shoulder of the highway. Gotta brag a little bit. Bugsy went back and had another bass of 24 inches and a bunch of bluefish with his friend. We hit up late night about 10 p.m. to go for big bass, using bunker chunks and clams. Bunker was about 4 days old, too old methinks, because it was rotted enough to only catch three skates and a dogfish.

Fresh bunker is a must if you are serious about targeting bass. If it's a two- to three-day-old specimen, with that slimy, brown kind of mucus on it, it just ain't gonna bring in the big bass. Freshly caught bunker placed on ice, kept firm and fresh, will always be your huckleberry to score a striper. Don't cheat yourself; if you think you need fresher bunker, go get it!

June 13

Hit my beach at 9:30 p.m. with Heckel with some frozen fresh bunks from a week ago and put Bioedge potion on it for bunker smell. Landed small 2-pound bluefish and big smooth dogfish 10 pounds or so, had a big bass knockdown, and a few skates. Fished till 12 midnight, seas 3- to 4-foot, east winds, new moon tides, high at 8:30 p.m. First real words of some thresher sharks around. Oh, and whales around blowing spouts last three weeks, saw two of them only 200 yards off my beach two days ago. Also was a dead seal on Mantoloking three weeks ago and dead pygmy sperm whale.

Cool, more whales, and there are always the local beach red foxes that inhabit the central Jersey beaches. IBSP is notorious for those ragged-looking sand foxes, and the Barnegat Barrier Island also has its fair share, maybe about six of them prowling the night hour beachfronts, but they only come out at night. Sometimes during the daytime, when you set out to go sea glass–hunting or beachcombing, you can see the fox tracks in the dunes. They're the stealthy red ghosts of the barrier island.

June 14

Albertson Ave. High tide 9:30 p.m., seas 3-foot, southeast 5 knots, 3% of new moon sliver in sky, clear and starry since it's so dark out. Fished 8:30 p.m. to 11:30 p.m. All dogfish tonight, some big ones though to about 10 pounds, also had a small dog and a monster nuclear-sized spider crab hanging on my bait at same time, ugly! Also, sand fleas or lice? Weird white maggoty bugs eating up bunker from the inside out, nasty-looking little things in the water. Highlight was a small, beady-eyed little fox the size of a cat, who kept stealing my bunkers behind my back when I went to the undertow cast!

I made a step forward to the wash, he made a step forward to the bait. I made a step back to the bait, he made a step back to the dunes. He claimed 3.5 whole bunkers that I know of, maybe more chunks! I nicknamed him Stealy. Steady bunker diets and salt air leave the beach foxes light bleached in color and mangy-looking, but they are just salty. Probably had that shiny, beautiful coat with a continuous diet of fish and stolen bunker from other night bass anglers, including me.

June 14

Hit Albertson at 8 p.m., high tide around 12:45 a.m., with six bunkers I snagged on Friday. Circle hook rigs and 3 to 4 ounces to hold in 2- to 3-foot east seas, kinda foggy. Water temp 64 degrees, warm for now, had one 3-pound blue hit right at 8:09 then silent for a bit, had two more blues, small 2 to 4 pounds, a couple of skates and dogfish bites, meaning the waters are warm for now. Taped Berkley Gulp glow-in-the-dark grubs to my rod tips to see in the darkness as I ran out of light sticks, didn't work too well! Mickey hit boat in Manasquan inlet at 1 p.m. They nailed monsters, about twenty 30- to 45-pound bass till 5 p.m. Bass moving north with warming water temps.

June 16

Insane year on bass fishing from Manasquan north, bass of 30 to 45 pounds every single day, joke fishing. Automatic from the boats. Anyway, full moon in two days, hit my beach 10 p.m., high tide 7 p.m., cast out frozen bunker I had. Immediately started getting hits with sand sharks and skates. Caught about 12 small, smooth dogfish and dropped a big one on a bunker head, it pulled and I fought it, it was wiggling hard on the line but don't think the hook was all in its mouth, big whatever it was! Ran out of bait 12 midnight, ran to JCBT to pick up a box of bunker and went back fished till 2 a.m., same action on dogs, think the brown sharks and big dogs will be here on the full moon in two days. Threshers reported in bunker schools.

Before 2006, there weren't the insane bass reports as we've had up until 2012 and counting. There was not much else going on in the June suds, besides some fluke and dogfish, like this.

June 16

Hit my surf from 7:15 p.m. to 8:15 p.m., southeast 15 knots, 2-foot, water grayish. Low tide 6 p.m. Went fluking with bucktail and teaser with white grub. Had one 15-inch fluke, very sandy brown, blended in perfect with sand at my feet and the darker waters.

June 17

Bunker chunked my beach 9 p.m. to 11 p.m., had 3 break-offs that were definitely brown sharky. Lot of dogfish.

And once again, those elusive weakfish show up when you least expect it. Though this next entry comes from the early years, around 1998.

June 19

Hit the hospital side of the canal at evening time to cast for weakfish. Like an idiot I packed all my bucktails and forgot to bring them. Had one chart/white bucktail I tied and a fins fish to cast around. First cast had a weakie on that shook its head in three seconds and got off. I had two more hits exactly the same, had to be weakfish. Hickory shad have been around the past few days here, but I lost my bucktail on a rather large something right near the bulkhead and then I was all out of ammo. The guy next to me had a few bluefish.

June 19

Fished Thunderbird, with northeast blow, heavy drift, too much salad in the water. They say this has been the best big bass season ever. Ever. Even compared to the old days. Schools of 30-, 40-, and 50-pound bass are patrolling from Shrewsbury to Island Beach, gobbling down bunker and clams and just menacing everything thrown at them. Stores are weighing in like 20 bass a day from 20 to 50 pounds.

June 21

Went to Princeton Ave. with one clam stick and one bunker stick. Got there 4:45 a.m. before sunrise and full parking lot. Walked south of stairs and set up. Sent out two rigs with 5-ounce pyramid sinkers, one on a fishfinder, one on a hi-lo rig. Brought my St. Croix to chuck black Bombers in the wash. Had a hit and started to reel in, head was thrashing left and right, I fought it like I was taking in a bass, but it didn't quite feel like a bass, got it to the surf line and it spit the hook. It was about a 6- to 7-pound weakfish. Casted another 20 minutes and hooked into another with the same characteristics. Same result, ripped through the papermouth, I must fight them more gingerly. Clam rod went off around 6:20 a.m., beginning of outgoing tide, and reeled in and saw a 12- to 15-pound bass surfacing on the way in. Fought him fair and square and released him. Left the beach at about 8:00 a.m. and went home for some shuteye.

Ah, man, this next one was a good day. Made me feel truly alive . . . and this was 2001, before the kayak craze hit, though if I did have a kayak, I'd have been out there every day for those bass!

June 23

You want a fish story? Finally beautiful sunny day temps at 85 degrees. High tide 3:30 p.m., flat winds, seas 1-foot to maybe 2, glassy. I went to the beach at 10:30 a.m. to surf longboard and saw a bunch of splashes about 200 yards offshore. Two boats pulled up to snag what was a huge bunker school. I watched them snag and catch fish for about two hours, pulling 40-pound class bass over the gunnel. I had enough. I walked to Ernie's, grabbed two bunker snags, a 2-foot Fluoro 30-pound leader, grabbed the old Lamiglas, and put the crappy Ryobi reel whose gears were shaky on the rod. One pocket had a knife and a pair of pliers. I went up to the beach and saw the bunker now moved almost directly in front of the T-Bird about 150 yards off. I grabbed the longboard. I leashed the rod off to it and paddled out to where they were. It was clumsy but I paddled submerging the reel and rod, but who cares! I finally sat up on my board, and cast out to snag two bunker right away, but they got off. Then it happened. I snagged a bunker, dropped it back, then felt a heavier weight on. It started to pull. Hard. My Lami bent and loaded and I was on for a ride! The bass I hooked into was pulling me out to the deep, about 200 or more yards off! My drag was set light. I started to reel, and it worked for about two minutes, until the gears shot and the reel crumbled in my hands. I decided to beat this beast, I would paddle to shore, I began paddling, rod in left hand and kept tension on the fish. As soon as I was gaining ground, she felt the tug, my rod bent backwards and took off for the Canyon, turning me 180 degrees and spinning me around! I kept the drag loose, and continued to paddle. Finally I got in far enough so I could stand on the high tide. I finally could touch ground, and ditched my board. I kept tension all the way walking to the shore. Once onshore, I realized I couldn't reel in cause the reel was busted. I gave the rod to a kid to hold and hand-over-hand, handlined the bass another 80 yards through the surf into the wash! She careened through a wave and I saw her ride it using the leverage. I played the line with hand drag, and finally she came into the suds. A wave brought her up the beach for a second, I ran down, grabbed her and hugged her tight, picked her up and carried her onto shore! She weighed 28 pounds and was 41 inches long! Everybody was clapping and cheering! She might have weighed more, it took me a good half hour to get her to Ernie's. Everyone who passed me on the beach congratulated me, and even into sunset when I went to Bayside Park, people were saying, "hey, there's the guy who caught the fish!" When I did the walk of fame down to Ernie's, cars were stopping to check her out, and the electricity of this beautiful girl was felt all around the town, and then some. There is something truly ethereal in achieving such a lofty goal. It makes the time spent alive, well, feeling alive. I gave her fillets out to five families, all my neighbors, and she brought a smile to people she had never met. What a day, what a life. Thank you!

That was one of those glorious fishing days that truly defies description.

June 23—Evening

Bugsy and Rob wanted to go fish the beach, lent them the gear and my clams. They were out jackassing around, when I walked over to Bugsy's rod and just looked at it. Then I put my hand on the rod and it bent over hard and jerked roughly. With one hand I picked up the rod out of the spike and said, "Bugsy, you're on, man—here!" He reeled in a 31-inch striper and released it, it was cool to see him catch something and get all excited! The guys said I was good luck, was able to touch a rod to make it get hit, and wondered why everybody wants to fish with me!

June 23

New moon on 22nd. Hit surf at 5:15 a.m. Sun up pretty much already, water temps are way high for this time of year about 68 degrees, and this is the third wettest June on record! Northwest winds 10 to 15 knots, seas 4- to 5-foot, salad in surf, too tough to fish effectively. Bass may have moved onward except for a few sporadic schools. Barely a thresher seen this year.

June 24

Night high at 8:30 p.m. Guy, Austin, and I packed up for Island Beach where a slew of stripers in the 20- to 40-pound range have been caught with regularity. The bunker is pinned inside and there are sand eels, and all sorts of bait everywhere. Incredible year for bait so far. Stopped in at Betty & Nick's and checked log book to see about 10 bass weighed in today from 12 to 41 pounds, slow day. Set up at Gilliken's with light sticks. Caught about 8 sand sharks and 2 skates, and got beat up by the black flies. Full Moon today maybe threw it off. Visible lightning strikes near Barnegat Inlet raised caution. Tried throwing bunker heads out on fishfinder rigs to boot for the big bass.

June 24

Fished IBSP with Mickey. 4- to 5-foot, glassy. Hit it at 5:30 p.m., high tide at 9 p.m. Bunker chunks, Mick had immediate 4-pound blue before he stuck rod back in holder. Then I landed a 26-inch bass which I tagged, had some fun, stayed in Lavallette, stayed up till 4 a.m. prank-calling telemarketers. Yeah, we were drinking at the Claw. Dolphins all over now chasing bunker schools.

Sometimes, you just notice the plain, simple happenings of life taking place around you, and it burns a place into your memory, like this:

June 26

Four ospreys cruised the 15-knot south winds at high tide for food. One of them dove and pulled out a large bunker, which it gripped in its talons, and took off in a northerly direction. A big blackback gull chased it. The gull harassed the osprey into dropping its bunker. The osprey shook off his excess water in disgust and went about hunting again. The gull grabbed the bunker in its beak and flew off casually to dine on its meal. Another gull followed. He thought of harassing the gull, but declined at the last moment. The gull carried the bunker to the washline and dropped it. He picked away at it until he was sufficiently pleased. Bunker are thick enough that ospreys are banking on hunting them off my beach. The waters are getting warm now with the 90-degree weather, and the water temp is around 67 degrees now. The bass bite has slowed considerably due to the warming temps.

June 26

Larger bass being taken the last four days, but I was in Cabo. Today, fished high tide 9:06 p.m., southeast 10 to 15 knots with a strong south current, and kelp and string grass in the water. New moon tonight, but hit Mount Street for first hour of high, nothing but weed and bunker heads getting picked apart. Then packed in and went to Princeton where not as much weed, but stronger current, beach is south cut again, and I even fell down cause I didn't see the dropoff on the first cast! Bunker schools off Manasquan and Point, Cali had three bass to 36 inches on shads three days ago. Water cold again at around 60 'cause of south current alongshore.

There are some days when it doesn't matter if the bass bite is going off bananas at the crack of dawn. There are other things that hold more importance. Like when your aging Pop doesn't want to wake up too early to fish for the monster surf stripers around as he has a one-and-a-half-hour drive, and would rather go crabbing off the docks at around 9 a.m. instead. There are only so many days we have allotted in our fragile existences to do the right things with the right people, and when you've got an opportunity to go fishing with your Pop, you just do it. No questions asked.

I don't know what drives him, but my Dad loves crabbing. Actually, it's not even a love, it's more of a passion that striper anglers usually have, but I get to look at it as an outsider, and see the lunacy of his ways. He flat-out lives for crabbing, and the process of it. The collecting of the crab traps and handlines, getting the frozen bunker from Ernie's Tackle Shop, and walking to the bayside docks. Now, my dad is a full-time big game hunter, for 400-pound black bear, monster whitetail bucks, and is the first guy on the ice to drill 24 holes with the gasoline-powered 60-pound ice auger, but he loves the simplicity of crabbing. And that's admirable.

June 27

Dad came down at around 10:30 a.m. to go crabbin'. We set up at Bayside Park in the pouring rain, like hurricane force, whitecaps and bay spray all over! We set up with 4 handlines and 2 traps, and pulled out 21 keeper males and threw back about another 24 crabs, smaller and females. Crabbed till about 2 p.m. and crabs everywhere after the full moon on the 22nd! The steel metal trap caught the most and the green-painted trap lacked a lot. We cooked crabcakes, had meat to dip in butter, potatoes, and the loin of bluefin I caught on Saturday dipped in wasabi ginger sauce. Excellent! What a day!

Ornery blue claw crabs make for some bayside fun off the local docks.

June 27

Full moon last night, red moon rising at 9:45 p.m., fished 9:30 p.m. to 11:30 p.m. with old bunker chunks infused with Bioedge Bunker oil, one big dogfish after another, up to 10 to 14 pounds. Couldn't keep baits in water. Joe O. had 7 brown sharks to 60 pounds two nights ago, but all dogfish last night.

June 29

Hit my surf early 6:00 a.m., dead-low tide, and bucktailed up a stargazer, good luck ahead!

If you've never seen a stargazer, they are pretty cool. They've got an under-slung jaw, rows of filter filaments that look like piercing teeth, a freak fish—blocky and ornery. With a constant facial expression like a mean ol' granddad.

June 30

People are still hammering big bass, more 30s and 40s caught this week than all year, two 50s too. Threshers are still being hooked by those livelining bunker, two hooked up yesterday a few hundred yards offshore. Woke up at 4 a.m. to fish the high tide around 3:45 a.m. Foggy, south wind 5 to 10 knots, dark. Casted a 3 1/2-ounce Driftwood, 10-inch big-lip swimmer into the suds for about an hour, nothing doing, fairly strong south current and some salad in the wash, but I know those big bass are there.

June 30
Chunked my beach again, all dogfish again. Had one brown shark–type hit.

Usually around the end of June, the bass have moved northward to Montauk and off Rhode Island, but stragglers do stay around so long as the bunker schools are present and the water isn't above 65 degrees yet. But now, as July kicks in, it's all about smaller fish in the suds, combined with many night excursions fueled with beer, beach fires, and bluefish.

5 July

AND THE LIVIN' IS EASY

Searing summertime heat permeates the air and lights up the hot sands during the month of July. Some summers are brutal, reaching the 105-degree milestone, though the morning offshore winds blow like a calming whisper through your windows if you live on the beach, soothing the oppressive uprising ball of crimson sun. July is peak season for Bennies, and all the hair gel and kooks that go with it are out in full force from sunup to sundown, though there is a quiet respite from 4 a.m. to 8 a.m., when you can drive or walk to the local WaWa in peace as you pick up a hot cup of coffee to perk the system up. Then you enter the darkness, where the waves lap on the shoreline in a splaying, soothing kind of way that makes the ocean seem just as relaxed as any visitors that come bask in its lazy summer beauty.

There's no real pressure to get up at the crack of dawn to surf-fish come July; you take it at your own pace. There's no anxiety of having to fall asleep just so you can get up four hours later to fish. It's simple moderation—kind of get up when you want to and get out there when you can. You can peer out the window as the alarm goes off at the crack of dawn and see the tourists walking their pooches on the streets to get a jump on the day's lounging. The songbirds, like robins and cardinals, are chirping furiously now, like they don't have a care in the world, piping about in their full summer plumage. Red-winged blackbirds perch atop the bayside phragmites, sounding their beautiful summer song to the world. The air is fresh and clean. There's no hard onshore breeze, only a gentle westerly light touch caress that wafts in between the houses as it makes its way to the beachfront, where it too seems to lie down and relax.

This is the time for surfsters to plink away at the little surf beasties that inhabit the waters—fluke, blowfish, weakfish, snapper bluefish, among plenty of undesirables like sea robins and small smooth dogfish to brighten up the day.

Every morning, afternoon, or evening jaunt out to the sands is implicitly and intrinsically wholesome and laid-back. Though make no mistake, there are ruffians in the waters, as brown sharks and cownose rays enjoy ripping rods out of sand spikes for day-trippers casting a clam or mullet out in hopes for anything. Ahhhh, July. Kick back and enjoy its offerings! Make no mistake, there are always surprises to be taken in July as well. It's sand in your bedsheets time. It's all about some old friends you haven't seen since grade school somehow looking you up to fish in the comforting summertime surf, chillin' out with a few brews and talking about old times, but also catching fish.

OLD FRIENDS, GOOD TIMES

July 2

Spann called the night before to come down and fish. I hadn't seen him since high school. We met at my house, and headed over to Princeton Ave at 6 a.m. He and his brother-in-law set up three rods and used clams and bunker chunks for bait. I bucktailed two sea robins in the dawn surf, and saw bunches of splashes outside the bar, probably weakfish or little blues? We had some fun with the sunrise, water warmed up to about 68 degrees, high tide at 9:30 a.m. or so. We caught over 25 sea robins in about four hours and left them biting, but the big news was when Spann's rod doubled over hard, and pulled out to the horizon—textbook big bass. He took out the rod and the sand spike came with it, and fought the fish down the beach toward me on the right, the other line got tangled in it so we cut that line, which I snagged later bucktailing and retrieved it, and fought about a 34-inch 15- to 17-or-so-pound striper onto the beach. Spann was shakin! And so was I, it was a nice fish on a bunker chunk. We then had sea robins the rest of the morn, I began to test my skills at holding the line and hand-hooking the fish, which was fun. It is a practiced art now that I am known for around these parts!

There's nothing like having fresh bunker for targeting big time bass, and there's a seriously noticeable difference in the hookup ratio of fresh bunker vs. old bunker and the quantity of hits and quality of bass you catch. One bait and tackle shop, Jersey Coast Bait and Tackle, owned by Tom, implements an honor system for fresh bunker, in which they keep a cooler filled with fresh bunkers outside their shop 24/7; you bag up your bunker and throw the money in the door slot to pay for what you take. Granted, there are the usual morons who abuse it, though Tom has cameras outside to peg the thieves, but the system as a whole works awesome, and you can get freshies at any given time of day or night, if you've got the hankerin' to go bassin'. It's pretty cool. That cooler has certainly helped me out when my insomnia kicks in at 1:30 a.m. and I'm rarin' to wet a line. Anyway, point of the matter is—Thanks, Tom!

July 2

Fished from 12:30 a.m. till 4 a.m. on my beach with Austin using fresh bunker chunks we picked up from JCB&T on the honor system cooler outside. Had 7 bunkers and wish we had more, as we beached two bass of 37 and 39 inches that went about 21 and 25 pounds, thick and fat, one bass Au kept had 24 fresh sand fleas and a digested sea robin. High tide was at 1 and most of the hits came around 2 a.m. to 2:45 a.m. Also dropped a big bass that wasn't hooked well. Reeled in a 5-½-foot-long sand shark, biggest I've ever had! Thought it might've been a thresher when it first came in, it was HUGE! Light west winds, seas 2- to 3-foot.

A KID'S GAME

July is the time to introduce anybody—child, girlfriend, dad, mom, anyone—to the saltwater fishing experience. Not only is the surf littered with small beasties to make for almost guaranteed hookups, but also the bayside is chock-full of crabs and juvenile fish species that hatch and grow, all with spirited full fervor to attack a bait. You remember the old red-and-white big bobber days of catching sunfish at the local pond, I'm sure, and July is the month to rediscover that feeling. It's kids being kids, catching small fish and letting them go to grow up together. I am one of those kids every time I wet a line, but it's infinitely more pleasurable to see somebody get the thrill of the hunt coursing through their veins as they connect to reel in a scrappy little treat.

July 3

Lauren [ex-girlfriend] and I went to Bayside Park to do a little crabbing. Packed up the crab lines, the net, the bucket, and the bunker, and hit the bulkhead, free of anybody around to disrupt our time. We were instantly into blue claws so thick it made my head spin, or was that the beautiful crabber girl who chose to hook her own bunker on the pin. We had over 40 crabs in an hour and a half, and had a ¼-bucketfull of males in less than an hour. Even caught one fairly large blowfish who sucked in and deflated to scare us away. Intense amount of crustaceans over 4½ inches (the legal limit), and up to 6 inches from point to point. We took them home, melted the butter, opened the Coronas and a few Amstel Lights and indulged in picking apart succulent rosy red crabs until we were sufficiently done and licking our lips, wanting more. But what we had was enough for us and it made everything worthwhile. I could not ask for a better way to spend some time. And the girl eating them, though distraught with the amount of meat she got from cracking them with fishing pliers and barely gleaning enough smushed meat to feed an ant, managed to spread a wide smile upon her face. I can't wait to do it again.

July 5

Crabbing with Shannon [girlfriend a few years later], her son Kyle, Maggie, and her son little Chris came down and we hit bayside dock with the crab lines and traps and pulled up small crab after crab and had five keepers in about three hours time. Had lunch and tons of fun though the crabs stayed far away from the traps once again??? Split some Dos Equis and everything was mellow and fun! Kids loved it!

July 12

Took Christine from WaWa and her two kids, Josh and Jasmine, out to fish my beach during the evening hours. We cast out one rod with bunker chunks, the other with clams. The clam rod got whacked and Josh reeled in a sea robin. Jasmine got to reel in a bluefish before we lost it in the suds and the other rod went down again for another huge sea robin. We had tons of fun and the kids keep bugging Christine to do it again!

July 13

Woke up at 5:30 a.m. and took Kyle down to Osborne Ave with the remaining bunker. Cast out alongside the jetty and Kyle reeled in a big ugly leopard skate. Had a couple of small bluefish hits, then Kyle beached a 16.5-inch fluke! Also had a sea robin, but noticed plenty of fluke biting out there, just had to have smaller hooks that I didn't have. Kyle loved it! Fished till 8:30 a.m. Most likely tons of fluke in that surf, got to hit it more often.

July 15

Took Kyle to Jenkinson's to surf-fish, but this entire week has been a washout with kelp and eelgrass flushed in from new moon flush out tides, impossible to surf-fish with clotheslined kelp on lines immediately. So went to inlet to cast squid/spearing combo to fluke with Bioedge squid potion. In an hour's time, Kyle and I landed 11 fluke from 10 to 18 inches, all great fish, outfished everybody there! He was stoked. And I did reel up a spider crab tangled in some braided line, along with a stargazer that hit my squid bait as soon as it landed on bottom. Rough seas again today, 4- to 5-foot, hard south/east. Kelp all over. Great white reported off Casino Pier, everybody's panties in a bunch, Seaside Beach closed with double shark sighting yesterday. No doubt browns or cownose ray fins breaching the surface. Lost this whole week of new moon sharking due to heavy rip currents and weed.

July 20

Eisenhart came down with his 5-year-old son Nicholas and we crabbed the dock with the traps. Nicky had a blast, he kept yelling "Haul 'em in boys!!" every single time as we pulled the crab traps. He'll make a great fisherman someday. We also had a few snapper blues on spearing.

July 26

Dad came down at 7 a.m., south winds cooled surf to 60 degrees again, fished till about 8:15 with no bumps, but bunker schools working just outside the breakers, west winds

5 knots, high tide around 8:30, water gray from Tropical Storm Beryl over the weekend. Dad and me then hit up Bayside dock with bunker and spearing and managed to pull four solid big blue claws till noon, and had tons of snapper blue hits, keeping 15 for the frying pan. Also had a 4-inch fluke and a blowfish on the Sabiki rig. Sunny day, 85 degrees. We went back home and cooked the snapper fillets in oil and 5 cloves of garlic, and steamed the crabs, picked a cup full of meat out of those 4! Got a salad from Beach Market and had a blast eating all the good stuff up! Dad was like a kid, reeling back and setting the hook big time on the bobber!

July 29

Hot as heck, past 103 degrees today and snapper blues are all in the surf with Kastmasters landing tons of 'em in the 3- to 5-inch range, kids are having a ball.

SANDERLINGS

I love these little shorebirds and they deserve the recognition of a subchapter. Along the sands in July, tiny, diminutive, pipsqueak sanderlings chase the receding waves, fluffed feathers and full of attitude as they "pip pip pip!" and stick their tiny bills into the sand, rummaging the washline for sand fleas and other assorted forage. A split-second wave washes up and sends them scurrying up the undertow hill, wings flitting and puffed, steps away from the oncoming waterwash, then they repeat the process like it's some kind of game of tag. Their American nomenclature is Sanderling, but the locals affectionately call 'em "lil Nasties" due to their ornery habit of chasing each other with fully puffed out wings as they territorially fight and peck at each other for the best poking spots for sand fleas when the tide rushes up. For such a small creature, they do pack quite an attitude. Watch these birds, and understand life.

FLATFISH FANCY

July means some serious surf fluking. It wasn't until about 2005 when people got hip to the idea that fluke could be targeted in the suds, and actually caught with consistency in the Jersey surf. Maybe it was done in the old days, but it's been a forgotten fishery, and it made a comeback as anglers around began to get smart about it. Fluking takes top billing in the surf nowadays, and a deftly cast bucktail in the suds over the first sandbar usually gets results. Paddling around surfing, you can see the fluke scared of the surfboard shadow, darting out of the sand and propelling themselves, leaving clouds of sand trails. Fluke are plenty thick in July, as they exit the backwaters and begin to move to deeper waters to cool off in the summer swelter, and they tend to exit the inlets and hug the deep undertow of the coastline, which makes for some pretty active surf fishing, during all hours of the day from sunup to sundown. Sundials, cousins of the fluke, also come to hang out, and windowpane flounder can be seen completely through their bodies when held up to the sunlight. Some years, the action is so good that you'll catch more keeper fluke from the surfline than you do on a boat!

July 7

Hit the suds at 6 a.m., dead-low tide, no wind. Bucktailed around some cuts and holes, not a hit. Water Grey Goose–clear. Schools of bunker were getting marauded about ¼ mile out, big schools, probably still by bass? And dolphins were moving through them getting them antsy as well. Little baitfish in closer to the beach across and on the bars, spearing, rainfish.

July 7

Fished the surfline for fluke with bucktails in the 5:30 a.m., dead-low, very low. The little rainbow-colored coquina clam shells are all over the place now, as well as mussel shells all on the beach, and I got bit by two crabs wading around out there. The jelly eggs are back, millions of them everywhere, are they bluefish or skate eggs, I dunno, but I wanna find out. Fluke are now in thick in the river and ocean, but 15 to 1 throwback ratio. Austin and Lido have been bagging them.

That's one thing I forgot to say. Summer surf-wading is an exercise in caution for your feet, as calico crabs burrow themselves in the sand and have no issues whatsoever clamping down on an unaware toe. I don't know if it's the actual pinching pain that hurts as much or the "anticipation of death is worse

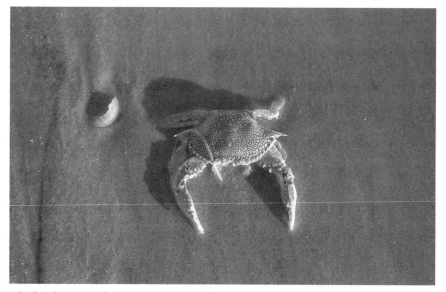

The land mines of the summer surf—calico crabs hiding in the sand aren't shy to pinch your feet. Get even and put them on the hook for bass baits.

than death itself" idea of knowing every step can be the one that hits the pinchy landmine. Whatever the case, crabs are there in July, and they are ornery, unforgiving beasts that let you know they are there with a swift, slicing cut from their claws. Ouch!

July 8

No fishing today, south winds strong at 20 knots and building, but one interesting thing to note. Went to the beach at 8 p.m. and saw some terns working the surf right on the beach in the washline. Went over and found a bunch of bay anchovies beaching themselves that the terns were picking off. Apparently, there are some bluefish in the surf, as some of them washed up in halves. Went over and immediately starting putting dozens of them in my pockets to bring home for fluke bait tomorrow. One guy on the beach thought I was nuts until I explained what I was doing. Probably still thinks I'm nuts.

July 10

Cast a bucktail on my beach at 6 a.m. to see if any fluke were around. Right down the end of the path had a bump, then felt like I hooked into a bowling ball that didn't move. I knew what it was. I steadily pulled back on the rod and eventually it came out of the sand and I reeled in with little fight but some weight. You betcha. Stargazer, big un too! He hit the surf candy teaser in the south winds high tide 6:30 a.m., but water freezing at 60 degrees still from incessant south winds. Stargazers are good luck!

It must be said that stargazers are one of the ugliest fish you will ever encounter, especially when you unearth them from the sands and see them at your feet, wobbling back and forth, with their menacing eyes and what look like minimal teeth, but in reality are just filters it uses to waft the currents and filter out detritus. But make no mistake, the northern stargazer has a deadly secret: a shock mechanism built into its forehead that will give you a good 9-volt electric current if you decide to rub its head! Which I of course have done many times, stoically, to get a good laugh out of local kids standing by, observing the odd-looking beast putting the hurt to me. All in the name of sparking a kid's interest in fish!

July 14

Hit my beach at sundown with a white SPRO and Fin-S. Fished at 7:15 p.m. in 10 knot southeast. Bumped around, saw a bluefish blitz in close, changed up to a Crippled Herring and had a tailor blue. Justin came up and saw my fish, along with two other little kids, was fun, but I couldn't cast back into the blitz since they were all asking questions and I didn't want to be rude! Then bounced around until I felt a tap-tap and a heavy weight on my rod. Pulled back on it and it seemed like I was snagged on something. I pulled back, bending the rod, until whatever it was seemed to pull out of the sand, I still had weight on then felt a few kicks. Got hit in the undertow and then saw a big fat ol' stargazer come up onto the beach wagging his tail! He was awesome! Swallowed my bucktail whole, but it was an easy dehook. I touched his head to try and get shocked but no dice. I released him promptly and saw him waggle away into the suds! Those guys are good luck!

July 13

Weed all over the surf with south/SE winds, 3- to 5-foot waves every day. Tried evening session fluke with bucktail, saw PJ hook into something with an AVA jig, he battled a cownose ray which was foul-hooked, broke off in the undertow. No bites, too much current.

A thing about cownose rays—when you hear of tourists spilling stories of how they got their rod taken away clean out of the sand spike and launched into the water from a monster striped bass, the rays are usually the culprits. Cownosers run in packs of hundreds and completely wreak havoc on leisure anglers' lines as they tend to their kids and wives and forget to pay attention to the rods. Cownosers come through big time in August, but can show up in July if the waters are warm enough. Many people mistake the schools to be vast shark schools terrorizing the beaches as their wingtips break the surface and resemble shark dorsal fins. Many a news station has made millions on the "shark scare" off the Jersey coast when in reality, it's just schools of the docile,

Cownose rays buckle down rods and snap lines in the summertime surf.
CHRIS LIDO.

homely looking cownose rays. But it's still fun to see everybody get into a dither over them.

July 14

Fished 5 a.m., my beach, with white bucktail and red sand eel teaser, dead-low tide, seas 2- to 3-foot, northwest, sunrise nice and warm, water's back up to about 71, where it was 62 three days ago. Had one windowpane flounder hit the teaser, wow, what beautiful white speck flakes on its brown- and black-spotted body!

July 17

Bunker schools still moving south, midday sunny 87 degrees, water clear as water. Bunker schools moving south, flipping and whatnot, smaller fish, rainfish in the suds too. Follow the ospreys, they were diving and pulling large bunks out of the water. Cownose rays showing up again, saw a pack of about 40 of them all huddled up in the breakers scaring everyone.

July 21

Cast around for fluke in the suds, water too dirty right now, we had a brown tide and a commercial boat spill his nets today to close our beach. Sands were rank with all sorts of decaying fish skeletons.

July 27

Cast a bucktail on my beach at evening time, light variable winds. Had a whomp and unearthed a stargazer from the sandbar, fat little guy, and a little girl came over to ask what it was. Just at dark fought what could've been a keeper fluke in the undertow in front of the T-Bird.

And sometimes, a little thing like a scrappy hickory shad can make the day—well, more than just a day.

July 28

One hickory shad. That's all I caught. Woke up at 4 a.m. Couldn't sleep, went down to beach to walk. About 5:30 I see shad jumping in the undertow, south current 10 knots hard and fast, dead-low tide at 6. Ran back, got 007 and white-green teaser and cast, had a bump after another 20 minutes had a Jersey Tarpon on! Unhooked and set free, after a few jumps of course. There is something I found out this morning. Such a sweet satisfaction comes over my body and being when I feel the bump, then hard pull of weight on the end of a fishing pole. It's a different rush, but just as good as sex, for real. When you've gone a long time without a fish in the surf, as I have from being lazy this summer, the rush fills you with emotions, of good times past, and of hope and fine times to come. That's one hickory shad.

HOT SUMMER SCHOOLIES

During the usually oppressive summertime heat of late July, people forget that resident stripers stick around and forgo the march up the Eastern Seaboard for warmer climes. Schoolies stay rooted when the waters have the predawn coolness, and early-morning or late-night sessions can have you into plenty of action on small linesiders.

July 18

Took a power nap and woke up at 7 p.m. Walked down to the suds with my Shimano 6-footer since it was already rigged up with a SPRO bucktail. Supposedly tailor blues and weakies have been in the surf. Fished for only about 45 minutes and had one hit that grabbed the Yo-zuri Emperor Minnow as soon as it smacked the surface. No other action, but calico crabs washed up all over, along with sand fleas. Calicos are the best bait for bass in July when they run through. Water is super clear and about 71 degrees.

July 19

Stayed up till 5:30 a.m. screwing around, swimming in the night surf naked. Decided to hit the suds. Casted a black Mambo minnow in the gray, glassy, 1-foot surf. Ended up tying into 10 cocktail bluefish from 1 to 2 pounds and two sea robins. Plenty of action, hoping to grab a weakie or two. Ended at 7 a.m. dead-high tide. Gave the fish to Andy Regn and Sean Wright to take home.

July 30

Got home from volleyball and decided to hit the suds at 11:45 p.m. High tide at 1:30 a.m. Casted a black Bomber for roughly 40 minutes until I snapped it off from a knot in my line. The moon crept over the black horizon, half-full, and hunter red. It was a sight to see, like the Phoenix rising from the ashes. I will try and find my trusty black Bomber in the morning since the high tide will probably wash it up in either direction, though I believe north is my best bet. The stars were clean and bright, and I felt alive.

SHARKS!

This—this is what July is all about. It wasn't until a fateful morning in June 2004 that I knew about anything other than bass that were patrolling the night waters during the summertime. Nobody in my era even fathomed that other denizens with mean dispositions and serrated, cut-you-like-a-Ginsu-knife teeth were out and about during the Jersey Shore's golden months. When I finally landed my first shark, all bets were off, and I was reborn into surf fishing once again. And when I finally dialed the whole scene in, through many times of trial and error, I was able to lay claim over night surf sharks.

Brown sharks, dusky sharks, blacktips and spinner sharks, the likes of which hadn't been around for decades, were back! My neighbor, Jackie Foulkes, and

A serious shark catch with Chris R. The look on my face says it all!

her father, Buddy, used to show me black-and-white photos of monster 6-foot sharks from the 1950s that came off my beach, and I thought they were just embellishing the "those were the good ol' days" fishing mantra, and had caught them somewhere else. I refused to believe that shark madness had once hit our shores. But now it was back again. After all, along these beaches were the 1916 shark attacks that inspired the movie *Jaws*. I wholeheartedly dedicated every possible night in July from 2004 on to targeting these beasts, to resurrect the good ol' days, and you know what? They cooperated.

July 6

Hit IBSP with Mickey and his friends and Surf Rocket Kenny. Set up to blast baits for sharks on full moon tide. Nothing doing but some skates. Fished 7 p.m. to 10 p.m.

July 8

New moon in three days. Set up for sharks on my beach at 8 p.m., high tide was around 6 p.m. Joe O and Tommy C joined me, with Mark coming later. Within first ten minutes had first break off! Then Joe, Tommy, and I landed 3 brownies up to 65 pounds in next 20 minutes, had a crowd of kids and moms on the beach! All astounded. Then through the whole night to about 11 p.m. landed 14 for 23 on browns and definitely blacktip sharks! Pronounced black pectoral fins and dorsal fins. Had one hit after another as we injected the Bioedge Juice into each chunk, creating a slick. Cousin Mark didn't catch crap only three blocks down! AJ from Normandy Market also came down. When I was changing out a rig, my rod got an impact shock like none other, then Mark's metal/PVC sand spike rod holder shattered with the ferocity of the immediate hit and my rod was headed fast for the surf, you could see the Cyalume light going into the breakers! The shark snapped off when AJ picked it up, had to be a 200-pound-plus thresher or even that huge great white that has been seen around here! Freakin' awesome!!! Seas were 3-foot and east winds, heavy water on the inside even on lower tides, no dogfish, water about 75 degrees now.

I did say great white shark in that last journal entry. In the summer of 2008, at least a half dozen great whites up to 6 feet long were boated off of Normandy Beach and Seaside Heights by anglers fluke fishing and trolling for bass, and reports had monster great whites of over 12 feet long hanging off the Casino Pier in Seaside Heights that summer. There is no doubt in my mind that the shark that hit that bait and bent a metal sand spike was one of epic proportions. That shark haunts me to this day.

July 12

Heard of some good bassin' off Mantoloking today so hit the surf at night. High tide 6:30 p.m., got there to fish 9:30 to 10:45, had one crushing hit on the wire, with 130-pound mono set up for threshers at dusk and it had whacked erratically and it was gone, broke at the braid!??? Thresher or big blue?? I dunno. Fresh bunker chunks for bait. Some big bass taken off the beaches of Avon and Deal, 20 to 45 pounds the last week.

July 15

Hit my beach with Heckel at 9 p.m. until 1:30 a.m., casting clams and old bunker to catch sand sharks and skates all night long. Was fun and relaxing.

July 16

They cleared out Brick III today at high tide, 12:30 p.m., because a big shark was inside the ropes and a helicopter spotted it and stayed above it. Thresher most likely. Saw the beach at evening time around 7 and saw six bunker schools about a half mile to a mile off getting slashed through by threshers! Ran to Grumpy's to get 12 fresh bunkers and hit my beach. Paddled out on my surfboard with the bunker and wire leader in my mouth to drop it out on a balloon. Tough to do at low tide as the current takes the bow in the line to the beach, has to be at high tide. Fished until 12:30 a.m. and pulled in two horseshoe crabs mating. That was it, because I didn't have the right setup to get it out there far enough. Threshers around now though!

And then, that night . . . .

Fished tonight for sharks off my beach. Paddled out with a bunker between my teeth on my surfboard with a balloon on it about 200 yards out. When I finally paddled out far enough under the darkness of the moonless, midnight sky, a monster tail thrashed around me on the bunker school and all I could see was bunker scattering in front of my eyes, with whitewater splashing and ripping around me! I spit out the bunker and paddled in as fast as I could, not to splash around attract whatever that was—probably a thresher!!!!!

Tommy C. with a monster bull shark wrestled in off my beach. The 200-pound beast had to be tail-roped.

Yeah, I had to change my pants when I got home that morning. Don't think I'm paddling out shark baits on a surfboard during the night hours again anytime soon.

July 19

Hit my beach with Mick and Lin to shark at 8:30 p.m. to 10 p.m., dead-low at 10, 3-foot seas and kelp. Sucked, thought the kelp was gone but guess not. In other news, I definitely created a monster writing about beach sharking in all my fishing columns, as everybody seems to be talking about it and doing it now up and down the coast. Hope it doesn't turn to bite me in the ass losing shark spots in some way.

July 26

Night sharking by myself. No luck.

July 28

Sharked with Joe and Tommy, Amos back in town came up too. Went from 9 p.m. to about midnight, had total of 5 break offs, landed one huge stingray. Cool thing was Joe was paddling baits out on the lifeguard kayak and I was greasing the kayak with the Bioedge fish chum all around the hull to drag out a chum slick! Funny stuff, and he was also dropping chunks out when setting our lines out, fast and efficient but Joe fought one to the waves, but broke off, pulled hook, might have been another stingray. Water temps got cold with south winds now 64 degrees, too cold for sharks, has to get warmer. Sharking getting big here now, everybody's talking about it. I have a shark fishing seminar to do at Fishermen's Supply tomorrow, too. A 6-foot blue shark washed up on the beach in Seaside two days ago, alive, and propelled itself back into the water. Two of them, in fact.

That was funny. The lifeguards never knew that we were using their life-saving kayaks as instant chum dispersers, though they probably thought something was amiss when they got a whiff of the nasty bunker potion while doing morning paddle-outs in their kayaks.

July 29

Unbelievable! Reports of brown sharks all over the coastline in the surf. Hit up Ortley Avenue, high tide 8 p.m., got there at 9:15 p.m., north side of the jetty. Had one awesome whack. Guys to the right of me on south side released two shadows that looked like browns. They moved at 10 p.m. and I claimed their spot. Then everything broke loose! I got 14 knockdowns that ran to the horizon! I battled shark after shark and dropped a lot of them with the treble hooks, made the switch to a 10/0 offset octopus hook and started letting the sharks run with the baits as their tails whacked at it you could feel them up and down the line. Finally I started beaching the sand sharks, smooth dogfish, had a few 4-footers. Then at midnight, under an almost full moon, clear waters, 1-foot surf, let the shark run with it and I stuck him. I saw it jump out of the water of the 2nd bar and fought it for 10 minutes, spooling line back and forth. I finally got it to the undertow and grabbed its tail. A 60-inch dogfish! Definitely beat the state record and world record is 58 inches, so think I broke that one too!!!!! Released her back to the surf. A stray cat came up purring and meowing and I gave him some bunker and my rod almost got pulled into the surf—again. I named him El Gato. Fished till 3 a.m. when I ran out of bait.

A big-boy brownie gives the life-guards something to think about tomorrow.

July 30

Hit Ortley again with Tom from JCBT, brought the chum bucket and slicked it up. Water brown and south 2-foot, crappy conditions and fished from 8:30 p.m. to 2 a.m. with only one real hit. Reports came from Sea Girt reef that makos, threshers, blue sharks all being caught 2 miles off the beach! El Gato came back and ran off with another one of my bunkers.

July 31

Went to Holgate to fish with Mickey night sharkin', he had caught 6 monster stingray with 4- to 5-foot wingspans along with big smooth dogfish. We set up around 6:30 p.m. began to pull on a few smaller dogfish, drank some whiskey, beers, and rum. Night fell then the bigger dogs came in. We weighed them to 14 pounds. One fluke, one stargazer, pretty wild night of constant hits, then went to Sea Shell and home to Mickey's house and got nuts there drinking.

6 August

SUMMER'S LAST GASP

ugust. The final days of the summer. Sultry nights are dotted with cloud-less starry skies, sweating it off in 85-degree weather with the humidity so thick you need to jump in the ocean to get dry and feel clean. August days are lazy. You can hear the ice cream man's musical jingle playing his catchy "Entertainer" song at all daytime hours as he pulls up every street, and kids flock like seagulls to free bread, handing out dollar bills and emptying their pockets of loose change to grab an ice-cold treat. The Nutty Royale ice cream cone is my particular favorite.

Sun tan lotion scents permeate the air from sunup to sundown, and even the seagulls are lazy in the 100-degree-plus heat as they wait until you are only a yard or two away before they feel the flight or fight syndrome and inevitably flap their wings just enough to get off the ground and land 10 yards farther away. August is definitely the month where everybody—and everything—just wants to chill out and conserve as much energy as possible.

The surfcaster also saves his energy, because he sure as heck is going to be chasing down rods and trying to stop his reels from getting spooled by cownose rays as they litter the surfwaters. Fluke are a dime a dozen in the undertow now, and cocktail blues, the ones that were just snappers only two months ago, are now terrorizing spearing schools in the suds, as their 1- to 2-pound bodies are equipped and ready to fearlessly attack larger baitfish now, and they have left the fear associated with their snapper-sized bodies back in the nursery of the bay waters. August is also the time when the garbage fish come out in full force—sea robins, skates, and smooth dogfish—enough to either piss you off, or give you plenty of smiles, depending on what your expectations are when walking up to cast a line in.

The end of August signals the start of the summer speedster run, when tropical-type pelagics like bonito, false albacore, and Spanish mackerel trickle up into the area from southern climes, waiting for quickly drawn metals to cross their faces, as they attack and light up reels with blistering, line-snapping runs. It's the last official month of summer, and you better get while the gettin's good. Long after the lifeguards take their whistles off and all the kids go home to eat dinner and take naps, far more fearsome fare enters the surfwaters in the form of primordial predators: sharks! But as a whole, August is all about kicking back and enjoying the fruits of the Atlantic in a laid-back way.

COCKTAILS, ANYONE?

A day trip to the beach under the bright yellow summer sun isn't complete without a fresh adult beverage in the hand, soaking up the sun's rays and enjoying a numb, elated sense that everything is all right, no matter what. Top it off with non-stop fun, fantastic action with small 1- to 2-pound cocktail bluefish, and the recipe is right for a smorgasbord of good times. Old friends and family get along and pull on bluefish after bluefish. These are the days that cocktails are meant to be either drunk or caught or both.

August 1

Big Irish came down. We fished the evening session with a high tide at 3 p.m. Cocktail blues are everywhere, and I mean everywhere. Birds are working like I've never seen in mid July. There are sand eels all over the place, up to 7 inches big. Irish and I casted out 007s, one plain and one with a yellow tail. We had over 30 fish each in about an hour's time. It was so hot, we said that if we casted and didn't get a fish after three casts, you had to pound a Yuengling. Not many Yuenglings got pounded, unfortunately. I brought out a Mega Bait treble hook jig to possibly tie into one of the cownose rays that have been schooling through. These brown-and-white rays run up to about 70 pounds and have a whiptail with a stinger, it would be a blast to tie into one.

August 18

Fished the morning surf 6:00 a.m. from my beach. Cast around, tons of sea lettuce in the wash. Made a few casts, finally saw terns working and bluefish blitzing. Cast out the only metal I had which was an A17, a little big, but connected with five fish, 1- to 2-pound tailors. Could've had them for about a half hour but didn't bother chasing with such a big lure. Filleted them up and salted them down for strip baits for fluke, possibly for mahi trip tomorrow.

August 18

First time hitting surf in summer morning, I hadn't seen a sunrise in so long and that had to change. Beautiful crimson sun, no wind, glassy flat. Cast bucktail, had two sea robins and a few bangs from fluke. Rainfish and snapper blues all over surf. Snappers chasing little baits around. High tide at 10, fished 6:00 a.m. to 7:15 a.m. Water temp 72. Cownose rays are apparently here too.

August 26

Fished Princeton Ave. High tide 6:06 a.m., dead on. No wind, 1-foot tops. Reports of Spanish macks jumping everywhere turned out to be true, I witnessed at least five jump anywhere from 15 to 60 yards off the beach; they vault in the air with purpose. I threw out a bucktail to begin with before sunup for some fluke, had two sea robins. Switched to a 007 with a 15-pound Fluoro leader for the macks. Had a robin, then missed two hits, then saw birds working at the end of the path. Saw swirls in the water all around. Boom! Bluefish everywhere, working just like it was fall. 3- to 4-pounders too, good muscleheaded runs. I had about 4 of them, they were gorging on the bay anchovies, and little tinker macks all around, which were breaking water everywhere you looked in the undertow. As I recasted for macks, I looked to my left and saw the huge brown thing wash up two feet away in the high wash, it was an inquisitive cownose ray who seemed to be playing around in the washline, checking me out! He looked goofy, and reentered the water in one ebb. Finished up casting, and had a hit like none other. I was reeling fast when my 007 got whacked so hard with the pull of the lure, I felt the explosion then it went slack. He hit it coming in, but not the hook, he actually knocked my knot sideways he slammed in so hard, had to be a Spanish. We'll see, give me the Spanish mackerel, I'm waiting for you.

COWNOSERS

It was 2006 when they first showed up in the surf, and they came to really fool with the day-trippers. Picture this: family comes down to the surf, a bare-chested man in Bermuda shorts pulling a big, bulky, inflated-wheel surf cart, spilling beach balls, sand shovels, and all sorts of colorful toys, while wife and kids are trudging behind, trying to keep up. The man sets up camp, pulls a rod out of the cart, hooks on a clam, and sets the rod in the spike. He turns around to finish laying out the beach blankets and turns around again to check his rod. It's gone. Nowhere to be found. He frantically runs into the water searching for it, asking bystanders left and right if anyone saw anything. Chalk it up to another cownose ray bandit. That rod is long over the second sandbar by now, dragging in the sand as the ray takes off for the deep water. That scene has played out in the August surf more often than not since the cownose rays moved into town.

August 2

Mission freakin' accomplished. Me and Irish had our fair share of cocktail blues again, but they were hitting the 007 with tails more since the southeast wind had the water a bit dirty. But enough of that. I cast out and felt a little dead weight on the end. Then it started to take off. I hooked into a cownose ray, and it was melting line off my reel! I looked at Kelly and he was on with the drag singing! We must have hit the school of them. Kelly fought and lost one on 30-pound PowerPro that broke, and I fought my 50-pound ray until I got it in the undertow. Kelly grabbed the pliers and pinched down on the 007 stuck in the ray's wing. It splashed and tried to fly viciously with its tail whipping on the sand. A gust of a wave came in and he was pushed into us as we ran like little girls to avoid his whipping tail. We unhooked it and he glided away. What a freakin' fight!

August 2

Casted around for the rays with a Crippled Herring but no dice, saw them everywhere in the wash at around 3 p.m., seems like they come out from 3 p.m. onward. Guy next to me hooked up with one and fought for about 25 minutes, kept trying to land it. I saw him struggling and leadered the thing using my hat for a grip, brought it up, about a 25- to 30-pound ray. Was so cool, he grunted like a little pig and really was a sweetheart! They have two spines just above their tail, two black almost knife-like spines one on top of the other. We let him go. Turns out I knew the guy who caught it, he was Tasker's friend.

August 8

Didn't fish yet today but probably will. There are so many cownose rays in the surf it is like a brown-and-white thundercloud is omnipresent in the undertow. I must have seen over 300 rays move through in a half hour. The cool thing was that they would swim up to us standing in the undertow then around us, like splitting the brown sea. It was an interesting experience seeing a pack of underwater creatures aiming dead at you and then turning away at full speed. One ray even got beached behind me and flapped around in the thin water of the washline until it swam frantically toward the ocean and bumped me in the legs and continued on his way. It was like I was the prey and he was the predator.

Now the interesting part. Jeff Durocher landed a fish and everybody on the beach went over to see what it was. I assumed it was a ray, but decided to check it out. It was a 4-foot-long, 60-pound sandbar shark caught on a mullet rig in the surf. It was a shock at first, because I thought it might be a bull shark since they almost look exactly alike, but it didn't possess the jagged teeth of the worst man-eater in the world. Anyway, we walked it to Ernie's to weigh it and take pictures, and I had the thing slumped over my shoulder on the walk back to my place. You should have seen the looks on all the people driving by in their cars, this silvery brown beast draped over my back, jaws open, drooling, and it reaching the small of my back. Wild.

I can only attribute these happenings to the warm water temps that are in the low to mid 70s now, and there are schools of bait roving through, they might be small blues, I'm not sure, but they are right in the undertow. Anyway. I'm going to try for sharks from the surf now.

Brown and bull sharks patrol the summer bay waters.

August 10

Rays. Water now at around 74 degrees in the surf, cownose rays are in again, saw them in my wave when I was up riding a wave surfing, six of 'em coming right at me and it broke my concentration and I fell off the board mid-ride.

FLUKE FRENZY

Deep summer fluking continues on in August, and most years, Jersey regulations call for an end to the season by the first week of September, which has encouraged many surfsters to make it a priority to ply the surfwaters for flatfish fare in the last decade.

August 1

Hit the beach in the morning and evening to cast for fluke, but an easterly push has swamped our beaches with eelgrass and sea lettuce as far as you can see. The jelly eggs are back too. And the cownose rays are here again! In the hundreds!

You know, I've never really figured out just what those jelly eggs are that wash up after a full moon tide in the late July, early August surf. I've asked some pretty knowledgeable people, and the best I could come up with is that they are salps, a jellyfish-like creature. Heard they might be squid eggs or skate eggs, but damned if I know what they are. They are clear jelly with a tiny black dot in the middle of them.

August 3

Hit my beach again. High tide at 7:45 p.m., hit it at 6:30p.m. and on, water 69 degrees. Cast a bucktail with a white teaser for fluke, nothing doing until the end, when the light went behind the houses and I got thwacked by a 16.5-inch fluke which I beached. It hit the teaser. Waves 2- to 4-foot, light southeast breeze, water pretty clear. A guy had on a ray to my left, but lost it when the line snapped like a gunshot, must've been 50-pound line the way it sounded! Fluke more prevalent in the suds now, and I swear I saw some things in the evening surf that weren't rays, I saw fins or something like permit, maybe a brown shark? Milling around just barely breaking the water's surface . . . ?

In retrospect, that errant large fin might've actually been a mola mola, or ocean sunfish, as I have seen them outside the breakers in summers past and since. Normally pelagic, they sometimes get lost inshore and actually even traverse into inlet areas and back bay waters, giving onlookers quite a thrill, as they usually are 6-foot-plus top to bottom on their very vertical bodies.

August 4

Hit Princeton Ave to cast the bucktail and teaser again at 6 a.m. No wind, glassy, 1-foot, high at 8:45 a.m. In a few casts had a short fluke. Then saw bait flipping, and on one wave got to witness almost Guy Harvey–like painting of a 7-pound bluefish chasing the bait through the glass of the wave, was awesome! Cast out again and got absolutely hammered by something so large and in charge. Immediately I felt weight and my rod bent, then I saw what I believe to be a cownose ray jump clean out of the water with wings flying, and it took off screaming drag for about 100 yards, I fought it until the hook pulled. Had to be a ray, but from a quick glance, maybe a sunfish?!? Kept walking south and found some holes to pull out two stargazers, those little stinkrats! Also managed to pull out another three fluke up to 16.5 inches. One fluke followed my buck the whole way in and whacked it dead in the undertow, I set back, pulled him in the air onto the beach, and released him all in one shot. Then fished on the north side of the entrance for a minute or two to pull out an 18-inch fluke. Five out of six fluke hit the teaser!

August 9

Hit my beach at 6:20 a.m. High tide 5:30 a.m., sunrise around 5:15 a.m. Bucktail with small white teaser tipped with 2-inch gulp minnow. Had one sea robin on the bucktail then fished in front of third set of windows in front of T-Bird. Went 7 for 9 on fluke all about 10 to 13 inches long. Sea robins then came through, actively feeding on the surface. Ray was down there and had a huge stargazer on a gulp strip. Apparently he saw some tunny yesterday in the wash. Water clean, 2- to 3-foot, light north wind. All the fluke hit the teaser, must be small rainfish in the wash.

August 16

Water is still gin-clear, and there is bait all around, spearing, tiny, look like neon tetra tropical fish, and all sorts of exotic little ones around. The water warmed up to about 71 now, bringing in all warmwater species. Saw a school of what looked like peanut bunker getting worked out past the low tide sandbar. Saw two bass about 18 to 20 pounds swim by my legs while wading in the mid-afternoon.

August 17

Hit the surf at 6 p.m., dead-low. Light east wind. Thunder showers. Bucktailed with a ⅜-ounce yellow/white with a rainbow trout Fin-S on the back. Water is white grape juice-clear, you can see everything. The coolest thing started when I saw a sea robin from about 15 yards out following my bucktail in. He trailed it furiously, but didn't bite. I casted back three more times and he did the same thing. Could see him visually getting frustrated and pursuing his prey, awesome! Next, I casted out and saw a grainy shadow following my buck into the undertow about three feet out. It rose, sank, followed, rose, sank, followed. It was a 16-inch fluke that when I jigged rapidly and twitchily in the undertow, he pounced on it right at the breakline. Had a few more sea robins, then fished by the new house in Normandy, and got walloped by a huge thud. Fought it in, it pulled drag, and ended up with a 20-inch fluke on the sand! Nice fish, wonderfully sandy colors. That was at about 7:50 p.m., just at dusk, low-light situation and it seemed the bite turned on hot for about 15 minutes between high-light, transition to low-light, then shut off at too low of light. That little window seemed to trigger a bite. Spearing all in the wash.

That's one thing I really learned while surf-fluking. Fluke are ultra-aggressive predators, and they have no qualms about chasing down their prey, many times coming off the bottom and launching 6 feet up to the water's surface to pop a lure on the water's top!

August 18

Fished 6 a.m. to 8 a.m. Dead-low 7:30 a.m., light northeast wind, seas 1-foot. Bounced the buck again. Had a few hits past the T-Bird, but did not connect. One was definitely a blue, took some bucktail hair with him. At around 7:45 a.m., when the tide changed, I changed up my Fin-S fish and put it on upside down. I got whacked on my first cast back by a 14-inch fluke. I think they like to see the dark side down, since they hunt gazing skyward. I now know why they call them rainfish too, by the way, a school of rainfish moved through and when they nose the surface, it looks exactly like raindrops hitting the water. Bunker boats working outside, I think they are, they had a spotter plane out there, tuna? I also think the influx of those beautiful little tiny clams that come around in August have something to do with the clearness of the water. There are so many, do they filter it in August?

Those little technicolored coquina clams are truly beautiful. They are about a half-inch in length and sport white, light blue, light orange, yellow, and red hues. They seem to unearth themselves by the millions in the August surf, right in the tide line, rooted down and hanging out their brown bristles to intercept plankton and feed. When the water recedes, they dig down quickly into the sand and vanish, until the next wave comes and they come back up again.

August 20

New Moon tide, hit surf from 7:30 a.m. to 9 a.m., dead-high, Hurricane Bill swell building now, fairly glassy, shore break 4- to 5-foot. Water about 78 degrees, water a bit off-color brown. Cast out a chart/white buck tipped with chartreuse grub and landed 6 fluke to 17 inches and dropped another 4 or so, also had snapper blues biting tails off my teaser grubs, a sea robin too. Apparently some Spanish macks around. Me and Bugsy spent rest of day seine netting the Manasquan River by his house; in two pulls had a 3-gallon bucket filled with spearing, had small kingfish an inch long, four tiny 2-inch fluke, and some unidentifiable little critters with tiger stripes, and other fat and pudgy ones, little green crabs too.

Seine netting is one of the most interesting things a person can do, especially during the summer months, when all sorts of fish that have spawned out as yearling fish inundate the back bays. Many "aquarium" tropical-type fish not usually associated with Jersey waters, such as moonfish, strawberry groupers, and pompano, can come up in a seine, and it always makes me feel like a little kid to see just what surprises get caught up. Usually it's a bunch of tiny kingfish, killifish, spearing, blowfish, seahorses, calico crabs, pipefish, sticklebacks, and snapper bluefish, though there are always other oddities, such as the 26-inch striper we once caught! If you've never seine netted, take a kid and try it out. It's well worth the entertainment and will provide hours of endless fascination.

August 24

Low tide 8:30 a.m. Couldn't sleep, so woke up at 4 a.m. and got gear ready. Went down to Princeton Ave. Cast a Megabait plug in the dark wash to no avail, but some bass being caught in the predawn from Ron at Fisherman's Supply. In the darkness I witnessed a wake of water about 15 yards off the beach, looked menacing, made me think twice, then saw three huge fins breach the surface—dolphins, the closest-in I've ever seen! A whole school was moving through, literally 15 yards off. I let them pass, tried to do a dolphin call to let them know what was up. Predawn light was out and I was in the washline casting when I saw this thing rise up about 5 yards away, looked like a pointed sunfish, was large, scared the s&%# out of me. Couldn't figure out what it was, but eventually figured out it was probably a baby dolphin, they are running with the moms now. But he came in that close, literally in the undertow! Eventually went to a popper, no action, then went to a bucktail. Walked north and had three bangs which I couldn't convert, since I'm not used to the Penn 5500, tried-and-true is in the shop getting a new pin. My retrieve is too fast with that reel, thus missed the strikes. Had two more hits that raked the Fin-S on the back of the bucktail then one hit took it clean off, bluefish-style in the undertow. I did catch a line, and when I pulled it in, it felt like something was on it, in fact I saw a boil in the water, but I reeled in a three-way swivel and a 3-ounce pyramid with no hook on the leader. Nothing to put on the beach, but I did see two fine ladies in bikinis come up to see the sunrise!

August 25

Hit my surf sunrise at 6:20 a.m., high tide 3 a.m., southwest 10 to 15 knots early, water crappy brown. Sunrise was hot pink and wonderful. Only fished for about 30 minutes, due to lettuce in surf. Water temp about 72 now. Supposedly small fluke, cownose rays in surf, haven't hit it in a while.

August 27

Fished 6:15 a.m. to 7:45 a.m., landed a keeper 18-inch fluke on a Vision Rain Fish teaser, and dropped another two big ones. Surf glassy, light northwest winds, stuff like shells washing up from nor'easter and those clams freaking bang on my ankles in the wash! But now 5 bunker boats and two spotter planes off the beach sucking up those bunker schools, man does that suck. So much for sharks or bass around on bunker schools now. Feelin' like fall again, high 50s at night, but 85 during day, water temp 78 degrees, but morning sun was crisp and clear, a muted yellow-orange that tells of an impending September fall.

August 31

Four days left of fluking so high tide 5 a.m. hit my beach 5:15 a.m. to 7:30 a.m., seas 3- to 4-foot, light north. Walked down to sun house and ⅜-ounce bucktail white-chartreuse gulp teaser beached 14 fluke, mostly shorts but had two of 18 and 19.5 inches—two keepers! Probably lost just as many. Three sea robins too, actually released one then cast out far and the hook freakin' had to land right on him, it hooked his tail and I reeled him in again—same exact one! Unreal. Then at sundown around 7:15 p.m. Saw tunny, bonito, and/or Spanish mackerel working over bait schools about 200 yards off. Excellent to nab a two keeper fluke in the suds! Sundown was beautiful and you can feel the September push of weather beginning to move in. The sunshine looks a little cooler and washed out now, sunset through the houses was ethereal too. By the way, a kid kayaked out a bait and beached a 5-foot hammerhead this week.

HARDHEAD HAPPENINGS

It's a pretty rare occurrence when croakers come up into the central coast area, as they usually stay south of Long Beach Island, but one year in particular, 2004, the hardheads came into the suds in full force during the evening hours for a week straight. These little grunty fish put up one heck of a fight for their small, big-headed stature, and a pound croaker will put a bend in a 9-foot surf rod to make you think you hooked into something with some shoulders. You never really see them north of Barnegat Inlet, but this particular year, they rushed the surf.

August 28

Light east winds. Muddy waters. Water temp about 71. Giblin and Shelia came up to visit from Baltimore. Hit my beach at about 7 p.m. and on the way up, two kids came down my street saying they were slamming fish up there, but didn't know what kind. Croakers I thought. Set up with fishfinder fluke rigs and squid strips. On my first cast out, couldn't even get the second rod in the water, the rod buckled over. Shelia reeled it in and a croaker came up to the beach. Then, seriously, it was nonstop action. We totaled about 35 croakers in an hour and lost just as many. The hardheads were everywhere and they were up to about 16 inches long, pretty fat ones. They are hard-fighting fish that don't get much credit in the surf. On one fluke rig, fixed with a rubber squid, I had caught two weakfish of about 15 inches. There had to be more weakies underneath the croakers, but you simply couldn't get past them. We had tons of fun bailing the grunters and a harvest full moon rose over the ocean horizon like some wicked alter-phoenix. It was pretty intense! We also caught a large skate that Shelia wasn't having any of.

August 29

Hit the beach again with Heckel at a 6:30 p.m., evening session for the hardheads. Same philosophy with squid strips, but no real whacks from the croakers. We did have about 6 bluefish from the surf, tailor size on small metals and our squid baits. The surf was about 2-foot when we got down there, water was muddied up. I cast a bucktail out with a Fin-S on the back and got banged in the undertow a few times, but no hookup. Finally slowed my retrieve and set back on a hit. Reeled in a nice size croaker that inhaled my bucktail. Shows they are aggressive when they feed! Then at dusk, the storm surge from Hurricane Gaston moved in like an instantaneous surge front. The waves went from 2 feet to about 4 to 5 feet in the undertow in a matter of minutes! Combined with the ebbing tide of the harvest full moon, it was pretty wild!

That's one thing I remember about when the croakers were in the surf that year: the harvest moon. It was a shining, spectacular beacon that rose off the horizon, larger than the sun at sunrise coming up over the Atlantic. Bright crimson red, with tones of orange and purple, it looked both menacing and spiritually calming all at once. I haven't seen the croakers back since that year.

SPEEDSTERS

The golden goose for August anglers is getting the first taste of the summer speedsters—bonito, false albacore, and Spanish mackerel—that move in some years, mainly in late August and the beginning of September. Spanish mackerel are not a mainstay in the Jersey surf; they are a once-in-a-lifetime catch, to be quite honest, and bonito, well, they are even harder to lay claim to. But some years, Lady Luck shines on you and you are in the right place at the right time on the right day. But more often than not, consider yourself lucky to even see one that is close enough to cast to in the surf.

Dad reels in a sweet cocktail blue caught on a mullet rig.

August 7

Hit Bay Head to try for some bonito, but south winds and lots of lettuce prevented me from hooking into anything. They are catching them, though, Steve from Reel Life had nine the other morning.

August 13

Hit the surf at night, cownose rays in here full force last week and a half. No dice. Evening tide with high around 10:30 p.m. dirty water again, east blow. I did cast into schools of what looked liked bunker or snapper blues tons of pods out there as they exploded when the Crippled Herring hit the surface. Water temp around 78 now.

August 31

Hit the morning surf in Bay Head to try for albies. Saw terns picking at the surface a bit offshore out of range, but no surface breakers. Walked from Bridge down past Johnson, a dragger must've dropped his nets, as some dead striper and dogfish skate carcasses were washing up. Nothing doing, though beautiful sunrise.

August has never been my lucky month to find Spanish, albies, or bonito; September is a different story, as you'll see later. But damned if I ain't gonna keep trying every August from here on out to land a surf Spanish.

BAYSIDE FOLLIES

There are four times when you should go to the Bayside Park dock to go crabbing—when you have kids down, when the east winds are blowing hard and unforgiving, when family's around, or when you just want to kick back and screw around. Now that I think about it, I can give you five, ten, twenty different other excuses to go to the bayside and crab.

Bayside Park in Brick Township was erected in 2002 after the Osborns sold the lot to the town of Brick in order to build a park that the community could rally around and get some good old family nature time in. It's not the place to catch the trophy fish of a lifetime, but it will make memories that will last three lifetimes over.

Bayside Park sits on the upper edge of Barnegat Bay; it's actually a little bay in itself, designated Silver Bay, and it's the budding nursery for just about every nearshore species that calls the Atlantic home. Blue claw crabs crawl about the bottom by the thousands, picking up scraps of dead fish and small baitfish, and at any given time, there are dozens of crab lines and traps set out to trick the crustaceans. Blowfish are cyclical and choke the bay some years, not like in the 1950s, but there are signs of a budding population rebounding in recent years. Kingfish, small black drum, juvenile weakfish, small fluke and needlefish round out the summer bay mix, but by far the most sought-after species for old and young alike are snapper bluefish.

The diminutive demons of 3 to 5 inches long run about in terror schools nipping away at anything in their path, and a simple bobber cast out with a 2-foot leader rigged with a spearing will put you into all the fun you can possibly handle, no matter if you have fished for black marlin in Australia's Grand Banks or battled goliath grouper in the Florida Keys. Once you see that little red-and-white bobber go *ker-plunk* under the water surface, all bets are off and you become a kid again. And that's why you bring people to experience Bayside Park.

August 16

Dunsby and his family down, took his little kids, Gavin and Lily, to Bayside Park to toss crab traps and catch a few pinchys along with snapper popping with spearing. They had a blast! Dunsby, ever so smart, tossed my crab trap in when it wasn't tied to the dock and I had to cast out a handline to search around and eventually hook it to bring it back in—with a crab in it! Dunsby's not allowed to toss the traps in any more.

August 28

Dad and Brother Billy came down and we set up at Bayside Park with spearing and bobbers. I was bucktailing up a few 4-inch fluke! Billy landed two needlefish and Dad was all over the snappers. Crabbing was very poor, but we then also had a kingfish Billy reeled in, a blowfish, sunny day out lots of fun. Billy and I went to arcade afterwards to relive some of the good ol' days—Frogger, Sinistar, Satan's Hollow, and Joust! Just two mid-30-year-olds playing arcade games and eating ice cream like we did in 1987. Dad cooked up the snappers, little bony though, but good with barbeque sauce!

And to add a little spice to the summertime vibe, there are still tog to be taken in the canal, though most summertime tog are small "toglets" or "chocolate chips." Nothing to go home and brag about, but sure as heck fun to pull on.

August 25

Full moon tide yesterday, nor'east seas 5- to 9-foot, so decided to go to the canal to find tog at high slack at 11:30 p.m. Had a dozen greenies and pulled on one toglet after another till I ran out of bait at 12:45.

YEAR OF THE SHARK!

There was quite possibly no other month like August 2009. Sure, we had the spring shark fishery, with browns and occasional threshers streaking bunker baits and stealing rods and snapping lines. But when the hot sultry weather really laid upon us, something triggered in the migratory habits of all sorts of sharks. Browns, duskies, spinners, threshers, hammerheads—they were all here in the suds, and they were punishing our lines on a nightly basis.

A beast of a brownie, weighing in at 130 pounds, unnerves the lifeguards standing behind it.

Heckel looks down the barrel of the FOF Bait Blaster pneumatic air gun.

August 2—Night

The guys from Far Out Fishin' showed up to fish with their pneumatic, homemade bait-blasting device that shoots out shark baits over a quarter mile into the surf. We blasted baits on my beach and had some large, smooth dogfish but had a lot of small tapping on the lines, too, possibly croakers or fluke?

Ha ha, I gotta explain that last entry. I met my buddy Dan Triano at the Saltwater Fishing Expo in Somerset, NJ, one year, right at the beginning of my passion for pursuing sharks from the surf. When I walked up to his booth, a 7-foot PVC tube attached to an air compressor stared me in the eyes, and I knew I had to have one. He explained to me that he devised his "bait blaster" so you can "reach from the beach." It was everything I wanted in a surf shark gun and we put the son of a bitch to use plenty of times, finding those sharks way past the breakers.

We've definitely had our fair share of cross-eyed looks and raised eyebrows, and even one or two helicopters circling back around to see what kind of terrorist activities we were up to. Probably the funniest time was when my buddy Captain Bob Bogan of *The Gambler* was fluke-fishing on his 90-foot vessel about a half mile off the beach and I called his cell phone to watch for the big splash off the bow of his boat. He said, "What splash?" I said, "Look in about 5 seconds," and *Splash!* He laughed and thought we were nuts. He was right.

August 3

Fished with Far Out Fishin' Dan. Blasted baits off Mantoloking pipe pieces and had skate after skate. Hooked the wreck off Mantoloking pipe on the last reel-in, too, so I know we were in the right area.

August 3

Hit my beach with bunker heads for some night sharking. Low tide around 10:30 p.m. At 11 p.m., had a screaming hit on the 60-pound braid, 11-foot rod that ran like a tuna, literally, couldn't stop him. Fought for about 5 seconds then he threw the hook. The mass was all of 100 to 200 pounds and I felt the power of it—no doubt a thresher shark! Ran out of bunker heads, and I don't know if I could've stopped it if it gave me a chance . . . we'll see for next time!

August 3

New moon passed on August 1. West winds 10 knots, 1-foot. Hit Lavallette with Heckel, set up 7 p.m., high tide 10, with big stinky bunkers from Betty and Nick's that were put in the bucket with a dozen Miller Lites. Set up and had a monster whackdown at around 8:15 p.m. that with sheer running force snapped my Albright knot at the braid connection, had to be a thresher with that kind of power! Now know to have drags set kinda loose for a baitrunner clicker-type appeal. Sundown began to pull on dogs, had some large ones again, but then Heckel said he started feeling sick. By 10 p.m. he was puking all over the beach, found out that the beers were sitting in the bucket with the bad bunker slime and he must've drank some of that! Never mix your beers with bunker! Ended up having to leave because he was throwing up constantly, left at 10:45 p.m. but still was getting big time whacks. Finished up at my beach where I got whacked by smaller dogfish until 12:15 p.m.

I can't tell you how funny that was for me to see Heckel on his hands and knees on the beach puking up every ten seconds, but I know he didn't think it was funny. A true trooper, Heckel said I could keep fishing, until about a half hour later I saw he was lying on his stomach, face in the sand, almost comatose, and I told him we would be packing it in, even though I knew the sharks would be biting. We came real close to taking him to the hospital. Never, ever mix your beers with old, rotten bunker in the same bucket. Lesson learned.

August 6

Fished with Mickey, Marc, Chris, and Ken from the Surf Rocket guys at IBSP area 10, drove on. Got there at 7 p.m., no bait so cast out gulp to catch some sea robins, filleted them for use as shark baits. Sundown, light west winds, seas 1-foot, high tide at 1 a.m. fished till 11:15 p.m. Now, Mickey had four knockdowns that cut him off or chomped the baits to the heads, after we launched chum out. Finally Ken's friend reeled in a small

Spinner sharks add to the summer shark mix.

35-pound class brown shark which I released and snapped my knee doing it. Fell into the water with it, with it snapping around my face in the water! Then my rod went straight out of the spike like a rocket, and it was hauling ass into the water so fast I can't even describe it. I ran after it 40 yards and slid into it like second base and reeled up and set on the circle hook and the fight was on! Took me down to my 20-pound backing running, pulling line and could feel the shoulders on him, got him into the low tide sandbars, and saw his dorsal, big fish! Finally played him in; after spirited runs, he had no more water to run in. Mickey leadered him and got him 75 pounds of brown shark!!! Released him and then Mickey caught next shark, about 40 pounds, but it may have been a bull shark with large teeth??? Great fishing, left to Crab's Claw to do tequila shots and a few beers. Wild time in the surf! Water temps finally moved up to 72 degrees now from 58 degrees days ago.

Three and a half years later, from that trip, I found out I completely tore my ACL in half, as well as tearing through my meniscus and LCL, and had to get reconstructive surgery on it. It happened when releasing that 75-pound brownie as I stepped in the undertow into a pothole and heard the loud *snap!* inside my knee. Commitment, right? All in the name of surf sharking!

August 7
SHARKING BUT FORGET HOW MANY WE CAUGHT!

Mickey and Kenny carefully unhook a brown beastie.

That was a day I will never forget, but was too excited to write it all down. We must've had over 30 sharks that night. It was so red hot and I was so amped up, I couldn't even write it down.

August 9

Dan from Far out Fishin' came down and we blasted baits on my beach from 5:30 p.m. on. West winds, 1-foot, high tide at 3:30. One after another smooth dogfish; had 4 that were 15 to 17 pounds, 2 pounds shy of state record! Only had 18 baits, 6 which were spot, lost one fish that was brownish. Elmo, Jackie, Dennis, Sue, Justin, Glenn, and Mark were all there, including tons of random kids that loved to see the sharks. Abby my labby was there too! I taped a night light to her collar to keep track of her in the darkness, then a kid gave her a pink night light bracelet to tie on her collar to see her. She barked at every shark and tried to bite them!

August 9

Here it is: SHARKS! Full moon tides. Finally, everything lined up right. Mickey came down and it was all-out bananas, seas flat to 1-foot, west winds, full moon high three days ago, high at 11 p.m. and it was freakin' on! Mickey and I went 15 for 21 on monster browns, duskys, and spinner sharks to 110 pounds plus! Light southwest wind, water clear but a little off-color. It was insane, using 65-pound braid to a three-way, 3-ounce pyramid, and a long leader of 100- to 130-pound mono 10/0 gammy octopus or big

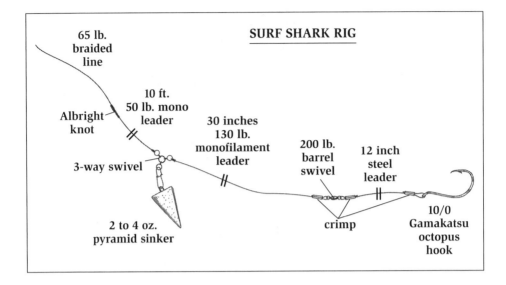

SURF SHARK RIG

65 lb. braided line

Albright knot

10 ft. 50 lb. mono leader

3-way swivel

2 to 4 oz. pyramid sinker

30 inches 130 lb. monofilament leader

200 lb. barrel swivel

12 inch steel leader

crimp

10/0 Gamakatsu octopus hook

river hook on end. I got stripped and spooled clean by three sharks I couldn't stop that bit me off or pulled the hook, probably makos or threshers with tuna-like runs. Landing them in the surf, you need to pull them up onto the washline sand, and need a tail man and a leader man. This was unreal! Fished till 2:30 a.m. Bite started at about 9 p.m., slack tide slowed up.

August 10

Like it couldn't get better. Mickey's friends came down. Shark bite was from 8:30 p.m. to 1:30 a.m. until I had to leave and they were biting past that, I was completely out of gear and tackle. We went 24 for 41 on sharks! When moon came out of the cloud cover, the sharks seemed to bite best at 11 p.m. right before high tide, seas 1- to 2-foot, heavy water inside. Some baits were cast out, hit the water, and immediately split-second got hit, which means the sharks were so thick, and feeding actively on the surface! Before rod could get in the sand spike, sharks were pulling it out of my hands. Little kelpy out, but not enough to stop fishing. INSANE SHARKING! Shannon and Kyle, Mark and Glenn there. Kyle reeled in dogfish along with Shannon. Perseid meteor shower going on.

August 11

Fished with Nicky Ianello and Chris Z and went 6 for 15 on sharks again in the 40- to 65-pound class, light southwest wind, water clear with a little brown to it, bite started at 8:30 p.m., then slowed up from 10:30 p.m. to midnight, but got one just as everyone leaving, stayed to midnight with Joe O and Tommy Cangliosi. They've been fishing every night, too. Had a few hits, simply couldn't stop in time to set the hook right or cut off. Meteor showers last three nights too, some wild shooting stars!

August 12

Hit IBSP with Mickey and his friends. Set up around A12 at about 7:15 p.m. with fresh bunker again and it was a nonstop dogfish festival with 38 dogs to 15 pounds. Mickey also had four break-offs that were very sharky. The backs of the sharks cut right through braided line as we saw one dogfish do. Chumming works very well to get a bite going. Ended about 11 p.m. High tide 4, so fished the dead-low, basically. Did see a nice harvest moon rise over the ocean.

August 20

Fished Holgate with Mickey and his family, tons of fun. With 20 fresh bunkers, live spot, we fished from 7:30 p.m. on through till 11 p.m. and cleaned up once again on big dogs to 16 pounds, had 15 break offs again, big sharks again. Next day Mickey had a 100-pound stingray, said 5-foot wingspan. Went out and got drunk at the Shell again, poured vodka over Ol' Jonesy, the Penn 5500 reel he's had since he was a kid, and Mickey slept with the reel for good luck!

Though August has a solid spread of surf activity, there is no doubt in my mind that surf sharking takes the cake. It's what keeps me up at night, and tired during the day. Then, out of nowhere, September hits, and the focus shifts to barrel-chested fish with long, thin, black lines running along their flanks, and unforgiving chopper bluefish.

7 September

LOCALS RULE

Break out the long sleeves. It's truly like somebody hits a switch come Labor Day. It gets cold—fast. The hard-charging partying of the Jersey Shore crowds is gone and forgotten. It's like a hurricane just ran over the entire coast Labor Day weekend, spreading trash and debris everywhere, and then it passes, as the clean-up swell hits the coastline the Tuesday afterward. The rod racks are now bolted back on trucks, silence is the norm and not the exception during daytime hours, and a sense of calm hits the area. Everything reverts once again to the shore's slow, lazy pace that the seagulls ride on.

September is hurricane month in Jersey, when we get the most activity from the roving storms up the Eastern Seaboard. Fresh, cool breezes flow through the cracks in your windows now, edging and pushing their way into the house, letting you know it's time to put the air conditioners away, tape up the windows, and fire up the gas heater. Mullet know this change in the season. Mullet are the driving force of the Fall Run.

Thoughts turn to striped bass now, as all the beach balls, light tackle rods and reels, and candy-ass gear gets put away, and people get serious about their fishing. The beaches open up to 4x4 traffic, and when bass are exploding on mullet schools, the beachfront resembles the traffic mayhem on the Garden State Parkway, making me question—do people have jobs anymore? Contractor trucks with constantly deflated tires roam the local streets, while other contractors and roofers pounding nails and laying shingles on beachfront homes are waiting and watching from the rooftops for the blitzes moving up and down the coast, primed to blow off work to jump down and make a few casts. The seashore smell is fresh, crisp, clean, and clear. If you could inhale light purple, muted orange, and red, and blend it with ultraclear blue, that's what the September surf would smell like.

You'll see more proper first names in the September logs than any other time of year as the hurricanes rumble through, and rough surf is the standard, with hard-driving easterly swells pounding the beachfront, followed by crisp, brisk clean-up winds and glassy epic waves. It's hard to choose between picking up the surfboard or unhooking the rod from the rack. I don't know, I smell it in my nostrils—the change of season—and it goes down my backbone and into my soul. The crisp, salty flavor and spirit of the Atlantic surf shines through prominently in September. It's a turning point month, and the electricity in the air is very real.

NEED FOR SPEED

Albies start to show up in August, but man, in September, all bets are off. For any surf angler that's put in his or her fair share of time, even constant bass, blues, and fluke can get repetitive, and you always search for that Holy Grail of surf fish. That's where false albacore come into play. Not only are they tough to trick, but surfsters have to have all their ducks in a row. Everything must be lined up—tides, winds, waves, lures, timing, and luck—to be able to land a surf albie or, if the Fish Gods shine upon you, an Atlantic bonito! Sure, it's easy enough to be lucky and spot a roving school; you see them from the terns picking away at the water. A quick albie back rainbows up out of the water and it's back down, then the spearing rush ahead, spraying forward, and you see the immense schools of dozens of albies breaking water and pouncing on baitfish schools like a shooting gallery.

Then they're gone. You have about a 15-second window to make your cast, then they are hundreds of yards up the beach on their 10-knot rush, out of distance, out of range, and you're out of luck. Even if you are in pursuit via beach buggy, it's near impossible to keep up with them, the best you can do is push the pedal down to 30 miles an hour on flat tires on the beach to get a few hundred yards ahead, jump out of the car and immediately start making casts, but by then, they've probably run over the second bar out of casting range, or have altogether gone ghost. It's run and gun fishing at its pinnacle, and most of the time, you are left in their wake. But when you do connect, all it takes is beaching one fish to make a lifetime pursuit worth the while. Sometimes, it's just best to pick a spot on the beach and wait them out. In retrospect, reading over these following journal entries makes me truly believe the pattern for albies to move in is the second to third week of September, on the dot.

September 3

Woo-hoo! Went up to the beach around 2:30 p.m. to read *The Rum Diary* by Hunter S. Thompson. West winds, water clear now, 1- to 2-foot. High tide. Looked off the T-Bird and saw some splash crashes, noted to be bluefish. All of a sudden, saw some little blips and pushes of water—ALBIES! Ran back to house to grab rod with Crippled Herring on it, and by the time I got back, the albies and blues were in an all-out blitz off the T-Bird. Ran into the water up to my elbows and cast as far as I could. Bam! Hooked up with an albie! He screamed drag off my reel and it took 15 to 20 minutes to land him. Got him in, released him at my feet, what a catch! Then cast again and kept getting bombarded right away by blues in the 6- to 10-pound class, big ones that took a good 15 minutes themselves to get in. Got in my Jeep and chased them down to 2nd Ave in Normandy, parked and ran up the beach, with only shorts on. Went right down to the water and hooked into three big blues again, but saw albies within the mix, just that the blues got to it first. Had a little kid named Josh watch me catch fish and said that he catches fish. He was about 5 years old and was fun to talk to. Drove down to Ortley Ave to head them off but they never came down, though I did see them crashing the rainfish schools again, and some anchovies or round herring got beached onshore from the big blues' feeding festival. Got an albie though!

September 11

Reports of albacore have me up early at 6:20 a.m.—well fairly early—at sunrise, hit my beach. Landed two 4-pound bluefish, but man, bait every-freakin'-where, mullet schools, rainfish, spearing, you name it, it's there. Snapper bluefish, which I snagged inadvertently on a Crippled Herring cast. Ray was castnetting mullet. Went to Lavallette, President Ave at 7:30 a.m., saw albies breaking surface out of casting range, only for a minute or two. High tide 10:30, water temp 74, light north winds, seas 1-foot, beautiful and sunny. Going albie hunting all day, hope to find some! Some guy also had a few fluke in the surf in Lavallette.

Later

Went up to my beach to sit out the albies. When I got up, there was a hundred-yard-long and -wide school of albacore busting up baitfish! Winds now were light, 5 knots northeast, very fishy, and the tunny showed up big time! I hooked one then dropped it. BK (Brian Keating) was there too; we followed them up to Brick 3 but moving too fast. There were sporadic little shots cleaning up the mess too, but just out of casting range. Went to Brick 1, then Albertson, then Downer to catch up to them, but they barely made it within casting distance, about 20 yards too short! AHHH! But you could see them vaulting out of the water, rainbowing and pouncing on rainfish, amazing, then the boats made it hard to target them, as they pushed down when the boats would come up. The school kept moving out and north toward Point, but stopped following around 2 p.m. Water was pretty clean, greenish, northeasterly tinge, very fishy.

September 12

Hit my beach early again, overcast, 6:30 a.m. southeast, gray water 2- to 3-feet. Looking around, nothing, looking around for 10 minutes, then wham! Just to the south, albies vaulting out of the water, right in the low tide surf! Saw about a dozen hopping and rainbowing, completely airborne! Made a cast but one cast didn't connect, followed to T-Bird, no dice. Got in car headed up to Princeton as all schools have been going south to north, waited it out for 10 minutes when saw same exact thing, maybe same school? Ran down, made a few casts, no hook up. Looked at Lyman and Bay Head; people there, no signs of albies. Went to Supply to pick up Deadly Dicks and fluorocarbon. Went up to my beach around 11:30, saw Polish guy from down the block and we saw sporadic terns pinpointing albie schools, but super fast, only seconds long before they were gone. Haven't landed one yet! Will keep trying. By the way, weakfish in the nighttime surf on teasers, all spikes, but apparently a load of them in Mantoloking.

September 12

Hit Princeton at 6 a.m. casting bucktail and teaser combo. Low tide at 8:30 and the water has been really skinny lately. Had one hit to the left of the pathway, and saw tons of rainfish out beyond the breakers. They were getting worked by something, bass most likely, since I didn't see any splashing and slapping on the surface and no albies came up greyhounding. Chased them for awhile to no avail. Did see a bunch of slap splashes about a quarter mile out, most likely blues, but hoping for albies. West winds 10 knots. Only break in the weather we've had in a week with 3- to 5-foot seas solid north, east, and south. Ophelia supposed to maybe hit us on Thursday, we'll see.

September 13

Hit my beach at 3 p.m. with my pup, Abby, just walking and casting to 2nd Avenue. Some bird tern plays on schools of albies or blues? Water greenish blue, straight east, sunny skies, 80 degrees out, water at 73, lots of jellyfish eggs in water. Abby kept getting pushed around by the waves and barked me out.

September 13

Hit my beach again for the albies but south winds now hampered the beautiful water we had. Dennis and his 6-year-old son Justin came up and I threw out the Crippled Herring in the evening time underneath the sunset and had one hit, but the hook didn't set since a big blue broke the tip off the hook yesterday. Missed the hookset; when Justin reeled in, he came off. Oh well, I knew it was gonna happen. The tide was low as Justin practiced casts, and he saw something on the sandbar. I walked over to it; it was a stargazer. I picked him up and held him underneath his body and put my thumbs above his eyes and for the first time ever *I Got SHOCKED!* Felt like when you put a wet finger in the electric socket! But it did shock me! I let out a *whoop!* and let him go back into the water, where he submerged and buried himself in the sand. Justin thought that was neat.

Stargazers are cool customers. Shocking to say the least!

September 14

Me and Bugsy got serious and set up for albies on our beach, looking from the "Tunny Tower" on the lifeguard stand. Saw some albies busting and ran to cast to them, but couldn't keep up, ran all the way to Brick 2 almost. Bigger albies about 10 pounds or so vaulting and rainbowing out of the water. Then later in the day about 2 p.m., had another two shots at the albies, chasing them south this time and not hooking into any, it was a one-shot deal and they were gone as fast as they came. Was funny, we ran away from Jackie and Elmo right in the middle of the conversation, same with Jon Harvey earlier in the day, what a conversation breaker albies can be!

That's the thing about false albies. Chances are if you see them, you are already too late to chase them down from the sands. Some days, I have my Jeep parked at the street's end, at the ready to jump in and gas it a quarter mile down to intercept them. Unless they do an about-face and head the other way, it's too late. Man, albies drive me nuts.

September 15

Northwest winds 5 to 10 knots, 2-foot, flat and blue, air 74 degrees, water about 70. Sunny skies, wonderful-looking September day, high tide at 3 p.m. Checked surf at Princeton seeing tiny pops of albie schools out of range. Hit my beach for 1.5 hours from 11:30 a.m. to 1 p.m. deep water, spearing, snapper blues, rainfish, and mullet everywhere, can see them in the waves, only saw an albie or two pop up once for a second and swirl, casting with Deadly Dicks. All albie schools I have seen have been moving south to north.

September 16

Hit my beach, beautiful conditions out, sunny, 84 degrees, glassy blue-green water, light northwest winds, high tide at 3:30. Casted about 4 hours or so with metals to try and blindcast albies, saw occasional swirls and bait spraying, went for a little swim midday, then casted up little snapper blues hitting my Deadly Dick, then went to Manasquan Beach, had two grounded hits from possible fluke by the jetties.

September 16

Hit the suds in the evening at Osborne Ave in Bay Head to see what's up. The water was a brownish color from plankton, or the steady 15-knot south wind that made conditions unfavorable. I did however see a bunch of little tunny working between Osborne and North Ave out past the second bars. I casted as hard as I could, but could not reach them. I even set up on the south side of the North Ave Jetty since it stands out about 40 feet farther than its north side, to give me the extra distance, but they did not come that far down, unless they just didn't like my A17 with no tail. Apparently, croakers, sea robins, small blues being caught on clams and mullet in the surf. High tide 4:56.

When gearing up for albies, if you can load up with light line, like a 20-pound braid, you'll increase your casting distance by a good margin. Any extra foot helps to reach the schools, as it can be a 5-foot differential between getting a hit and blanking out.

September 17

Finally! I set out at 5:50 p.m. or so to check the Bay Head surf, just had a good, clean feeling about it. Started at Osborne looking for bird play, then Bridge, nothing. Then went to Johnson and saw a few gulls picking away right in the undertow to the left of the walkway. Set up with a Megabait jig in blue, green, and silver, 1-oz., the one that looks like a Crippled Herring, and started casting. Had teeny bites and slowed it down enough to finally snooker into about 7 bluefish of about 7 inches, real small. Went to a popper to have some fun, then saw the magic dance up close. Three little tunny galloped and rainbowed out of the water right in front of me. I hucked the popper out once to try and get them to strike. Once I reeled in, in no time I put the Megabait back on. I started casting out as far as I could, and reeled as fast as possible, minus a notch. WHAM! Finally! The false albacore stood me straight up, and then peeled drag like I've never really felt from the surf. He ran, stopped and ran for about two minutes, paralleling the shore all the while pulling drag, breaking the surface three times, until he ran out of juice and I played him onto the sand. A beauty of about 7 to 8 pounds, and he was pumping! You could feel the little, tight, short tail bursts as he fought in the water, different from a bluefish's moderately quick thrashes. I gave the guy next to me an AVA 17 to try and he hooked up. I kept throwing and managed two more tunny. The bite happened around 6:30 p.m. and the sun went down behind the houses at about 6:45 when the bite subsided. I think tunny like the sun, though I did grab my last one at about 6:58 or so. Damn! Tunny are fun off the surf, I know now that I should oil my drag a bit, since it was a little too herky-jerky after the second albacore. They were puking up rainfish of 2 to 3 inches long. And they like to bleed when hooked. Gimme more. Took one dead one that washed up home and stripped him up for fluke bait. My drag still hurts, but not my pride. I'll have to take my Fin-Nor out for some nice oiling, greasing, new line, and some praise to thank him.

Atlantic bonito are pelagic customers and they rarely come close to the surf off Jersey. Truthfully, we barely get to see them, if we are lucky, for about a month, and that's only if summer water temps are high in the 70s and the clarity is gin clear. To find them by boat is an accomplishment, but to find them in the surf, well, that's monumental. This one morning in particular was something special to me.

An impressive and rare feat—my first ever surf-caught bonito, hooked in the Bay Head twilight!

September 24

Abby is new and in town and she kept me up all night. Left Shannon's at 8 a.m. and went to Johnson Ave, where I saw bustling off the jetty. Went running down to surf with Crippled Herring 1-oz. I asked the guy next to me if he caught anything; he said, "Yeah, albies, but didn't bring one in." Cast out and then felt a fight, like a big blue until it got to surf undertow then tail pumped in a boom-boom-boom-boom quick tail bursts not like a tunny and reeled in a . . . Bonito!!! Northeast winds 10 to 15 knots 2- to 3-foot semi-blue-green water . . . then caught three others of 4- to 6-pound class and called Ristori down to take some photos. Unbelievable!!! Once in a lifetime!!! Tried to follow them to Lyman, made a few casts, but they were breaking up on top of surface with birds working it all. Could've probably gotten them on poppers, they were so aggressive!

I've never repeated that feat since, or even come close with conditions all lining up, and truthfully don't think I'll ever have that opportunity again. All I know is that I had that gut feeling when I woke up that morning that something was going to be a little off-kilter, special. Abby's little 7-week-old puppy squeals wouldn't let me sleep for a reason. Thanks, Li'l Boo!

STORM SURF BASS AND BLUES

Remnants of all the hurricanes and tropical storms coming from the Caribbean usually roll their way up to the Jersey beaches in September to meander and hang out for a day, dumping rain and stripping some roof shingles and siding off houses. Some years we'll even get punishing head-on hits like Andrew in 1992, Camille in 1962, or Bill in 2011 with the Category 2 eye running directly over my house in Normandy Beach.

A bruiser 80-pound brown shark hoisted by Mickey and myself.

November is prime time to score stripers on AVA jigs and teasers.

Nothing puts a smile on an angler's face like the first spring striper of the year.

One of many pig blackfish taken off a secret surf wreck.

When spring bluefish come rumbling through, it's a three-ring circus trying to keep up with all the knockdowns.

Legend Al Ristori flashes his iconic smile when he's out pursuing his favorite fare—bluefish. AL RISTORI.

A swashbuckling shot of James struggling to release a striper back into the IBSP suds.

The path home, headed up to the surf for a January striper.

A breathless sunrise over Seaside Park. This is what it's all about.

For the most part, hurricanes graze the coast a hundred or more miles off, and the residual effects are churny 6- to 10-foot seas. They aren't the messy chocolate milk seas a nor'easter ushers in, but clean, whitewatery bombs of waves that create massive cuts and sloughs and some insane striper structure.

Though water temps are generally still warm, in the high 60s to low 70s, any stripers in the area go on the hunt big time when the roiling surf unearths clams from their roots, smashing and crushing them along the surfline, providing a surf buffet line for any bass in the area. Add to that the cool nighttime air temps plummeting to the high 40s, and the presence of mullet, sand eel, and peanut bunker schools that begin their fall migration southward, and the combination is set up for some quality early fall season bass fishing.

Those skinny bluefish that came to the shores in spring have had a long summer of fattening up on fatbacks and all sorts of hapless fish, and now, equipped with sledgehammer sized heads and porky bodies to boot, they are primed to make their assault along the surf. Alligator 12- to 20-pound bluefish come crashing through as bait schools choke inshore waters, creating a combustible mix. If you've got the stamina to challenge the stormy surf with swashing currents and bombing waves, now's the time for some heavyweight fights.

September 5

Ernesto rumbled through with heavy 12- to 14-foot seas, then calmed down. Today high tide 5:30 a.m. Hit Princeton in 15 to 20 NE winds, at around 6 a.m., a guy there had five bass to 29 inches and a big 15-pound blue. I cast out an A-Salt mullet color with teaser, the plug took a 2-pound blue, had another bluefish on the teaser and switched up to a Crippled Herring, on which I had a strike and fought it to the suds where it got off, might've been a small bass. Another guy had a 27-inch bass on clams. Water warm, around 75 now, looks good for week ahead.

September 5

High around 2:30 p.m. Light offshore winds. Fished my beach today, with Hurricane Fabian's swell, huge breakers 4- to 7-foot solid, with occasional 10-footers coming through. Tried to fish for brown sharks in the churny surf. Extremely sunny, Bermuda high, casted out the Meat Stick with mullet and the Loomis with mullet as well. Had trouble holding with 8 ounces on a torrid south drift that had my baits in on shore in a matter of minutes. Managed two sea robins out of the whole deal, found out that the Hatteras sinkers didn't hold as well as the Pyramids.

September 8

Hit Mantoloking at 5:20 a.m. dark, sunrise at 6:35 a.m. or so. Leftovers from Hannah leave 3- to 5-foot surf, classy and slick like, peanut bunker schools getting sprayed,

Telltale signs of a deadstick outing—surf clams and bunker chunks.

though didn't see any visual confirmation. Lost black Bomber on second cast, no lures in the bag since I gave most away on my travels, cast an A17 out but no hits. Did see dolphins way far out jumping and frolicking. Lost Hi-Flier was on the beach with red flag, concrete anchor got washed in from the offshore grounds from Hannah's strong swell. Low tide 8:00 a.m. Beautiful pink sunrise.

September 9

Bluefish smackin' mullet schools at A10 IBSP, stopped by Bum Rogers later for beers, blackberry brandy shots, and chicken wings. Fished 2 p.m. to 6:00 p.m., high tide 3:30 p.m. All around the high tide were bluefish, 4- to 14-pound, and they were slammin' poppers and bunker chunks, but stayed off of mullet, though mullet schools were streaming up into the sandwash in unbelievable numbers! Mullet were running for their lives, Mickey and Marc had a blast.

Some interesting things always wash up after the hurricane blows.

September 11

Well, the nor'east blow that has been on us for 10 days straight finally culminated into 10- to 15-foot seas, nasty. Found rotting sea turtle on beach, along with hi-flier markers and a life preserver. Inlet absolutely flooded. Fisherman's Memorial too, jellyfish in the streets! Really deep bowls, cuts, and sloughs now, even on low tide.

September 15

Getting Hurricane Gordon's swell, and it's big: 6- to 7-foot solid in the surf and glassy. Hit the surf in the morning, west winds 10 knots, tons of water on the inside even at low tide, at 6 a.m. almost low tide, cast black Bomber, saw schools of medium bunkers getting worked, with bass boiling and vaulting out of the air like 5 feet to crash on them! Reached outside of the waves and in the whitewash on the inside got whacked big time, started pulling drag out nicely, three or four runs, then beached a 33-inch striper, fat and sassy. Bluefish were jumping around at my feet as well. There was a lot of action, and bait is everywhere, mullet moving out.

September 16

Hit IBSP A10 again, 2- to 3-foot northeast, had blues chasing sand eels, beached three blues 8 to 12 pounds, one coughed up 52 sand eels and two digested snapper blues! Seagulls were swiping at us as we threw sand eels up in the air. A few sea robins too. Got real drunk at Crab's Claw and UB's, then fished my beach at midnight, didn't catch anything, but passed out cold drunk on the beach for a half hour.

September 17

Overnight, the waters really cleaned up with a steady west wind in the dark. Fished at 6:20 in the morn at my beach, and the water really looked like a freakin' bass heaven: 2-foot waves, churning water, and mullet swirling in the undertow. But the temps are still around 66 degrees, a bit too warm, even though I heard of the occasional striper to 12 pounds coming up on clams. Cast a black Mambo minnow, and had two bluefish to 4 pounds. The blues are reaching chopper size now, and during the day, I witnessed schools of just over snapper-size blues schooling in the wash moving south. A guy had a fluke on a yellow Bomber and teaser combo around 3 p.m. High tide 6 p.m.

September 19

Woke up at 6 a.m. to fish my beach again, nice clean and clear surf, west winds, 1- to 2-foot, mullet getting crashed on now in surf. Cast out Bombers and teasers, had a hickory shad, then about 6 small bluefish and two taps from bass, guys had about another 6 blues on bunker chunks and clams. Mullet schools getting pushed around, bluefish had small 2-inch 005-sized sand eels in their stomachs.

Night

Hit my beach after we went to the Festival of the Sea and cast bunker and herring chunks out, plenty of little taps, had a bonfire with Amos, Eddie, Lauren, Jon, and Katie, no real hits except for one—I reel in what seemed like dead weight, but it took off north to the T-Bird fast. Eventually battled and landed a huge 50-pound southern stingray! Equipped with large barb and whippy tail that kept trying to whip me.

Released him with everybody checking it out around us. Ordered a pizza to the beach and had it delivered to us from Lenny's!

That was a classy move, getting pizza delivered to the beach. Lenny's rules.

September 21

After Hurricane Isabel and two weeks of constant 25-knot NE blow, hit my beach with Lido and Spann at 6 a.m. Mullet, spearing, peanut bunker have begun to spill out of the backwaters on the high tides now, and are hugging the coastline. You could cast net them in the suds today. They were getting worked by small to medium bluefish. Had one sea robin on a 3-ounce bucktail with a Bass Assassin. Surf was rough and wind stiff to cast effectively. Bait breaking and rippling everywhere. We cast out mullet rigs, NE 20-knot wind, high tide 4:38, and we caught 10 bluefish from 2 to 10 pounds during the day. Spann had the 10-pounder around 6:30 a.m. We also caught over 45 sea robins, fished till 2 p.m. Apparently, croakers in the surf as well, taking small clam strips. Constant action hitting the mullet rigs, plenty of cuts and sloughs from Isabel. Hit the evening surf too with Crippled Herring, went southeast, three strikes, probably small blues.

September 22

Full harvest moon tomorrow, first day of fall, too. Seas 5-foot, wind south at 15 knots, water brown. Tossed Bomber and AVA jig in surf 6 to 7 a.m. no hits, sunrise about 6:30 now, dead dark at 6 a.m. Bait everywhere you can see rippling even in rough surf, bass at IBSP this week on AVA jigs.

September 30

Hit A10 IBSP with Mickey again. Waves 2- to 4-foot, heavy water, east to southeast winds 15 knots. Low tide at 2:30 got there 3 p.m., had one fluke immediately on AVA jig, then Mick had a 12-pound blue on a bunker chunk. Lots of sea robins, then Mickey landed a 27-inch bass on clam around 4:30 p.m. I landed a 26-inch bass around 6 p.m. Fresh clams got all the bass. Later that night went to Broadway and ate wings, got bombed. Mick's friend James was there too to drive us. Got back to the house, went up to the beach to fish. Fished for hour and a half and I bagged two 27-inch stripers and Mick got another short too, all on clams. Some tiny smooth dogs out there biting, too, came back here and stayed up late till 5 a.m.

September 30

Tropical storm Nicole kind of here with 6-foot seas southeast 30 knots, kind of missing us going inland, water pretty clean, gray whitewater. Casted metals and bucktails in stiff south current, but no takers. Mickey had a lot of weakfish fishing LBI back bays from dock yesterday.

Decking sunrise stripers at IBSP.

BIOLUMINESCENCE

The guys up north of Jersey in New England call it "fire in the water," but it's more commonly known as bioluminescence. I've noticed it only really comes around our waters in September, but whatever you choose to call it, it's generally accepted that it turns off the bite in the surf as its presence sticks around for a good three days or so. If anything, it's a trip to walk the beaches at night and see every step you take light up like a floodlight underneath your feet.

September 22

Southeast winds still prevail, but I walked the beach at nighttime and saw my feet lighting up underneath me like some alien, magic! It was wild, my footsteps were actually glowing for a two foot radius around my feet with each step! I think it's what they call fire on the water, looks like minute phytoplankton, but I found a sand flea that was energized with this stuff, brought it back to my house and it glowed all night long from its inside. It was a green glow-stick type of glow. Weird stuff!

September 24

All the bait schools round, thick in pods off the coast, peanuts and mullet schools were getting roostertailed by threshers today. Saw a few schools with the white-water roostertail so I hit up my beach with bunker heads from 6 p.m. to 9:30 p.m., but no dice. Bioluminesence starting to show on the sand.

SCREWING AROUND BATTLING BEASTIES

Fisherman love consistency, the truth in knowing you can go out to a certain spot and a certain tide and pull on a striper or something to that effect. Applied knowledge is grand. But fishermen are also built with an equal drive to search out the unordinary, to be surprised, the need to do something different, switch it up a bit when the surf gets too rough to fish.

Sometimes, it's not even about catching anything, but just to cut loose and have some fun. Those fine times usually start out swilling a few brews with the boys, and end up trying your luck off the local docks to get your crabbing on. Or sometimes, after a night out at the local watering holes, you grab the nearest rod and reel, with no plan or direction, and stumble up to the beach to make a few casts in the darkness. Whatever the case, it always ends up being more fun than you expected it to be. It's not the size of the fish that matters, but the times spent goofing off and targeting creatures you wouldn't normally go after. Basically, forgetting about trophy dream fish for a little bit and just havin' a little fun.

September 2

Hit Emma's with Hukkanen and was ready to go to sleep around 5 a.m. when I decided to stay up and fish instead. Went to my beach with rod in hand and got comfortable by the bench underneath the stars, taking a snooze under Orion and watching the sun push up. Woke at 6:15 a.m. and decided to go to Princeton. Immediately started casting to the right and it was nonstop; out of 15 casts, I had 14 sea robins! Then a short fluke and a bluefish. Did see some fish working bait schools for sure, boiling. Finished up around 7:30 a.m. and finally went to bed.

September 5

Dad came down to fish and crab the bayside. We set out three crab lines, but before we could reel them up, we cast out bobbers with squid and spearing. Dad was fighting with small snapper blues and brought in three needlefish! I bucktailed up a small fluke, three black drum, and a tailor bluefish. Dad then had a blowfish. A wild array of species in the morning hours. Crabs were small and not pinching at the docks, so we went to the ocean to cast out three rods: one with bunker head that got really whacked hard once, another with bunker chunks, and a third with spearing, which I cast out and dragged back to bring in two little young-of-the-year dogfish. Though no doubt I also had a few fluke on that shook the hook on the way in.

September 16

Hit the Sand Bar docks to screw around at high tide 7:30 or so at night. Hotties all over the Sand Bar, but alas, I must fish. I cast around and got little taps, but nothing solid. Then saw by the dock corner some weird fish checking out my bucktail, they could've been blues, weaks but looked like something weird like jacks or something, bigger ones were hanging off the riverside of the dock and had them bump my bait a few times but didn't hook up. They really looked like some kind of jack or something??? Found out, I think they're spots.

September 18

PRE-Fiesta as Irish, Greg, Sophie came down to fish tonight with clams and bunker high tide at 8:30 p.m., dark already at 7:15 now, cast out and had about a dozen 1- to 3-pound bluefish and two spotted hake, which were grilled up at the house and had some good eats at 2 a.m. Pilot whales spouting 50-foot sprays all over!

Besides going toe-to-toe with a common skate, there's probably nothing more lowly than catching a wimpy 6-inch spotted hake in the surf. But they are rare, and kinda cool-looking, which makes them worthy in my book.

September 20

Bugsy, Elmo, and I hit the Bayside Dock to screw around with the tons of little fish around in the back bays. I threw out a crab trap with a 3-year-old flounder chum log in it to set up a slick. We cast out little size 8 hooks with clam bits on them and mercilessly got whacked by snapper blues, blowfish, and small weakfish. It was awesome! I even had a nuclear-sized eel slam into a clam bait and the thing had to go about 6 pounds! Bugsy hooked up to a juvenile black drum that he lost at the bulkhead, about 15 inches long. Elmo casted small plugs to bag two little weakfish and some snappers. Was fun all around. The blowfish were omnipresent, nipping at the baits, and I landed a few of them, they puffed up and got mad on me, it was hilarious!

September 29

Hit up Sand Bar with Cali and Willie for a few smoothies. Checked the slow waters by the gas dock at the high tide at around 10 p.m. and saw all sorts of mantis shrimp swimming around forwardly. I nabbed a few to check out and they were about 1 to 2 inches with their praying mantis–type claws, I think they were mantis shrimps? Then I saw a rippling on the surface, I shot my hand into the mix and grabbed a 2-inch fluke straight from out of the water! It looked awesome, so miniature with two bug eyes and breathing, I let him go and he fluttered down to the depths. Water still about 70, nights down to 43 now.

MIXED BAG

Though I haven't given them their due yet, it should be noted that sea robins are usually an unwelcome customer that will fill the bill when the bite is slow and a bent rod is needed to keep morale up. They aren't desired, save for a few fishermen that swear by the tastiness of their meat, which I do not doubt is succulent, as they are a delicacy in New Zealand known as gunards, though I can't recall ever filleting them for anything more than for use as fluke strip baits. Nonetheless, sea robins, with their grunty, fan-finned, brown-and-orange colorings, put up a decent fight on the beach, and are worthy of at least a few words. Other customers in the September grab bag include loads of fluke, kingfish, and weakfish.

September 1

Woke up at 2 a.m. Couldn't sleep, hit my beach at 6 a.m. Dead-high, just getting light out then, sunrise about 6:45 a.m. or so. Northeast winds 10 to 15 knots, seas 3- to 4-foot. Big sandbar, lots of water on the inside of it, found fluke in one pocket right in slough in undertow, found another group on the inside of the sandbar. Beached another 14 fluke, all shorts, but had one on that shook the hook—felt like a 3- to 5-pounder! Two sea robins too. Fished till 8, weird low clouds only a few dozen yards above me, Super Mario Brothers–type clouds. Best to let bucktail slack up and pull, twitch it, so long as it's on bottom, $\frac{3}{8}$-ounce could've probably used a $\frac{1}{2}$-ounce to hold better. Oh, actually had a doubleheader fluke on one cast! Low 60 this morn, first day of wearing long sleeves.

September 3

Fished the evening on my beach with a bucktail teaser combo. Had one nice hit by some fluke of about 2 to 3 pounds for sure that I dropped right in the undertow; he must've followed it in from the sandbar and hit right at the last second. Also saw a few sea robins chase my buck all the way in without hitting it. Big sandbar off my beach, no holes to let stuff in or out yet.

September 10

Hit my surf, starting to see 4- to 7-foot swell from Hurricane Florence now. Low tide 5 p.m., hit it at 6 to 7 p.m. Casting bucktails, had one hit that seemed like a nicer 2-pound or so fluke that shook and spit the hook since I didn't have a good hookset on him. Nothing else, but heavy water inside on the low tide, full moon was on Thursday, four days ago.

September 11

Hard NE winds still hammering the coast for the fifth straight day. Bermuda high still sitting on us with impeccable blue skies. Decided to fish the Manasquan River again. Headed out to the train bridge to cast a few. The cinder worm hatch is on full steam. It usually starts mid to late August, but is late like everything else this year. No action here, so went to the Brielle Yacht Basin gas dock. Heard and saw splashes, blues and weaks and bass slurping down the worms. High tide supposed to be at 9:38 p.m., but NE wind delayed it till seriously 11:45 p.m. for the slack, it was late. Saw spearing and tiny rainfish corralled in the corners by the end boats, tiny crabs and cinder worms all over. Had a bass come out and strike my ³⁄₈-ounce Fin-S fish, and I lost him due to the close quarters. I then opened my bail set the rod down and handcasted, jigging up the Fin-S like ice fishing. Boom! The bass hit again, and I handlined a spunky 16-inch striper up onto the dock, it was awesome! Had a few quarter-pounder bluefish, they were shredding my Fin-S. Went over to the canal to have few casts, too windy and dark for anything productive. First day after the full moon, it was a bit cloudy, so no real overhead light. The river is definitely alive with all sorts of species.

September 12

Went down to fish with Andy from Riptide at Brigantine Beach for Kingies, joined Gary Borne and Charlie Hollowel and we drove on to the bird sanctuary first to cast out small bloods and mullet bits to pull on small kings outside the first bar, along with spot, and small weakfish. Then drove to the north end just inside wreck inlet to cast out again to bag weakfish up to 16 inches and Gary had a 15-inch king. Fun to cast out far with small pill floats and size 4 hooks. Lot of skinny water there, though you can find holes on the north end with churny rips and swashing. Water a bit brown with heavy west winds, seas 1- to 3-foot. There is a shipwreck there too that Gary said he gets blackies off of, thinking about heading back in late fall!

September 13

Hurricane after the bad blow has been riling up our waters, steady east winds last week or so, made the water muddy and rough. But west wind this morn cleaned it up a bit and sparked some excellent activity. Got to beach at about 6:45 in morn and saw mullet and p-nut bunker schools all over the place. They were getting worked, I looked closely enough but only saw splashing at first, but kept persisting to determine the culprits and found the bait getting torpedoed—little tunny! Yup, they are definitely here now, albeit just out of casting range. I threw a homemade chartreuse buck with rainbow Fin-S and white-brown teaser and bagged a 14-inch fluke right down from the path. Walked south and saw a guy pulling a small bluefish out. Mullet was getting corralled and worked in all sorts of pods up and down from me. I bucktailed another short fluke of 12 inches right at my feet with a white SPRO buck this time. Water very warm at about 75 now, with the latest east winds, and sounds like the baitfish have begun to exit the back bays. The mullet run has started.

September 21

Me and Bugsy hit my beach with mullet rigs, hoping to bag a brown shark or something, high tide 1:53 p.m., beautiful sunny day, 75 degrees, west wind. Used squid on fluke rigs and fresh Ernie's mullet. Bugsy got a takedown at about 1:20 p.m. and battled a 4- to 5-pound blue to the beach. I got whacked on the big rod with a double mullet rig, and fought a 10-pound solid blue to the undertow where my crappy old Silstar reel locked up on the drag and the ensuing wave snapped him off rig and all. There were bluefish blitzing on the mullet outside the breakers and birds picking at the surface, maybe little tunny underneath the birds?

September 23

Hit IBSP A15 with Mickey, high at 1 p.m., fished 1 p.m. to 4 p.m., south winds 15 knots. Tons of mullet and sand eels in water, dolphin everywhere corralling bait and jumping around, also pilot or minke whales offshore spouting plumes of spray again. Nobody had any bent rods around us, sun came out, turned out to be a nice day, only had one snapper-sized bluefish that ate a Fishbite.

Standing in the surf in shorts in 48-degree weather when the surf is at 65 degrees, is pretty darn cold. It feels like a true baptism. Waders are not needed, yet they would be a creature comfort. That part of the Fall Run has yet to start and creep into the soul. Hardy, yes; comfortable, not so much yet. Two weeks from now, in October, waders will be a necessity.

September 25

Got home from Ocean City, and hit the beach at 3 p.m. to 5 p.m. Threw out some fresh mullet on mullet rigs, which, by the way, are annoying when the double hook falls off, they need to tighten that gap better. I only had about 14 sea robins on the day, nothing much else bit on the low and incoming tide.

September 29

Joey came down with his bud, Phil, and we casted out mullet rigs on the beach from 6 p.m. till 7 p.m. dark. Had not one bite, but threw back a few beers, and had a few laughs. Low tide 4:38 p.m., west winds, nice clean 3- to 4-foot waves, good surf variety. Have to change the line on my rod, it freakin' snapped two mullet rigs off, weights baited and all, too much UV damage this year I think.

September 30

West winds 10 knots. Low tide 6:30 p.m. The west wind pushed the water off of the bars, exposing the beauty of the clear, sandy sea. All sorts of mussels, clams, driftwood, horseshoe crab parts, sea glass, and other assorted maritime debris washed up. I strolled along with my 6½-foot Shimano, casting a ⅜-ounce white bucktail. I had tied into one sea robin that displayed his wings beautifully and grunted begrudgingly to my hook in his mouth.

This evening was something else. I smelled the reason for life on the salty wind. The orange glow of sunset on the clear and crisp waves was joyful. I was taken back to late fall at home in Clinton, smelling the sparks of a fire burning, the almost comfortable cooler temperature of the wind, wearing shorts, and life all around emanating the life

Matty Monogas's dog Brielle takes it easy during a lazy September surf day.

force of the collective soul, preparing to live full and live wild, and live free, all truly chasing the same dream to be at one with the Love of God. My collective string of memories sometimes eludes me, but on those rare occasions when I do catch up to it, I am truly in a place that I know in my heart is meant to be. I need to catch up to that more often.

TOG TIME

When nasty seas make for near impossible fishing, the local boys know we can tuck in and hit some backpocket sheltered spots on land to target one of the most daunting fish in the ocean—tautog, or blackfish. Blackfish are commonly thought of as wreck fish that you can only truly target by boat on the ocean grounds, but the bucktoothed brawlers stack up on any inside bay and inlet structure as well, and that's a well-guarded secret among many local anglers.

September 16

Hit canal for toggin' with Dave, they only bit on the dead slack again at 10 a.m. through to 11 a.m., lots of shorts, about 30 of them, and an oyster cracker! And two almost-keepers on green crabs and clams.

September 22

One full week of 15- to 25-knot northeast winds has the bass and blues biting better now with some teener-size bass hitting in the surf. I hit the canal at 4 p.m. high, slack

Ol' whitechinners love green crabs dropped off the pier.

using size 6 hooks, size 4 would be better there, fished the grass edge, other lot up from the marine police. In one hour, using green crabs, hoisted out 24 tog, 4 keepers to 17 inches! Awesome fun, all even before the true slack tide, water still running in when I left! Mullet all over backwaters up and down coast. Water temp 68 degrees.

September 24

Hit canal, claimed lots of blackies, no keepers though.

September 25

Hit canal for slack at 12:30 p.m., blackfish biting very soft, sunny, 85 degrees, beautiful day, they have been getting a few weakies and hickory shad in the surf.

September 26

I know blackies in the canal right now so hit up C—— wreck, which I believe is now the C—— wreck for tog, solid 15- to 20-knot south winds cast out on full moon low tide at 2:00 p.m. to try and get through the blow, had five sea robins. Had hit like tog immediately when it landed. Cut both my forefinger and middle finger up real good, sliced off from braid line guillotine, but will tape up and be back tomorrow.

September 29

Seany came up and we hit the canal marine police side, 2nd spot with greenies. We cleaned up on tog again, had about 52 or so, tide was 3½ hours after high at 11 a.m., though found the tog biting better when the tide was moving an hour before and two hours after. One guy had a 4-pounder, we had about 5 keepers.

September 29

Hit canal at 1:30 p.m., fished till 3:30 p.m. with Mickey, more tog actually hooked today, used small greenies, next to wall most bites, had them to almost-keeper size, lot of short bites and soft nudges. Other guy there had some oyster crackers. Spearing all over the place, seems like some bass or blues attacking them from below.

UFOS!

And this, well, this had to be included. It was Labor Day weekend, 2007, and my beach was the spotlight of all cable news networks, as a reported UFO crashed in the ocean a mile off the beach. Yeah, I said UFO. News trucks jammed up the sandy street with reporters shoving microphones into any drunk, wide-eyed tourist's face they could find for interviews that blanketed the news networks. Reports ranged widely from beachgoers seeing a fireball crash into the ocean, others dismissed it as a barge that caught on fire off the coast, or a military missile test gone wrong from Fort Dix, but there was never any official explanation as to what happened. The next four days, zillions of pieces of trash, medical waste, logs, dead fish, pieces of dock, and strange-looking plastic and metals washed up on the shoreline! Whatever it was, something destructive happened for sure.

September 2

Hit my beach waiting for Shannon for a Labor Day party. Cast out a bucktail, on which I had one small fluke in front of the T-Bird. Seas 2- to 3-foot, easterly winds. Last night a UFO crashed into the waters in a fireball and huge splash right off my beach! Made Fox news! They said it might have been a meteor! People were freaking all over the beaches getting interviewed by news channels. Then a live thresher shark washed up off Rockaway Beach, Long Island, and another thresher washed up in Ventnor, also a lone head of one off the Surf Club!

Just a bunch of weird stuff going down that day. Who knows what the heck it was all about. Weird!

8 October

THE FALL RUN

October. The first real crisp of fall arrives, not gracefully, but with immediate 35-degree night temperatures, an impending nor'easter always on the rise, and loads of sand eels, peanut bunker, and mullet in the wash. It all spells striped bass. The first rites to the Fall Run are elemental to living a surf fisherman's life. This is when it begins to get uncomfortable, including arriving to your workplace 30 minutes to an hour late and conjuring up a halfhearted excuse for your boss from sticking out a hot morning bite. Unforgiving, cold, and clammy neoprene waders are pried onto your legs predawn, the sock hat goes on to warm your head and ears, and the headlamp is donned to guide you through the night darkness, with twinkling stars high and sparkly in the black sky. This is most certainly the time, the first instance of the fall, when things can really pop. This is what you've been waiting for since the last spring days of those 20- to 40-pound bass in June. The surf awakens, prosperously.

Now I have the advantage of putting my Jeep on the beach to ride the sands to see what just may lie in the holes a mile or two down from me, or maybe 7 miles down. I do have all the required permits, which I most responsibly attained by shelling out a couple hundred bucks to outfit my Jeep with the required gear and assemblage of trinkets that are needed, including a car jack, spare tire, fire extinguisher, and first-aid kit, not to mention tire deflators and a good can of dip, and if I go into evening time, a solid six-pack of Yuengling.

Big bass are on the prowl, and I can't wait to redefine the recent norm of summertime doldrums, devoid of bass, to see just what this new cold front environment will bring. The air sends a chill down my spine now. It wasn't like this two days ago; that's how it happens. The switch gets flipped and fall hits immediately, with no warning. A crispness fills the nostrils when you step outside, and the stinging bitterness questions your motivation and dedication when you first step into it. The crashing sound of the waves reinforces your belief that you are doing something grand and real, something wonderful, even if you don't have tug on the end of your line after all your efforts. Noontime, I have to go back to work and write about this, but meantime, I look forward to the anticipation of what may come. I sound the alarm for all my brethren to head on down as fast as their wives, girlfriends, or jobs allow them to. I am the Paul Revere of the surf: *The bass are coming! The bass are coming!*

In the fall along the Jersey beachfront, there are no vibrant red, yellow, and orange leaves falling from maple and sycamore trees, just gnarled and bent scrub pine trees with prickly evergreen needles and brown pine cones falling off, while store-bought vibrant chrysanthemums bloom on front porches of beach bungalows. The textbook colorings associated with fall in the Northeast are absent all along this coastline; the beauty that shines through here is of a different kind.

Radiant orange and black monarch butterflies populate the winds all along the sand dunes as they get blown offshore in their migration to southerly climes; it makes for a surreal experience when you take the time to notice the thousands of them flitting over sand dunes between casts. Like broken church windows, crystalline shards of antique technicolored glass wash up from the hurricane swells uprooting shipwreck bottles—blues, greens, whites, browns, and even the hallowed red shards can be found washed up amongst the crushed shells and polished pebbles on the low tide. (Red glass is made with gold specks, and was only in use until the early 1900s.) If you're lucky, you can even find broken pieces of T&R Booth china plates and teaware, with striking blue engraving ink on milky white china, rounded and smoothed down from washing around in the sand for two centuries of tide and time.

Rolling sand dunes and their sawgrasses wave lazily in the winds, while black-and-white-crested bitter terns shriek as their orange feet plant in the tide line. The musty smell of beach foxes hiding in the dunes with their scruffy brown and red coats, looking for a free meal of cut bunker, leads me to follow their footprints along the tops of the sand dunes. Before I take a cast, I'll put the rod down, cup my hands for a full handful of sea water and inhale it into my nostrils, feeling the salt enter my system. It purges, it cleans, and it gives me life.

October holds a special place in my heart. As my Dad always says every year when it comes around, "There's so much to do in October, you don't know where to begin. The bucks are rutting, the bass are biting, the geese are flocking, turkey are moving, the blues are running. You just don't know where to start." He's right. If you don't plan your time out well in October, you'll end up doing nothing, running yourself in circles chasing your tail. You need to have kind of a rough plan to split up your fishing and hunting, so you can fit it all in during the 31 days of pure bliss that are October.

A CHILD'S DREAM

As a child, sitting around the dinner table in the Septembers of my youth, I remember vividly my Dad and Uncle Greg talking about the "Fall Run" of striped bass—this happening where you could go down to the beach and, from the sand, make casts to pluck hundreds of stripers out of the roiling surfwaters. The implication that this kind of dream sequence could happen was enough for me to nearly wet my pants, but thankfully, I was able to hold it together. The Fall Run, it turns out, is a real thing—not a mystery, but certainly magical.

The Run is simple. Schools of stripers migrate southward on their way back down the Eastern Seaboard, following the 58- to 63-degree water temperatures, as well as myriad baitfish schools, and they are always aggressive and ready to feed. If luck shines, bombastic bluefish will also be in the mix, and if Lady Luck is truly alive, weakfish will be in the melee too. It's a sunup to sundown, on through the night type of affair, and it cannot be defined as anything but world class. Some years are more productive and crazier than others, but there are always fish to be caught and stories to be born. And it's truly grand.

BOMBERS AND BASS—PLUGGING AWAY

Remaining mullet schools trickle into the undertow in the tenth month of the year, and in Jersey, the gem in the surf bag arsenal is the Bomber lure—a black Bomber Long-A or A-Salt, more precisely. These lures alone have claimed more fish in the 2000s than probably any other during this decade, most probably due to the media types like myself that have bought it, used it with success, and promoted it. The black Bomber's subtle swagger under moonlit nights and at times of predawn and dusk is something bass simply cannot deny. All you will hear along the Jersey Coast is black Bomber, black Bomber, even if some hot new lure comes out. The black coloring is red hot during low-light hours as bass hone in and crush the silhouette from below. Some variations, like the Mambo Minnow or Stillwater 5-inch Beach Runner, will work too. It's that mullet-type profile and coloring that have claimed more fish in the shorty to 33-inch class than I can count. Though when the going gets strong and the big girls push in, it's all about large, homegrown and handcrafted wooden plugs—swimmers, poppers, and darters—that Jersey is so famous for.

October 3

Fished from 5:15 a.m. on till 7:30 a.m. Light west winds, seas 1- to 2-foot, water temp around 65. Cast black Mambo out, had one strike in the undertow that exploded like a depth charge, it shocked me in the dark night, so much that I scampered backwards in thought of being devoured by a shoreline-hugging great white, but it ended up being a feisty 26-inch striper. He really whacked it, sitting about 8 feet in front of me in the undertow. Saw some incredible shooting stars, and then was privy to an ethereal sunrise.

October 5

Lido came down and we fished the Governor's Cup at IBSP. We waded along the shoreline, you need waders now, the morning air is in the 40s, seas 3- to 4-foot, and the waves were crashing in the wash, soaking us. Black Mambo produced a 26-inch bass smack dab in the undertow again at around 5:45 a.m. Lido hooked up with his shortly thereafter using a redhead and a sand eel-like teaser. His went about 24 inches and hit the teaser. I had a sea robin and a small tailer bluefish. We met up with Gary Cogland of *New Jersey Fishing Show*, and fished a bit with him, till about 8 a.m. Saw a huge beam piece of an old schooner shipwreck was around in the undertow, it had brass spikes and knobs on it. Met up with Austin, who had caught a spunky 18-inch bass on his teaser rig. Mullet being chased in the surf, the mullet run should have tapered off by now, but it is still thick in the surf. Got interviewed for *New Jersey Fishing Show*, and I was a bit out of sorts, delirious if you will, should be funny to see.

Came home and hit my beach at around 1:30 p.m. and cast out mullet and clams. Nothing to show for our efforts, the waves were 3- to 4-foot solid, west wind 10 knots. Saw a mess of mullet rippling out past the second bar, they kept coming by and around evening time, saw swirls whirlpooling around and under some schools. I cast out with a Yo-Zuri silver/blue plug but could not reach them, I believe they were bass. Deg and his family showed up later, and Deg grabbed a rod and cast, hooking up with a tailer bluefish, while his son Nicky watched. Little Nicky sat on the ground and cried "Daddy got to catch a fish AND he did a charter this morning," under a stream of steady tears. Well said, Nicky, well said.

Lido and I indulged in a few Yuenglings, and broke out the yellowfin and mahi in my fridge, headed over to Amos's and grilled up just about the damn best tasting tuna and dolphin I've ever had. I marinated the steaks in this Wasabi oil sauce from the Normandy Beach Market. Holy mackerel, was it good. The mahi fillets were wrapped in aluminum foil, draped in olive oil, crushed red pepper, black pepper, and a hint of garlic, basted on the grill. We all ate famously well.

October 6

Deg met me at my house at 5:15 a.m. We hit my beach, waves solid, 4-foot and glassy, wind from the west 15 knots. High tide 5:30 a.m. The beach is sloped and the surf is heavy on the inside since we have no more sand, since Isabel. It was fairly dangerous in the night morn hours, since it virtually sucked us back into the sea with its salty tongue. It's actually great for bait to get stuck in close in the deep slough now that runs along the inside. Cast usual dark hour plugs, and didn't hook up with anything. The sun came up with a Technicolor explosion of purple, blue, red, orange, yellow, and lavender-red.

Was beautiful. Saw another streaking shooting star crossing the bright Orion underneath the jet-black sky, sparkled with blinking starlight. We left my beach at 7:30, looked at Downer Ave, then made a few casts in Bay Head, then at the Pocket. Some guy had caught 6 fluke from the jacks, and said the little tunny came through on the Manasquan side, but we missed it. It was 9:00 now.

October 15

Couldn't sleep all night, woke up at 4 a.m., decided to hit Bay Head with my new black Bombers. Got to Osborne at 5 a.m. and walked all the way down to Johnson, plugging away. High tide around 9:30 a.m., waves 2- to 3-foot, no wind. Dark out, cloudy, new moon last night. Had only one hit on Mount Street at about 5:30 a.m. in the pitch black, small bass I assume whacked my plug, had him on for a sec, then saw him surface and throw my plug, probably about 20-inch bass. The bioluminescence is pretty much gone now, though it was here the last week or two.

October 15

Hit my beach again, this time constant 30- to 40-knot west blow, low tide 6:30 a.m., water like hot mocha chocolate milk, brown as anything, but yellow teaser showed up nicely in the dank liquid. Maybe throw yellow Bomber when conditions like this prevail. Hard west and low tide made water extremely thin, though 2-foot waves still making their way over the outside bar, filling up the inside with some water. Some clams washed up, no fish today though. 40- to 80-pound tuna being caught in the canyons still, sprayed clouds in the sky from solid west winds. Spectacular sunrise over the white-tipped waves of the morning, glassy and frothy ocean.

October 15

Hit the suds at 6:20 a.m., it was still dark out, the clocks turn back next week. The surf is still rough, 4- to 5-foot, and there is a lot of water pushing in behind the breakers. The sand bar is defined outside, where the beach got swept out about 30 yards. Casted a black Bomber to no avail into 20-knot east winds, which landed basically 10 feet out. Put on heavier darters, and Rat-L-Traps, but still couldn't really cast with any distance. Jimmer brought some clams up around 7:15 a.m. and had one little bite, then as we were leaving, he pulled in a 26-inch bass, nice colors, and healthy. Storm of 40-knot winds coming tomorrow, we'll see what it does for the bassin'.

October 21

Fished my beach casting black Bombers, poppers, from 5:30 a.m. to 8 a.m. with nothing to show. It got quiet real quick. Some bluefish in the 3-pound size were apparently caught, but the surf looked good with some cuts from the last storm. I think it still needs to drop a bit in temps. Some bait was getting scattered in the undertow when I would reel in the plug, but it all looked small. Went out in the afternoon with fresh clams from the suds and casted out from about 3 to 5 p.m. with nothing to show. No bird play or any sign of bait.

October 22

Fished with Jackson at Island Beach from 6:30 a.m. to 8:30 a.m. with Bombers and Rat-L-Traps. Nothing to show again. N/NW winds about 10 knots. The beaches of Island Beach carry a lot of water and there are some sweet cuts there, no wonder bass love to hang there. High tide 10:30. Fished area A21. Full moon.

October 29

Hit my beach and it was bananas! I came down and Jimmer already had 8 bass on black Mambos, Dave hooked up with an 18-incher, I went to T-Bird with black Bomber and white teaser in dirty water, and had a quality 15- to 18-pound bass on! About 15 yards out, he rolled on my rig and snapped the 30-pound leader where the teaser was! I had another two hits. Bass are moving in steady now, bigger ones being caught at IBSP to 25 pounds, Bay Head went off this morn with 20 per man up to 29 inches.

BLUEFISH BOMB

Anybody—I don't care if you are a super dedicated sharpie surfster or an armchair angler on the Internet—knows that October 13, 2008, was a day that will live in infamy as the most bombastic bluefish blitz to go down in modern times off the Jersey coast. It lasted three entire days and nights, and the school stretched from Sandy Hook down through Long Beach Island, and was a half mile wide, hugging the entire shoreline. Tales of this event were logged and recorded and put up on YouTube—check it out! I personally have never seen anything like it before or since. Numbers were in the millions of bluefish, and they were not pantywaist little blues, but nuclear-sized monsters that all went 15 to 25 pounds, and probably even greater.

I am surprised nobody broke the world record on this three-day stretch, as my personal best on October 13th went 48 inches long from nose to tail—a 4-foot-long blue that easily was in the mid 20-pound range. I was lucky enough to be on it right when it moved in, as it was a leisurely October afternoon, sunny skies, and not a wisp of air in the ultra-clean, soft, flat surfline. I simply needed to stretch my legs, so I left the house and walked up the sandy path to the beachfront when north of the Thunderbird about 300 yards, I saw what looked like Armageddon, or at least a tsunami heading to the beach. It was roiling, crashing whitewater as far as your eyes could focus, and it took me a second to actually internalize what I was seeing: a slaughter. Peanut bunker, round herring, and sand eel schools had their Judgment Day, and millions of them opted to beach themselves for a slower, less painful death, than to be ripped apart mercilessly by the oncoming hordes of razor-toothed warriors.

I ran back to my house, amassed every single bit of metal and popper in my arsenal, threw them in the surf bag, and ran back up to the beach just in time to hit it right when the bomb hit my beach. It was seriously the only time I've been cautiously scared for my safety, standing in the undertow to reach the schools that would pop in and out. Sometimes the blues came in so quick I was standing in the middle of the feeding schools, blood and ripped up carnage of silvery baitfish littering the waters at my feet. Twenty-pound bluefish were swimming maniacally with their mouths wide open, slashing and tearing apart anything in front of them. Looking back, wearing a swimsuit and only bare feet was probably not the best idea, but I was caught up in the moment, and no seconds were going to get lost in this once-in-a-lifetime happening. The low tide seemed to imprison the baitfish and force them to choose between beaching themselves and being eaten. Here's how the journal entry went down:

October 13

Holy S%@*! The biggest bluefish blitz I've ever seen hit my beach at high noon. Clean and clear water, light west winds, and water absolutely black with bait and spraying depth charge–like explosions caused by the vicious bluefish onslaught. Schools of 14- to 23-pound gorilla blues were all on the beach, it was black as night in the water and they were on top of each other! Insane! They chased rainfish clouds and spearing, one coughed up three whole butterfish and balls of rainfish and spearing. They hit poppers, plugs, metals, flies. I lost 6 poppers and three metals, they snapped my running line, bit through 60-pound test leader. You could fit three man-sized fists into their mouths, I taped one out at 42 inches long! I even hand casted an AVA 17 metal and got hit immediately. You could see them chasing the metal. It was more fun trying to keep it away from them as they pursued with their mouth wide open chasing it! They tarponed out of the water and ripped drags apart in quick sustained bursts. Unbelievable! I beached about 8 fish and lost twice as many more. No doubt had them to 20 pounds today. Under my feet saw small kingfish, calico crabs, little mullets, so much life! Water temps around 68 degrees. It was outgoing near low tide. The school moved south and stayed hot.

Truly, that was one epic stretch of three days.

October 17

Water like the Caribbean today: dead flat, crystal clear, and that blue-green, island-type water. Loads of spearing and sand eels in wash, fished around 2:30 p.m. around high tide. Zillions of snapper bluefish chasing my lures back on each cast in the undertow, some nipping Deadly Dicks. Water temp about 64 now, IBSP had monster bluefish and bass blitzing last day or so, 15 to 35 pounds, blues to 18 pounds. Today a little slower. No wind. Did see a large bunker school flipping through out of range and a couple of bass swirling on bait in close. Funny. Matty Monogas's truck battery went dead last

Lido and Nite present two chopper blues from a massive blitz at the Fish-N-Fiesta.

night when we were drinking at UB's. I had to bring over jumper cables and a battery to get him started at 2nd Avenue! Still holding the surf skunk on my back, sounds like Jason from Pell's is having the same problem as me!

Everybody at one time or another in their surf-fishing career gets the skunk on their back. One year, I believe it was a solid 7 days of surfcasting without even a sniff from a sea robin. But inevitably, you shake the skunk. Sometimes you can tire of catching bluefish, but this one made my day.

October 19

Bluefish blitzed my beach early around 7 a.m. to 9:30 a.m. I caught the next show at 10:30 a.m., the tail end of it, but finally ended my skunk! Tossed a yellow popper on the big rod, and popped up a 12-pound blue, with 4 to 5 others following it in. Casted back to those, had them blow up on it, hooked for a second then dropped, had 6 other boils, swipes, and misses. Russians next to me landed about a dozen big blues. Tried evening session at 4 p.m. to 5:30 p.m., seas dead lake flat, gin-clear water, air 65 degrees, so at

Wrist-wrenching bluefish can make any surf outing one to smile about.

5:30 sundown decided it was so nice I got down to my swim trunks and dove on in! It was 54 degrees and cold, but so gin-clear I could see straight to the bottom with all the shells and whatnot, rainfish, and snapper blues I could see, so refreshing, felt like a baptism!

October 19

Heard blues around at IBSP. Fished Top of the Mast 23rd Street in the Seaside Park with AVA 27 jigs green tails. Hard northeast, 6- to 10-foot, water relatively clean, but not a hit! Talked to three guys who read my column and I helped them release a seagull in their lines. Raining, 69 degrees out, water temp at a warm 67 degrees still.

October 20

Out early shift 6:45 a.m. to 8 a.m. or so. Dave up there, popped around, dead zone all over, though boats getting big blues and big bass half mile off. Waves still flat to 1 foot, mullet and snapper schools all over the place.

October 20

Yesterday was great in the surf apparently, with peanuts getting blitzed by bass and blues, but fished the nighttime with black Bomber on my beach, then Lavallette beaches from about 8:30 a.m. to 10:30 a.m. with nothing to show.

October 21

Aired down and went for a beach ride, casting poppers starting at Kittiwake, seas now 1- to 2-foot, was southwest so water got a brown tinge. Birds working from Ortley Ave down to seaside until 6 p.m., but the blues didn't come in close enough to get at. In Lavallette, I saw what was the largest bluefish I've ever seen in the undertow milling around, lazily hounddogging rainfish schools! It was so big I thought it was a shark, then a 30-pound bass, then saw its black tail. So I took my popper and trout-casted to him to get him interested, he came back on it to inspect, swirled under it but never got interested enough. He kept patrolling back and forth, ten yards north, ten yards south.

Ran up to jeep to switch to a 007 metal and shad, but he was gone when I got back. What a beast, truly a beast, had to be 25 pounds, maybe a world-record fish for real! Bullshitted with a kid named Jay past Philly Ave. Good guy. No fish though for anyone, except a boater who pulled a blue out of the birdplay. Oh, did see another seal today at around 6:00 p.m. duskish.

There was also one bluefish trip in particular that I took with Mickey that stands out. I include the excerpt from his log book in here, because this describes the story, well, perfectly.

October 14

Hit IBSP with Mickey, north winds 20 knots, air 39 degrees, water 5 degrees. I'll let Mickey tell this one.

"Today was one of the strangest days of fishing I've had in a while. I woke up at 4:30 a.m. and drove to the shore to meet Nick for some surfcasting. We were on the beach by 6:30. Not long after we got our lines in the water, one of my rods got creamed. I was fishing with a whole bunker head, a favorite bait of big striped bass. I had just respooled my reel with 30-lb. braided line and never set the drag, of course it was screwed all the way down. The line snapped and I lost the fish. The next 5 hours were uneventful except for a fluke that I caught on a metal spoon I was tossing around.

"Around 11 a.m., the waters erupted when a school of monster bluefish came raging through, this was more like it. We suddenly went from no action to mayhem, with two rods going down every few minutes. At this point, seemingly out of nowhere, 5 big, ugly chicks came riding up on horses, almost getting caught up in our lines. They went on their way and we continued catching big-ass bluefish. About 30 minutes later, I see a horse at a full gallop charging down the beach toward our lines again, only no one is in the saddle this time. This horse had apparently gotten tired of these women and bucked one of them off his back. The horse goes flying past us at about 40 mph and we are like 'what the f&%#?' 5 minutes later, one of the women comes galloping up on her horse and jumps off and screams at me, 'We have a runaway horse and I need your truck!' She hands Nick the bridle and says, 'Hold onto my horse,' and she jumps into my truck.

"Although I didn't realize it at the time, Nick has never been around a horse, but this woman was being pretty demanding so he takes the horse by a short rope and I jump into my truck with the woman. We take off down the beach (the runaway horse is no longer in sight at all) and I'm doing about 50 mph with this woman in the passenger seat, our heads are bouncing off the ceiling of the truck and I'm afraid we're gonna flip, but hey, there's a runaway horse on the beach and this woman looks like she could kick me and Nick's ass with one arm tied behind her back, so I'm just taking orders at this point. She informs me that the horse's name is Victory Lap, and he has just been retired from Monmouth Park Racetrack, and this was his first-ever ride on the beach. Apparently he didn't like being ridden very much, so he kicked off one of these women and decided to split.

"So I'm chasing a racehorse in my truck on an open beach, Nick is holding onto a horse while 4 of our lines are in the water during a bluefish blitz, and he's never been around a horse. It takes me about 4 miles to catch up to Victory Lap and 'Betty' (I don't know what her real name was, but let's just call her Betty) jumps out to stop this runaway beast. The horse is having no part of this s&%#, he's living the dream, running at full speed down a beach, far away and free from his angry handler. Betty stands in front of the horse to stop him but he ain't having it, he almost runs her over and keeps on charging toward Seaside Park. So back in the truck we go, back in pursuit of Victory Lap.

"F#$%!

"Betty curses like a trucker, except maybe worse. She's literally saying 'f#$%#n' stupid motherff#$%#n ' horse, I don't need this f#$%#n' bullshit,' etc. My mind starts to turn to Nick, who unbeknownst to me is having a shitty time with the other horse. This horse hates him and is using his head to try and bowl Nick over. I, on the other hand, am worried about my rods, I'm imagining Nick standing there holding onto a horse while my Van Staal gets dragged into the wash. Anyway, about 20 minutes later, we double team the horse and he gives up. Betty jumps on his back and ties a makeshift bridle on him and I begin the long ride back to base camp.

"I get back and Nick looks troubled, he tells me that the horse doesn't like him and to top it off there's some weird foreigner standing there babbling at Nick. Eventually Betty pops up on the horizon to take this horse off our hands. Nick and I start reviewing everything that just transpired when one of Nick's rods gets hammered.

"Only it's not a fish, it's a seagull tangled up in his line. I said '[Nick, let's get the f#$% out of here.' I had a feeling that if we stayed a minute longer we would get hit by a meteorite or some extra bizarre shit."

Funny stuff!

PEANUT PARADE

When the air temp gets just right, it sparks a mass exodus of peanut bunker schools into the surfline that have been summering over in the backwaters. It's yet another trigger in October that gets the Fall Run rolling. When the peanuts are in, it makes for some downright excitable action. Schools move in droves,

Snagged peanut bunker are primetime baits during the Fall Run. CHRIS LIDO.

usually from north to south down the beachfront, most of the time staying inside the first sandbar. The silvery little fatbacks plit-plat their way southward, and the telltale sign is the rippling waters as they quickly break the surface and wiggle their way down the coast. If you tune your ears in, you can actually hear the *plit-plat* of their silvery flanks slapping the water surface in the predawn darkness or night time. These are the 1- to 3-inch bunkers, and most experienced surfcasters will always have a snagging-type rig ready to hook into a bunker and then liveline it back immediately. As bluefish hounddog the schools, peanut bunker that have been casualties sink below the schools, where bass await to gobble the injured or freshly dead ones up.

October 23

High Tide 6:38 p.m. Went to work at Fish and Game. Slow day, boss gone. Rode to Point to check the canal for garbage pickup, nothing doing. Slow day. Said to Steve, "Let's check out the surf, on Osborne Ave." Last night the first real cold snap of the fall came in roaring, 34 degrees at night, 48 during the day. Solid 15- to 25-knot northwest blow. Water a sea green look to it. Knew something was up. Scrambled up the Osborne steps, and saw black pods of peanut bunker shadowing down the coast from Risden's Beach down. Saw one guy hook up with what looked like a 12-pound blue, some peanuts jumping around, seas 1-foot, not rough at all, but not glassy either. Came home from work at 4:00 p.m., checked Bridge, Lyman, Princeton, and Kupper. Action at Lyman. Got home, bought a pint of Johnny Walker Red from Beer In Here at Curtis's, tied up some snag rigs, 1/0 treble silver with 3-foot section of 30-pound Fluoro, and a 25-pound snap on the end to hook on the treble so I could then unhook and put on a single when I had a bait. Drove to Lyman. Saw to the left a pod of peanuts, went down, cast. Snagged a peanut, rehooked it on through the upper dorsal behind it. Cast out with bail closed. Walked with that pod down for about 400 yards, no hits. Finally cast out another fresh peanut just at the tail end of the school. Felt a little pull, little pull again. Thought that the bunker, 3- to 5-inch size, might have been pulling, felt stronger, reeled up a bit, felt a little more tension, reeled up a lot, and felt an anchor! Set the hook, my rod doubled over and line peeled from a sparsely filled reel of 14-pound test, drag pulled out hard up north. I walked then down south, textbook bass maneuver. After about a 5-minute fight, beached a 36-inch, 18-pound bass, put him on the sand for a second, to give my neighbor Frank something to eat, then picked him up and released him with fiery vigor, for a little bit of good karma on the fall run. First bass, for my last fish in January, or something like that. Chased that school down past Albertson, about 1 mile or more down, picked another slot bass of 26 inches from the mix, very light in color and had an open wound on its left side in front of the tail, maybe a snag? A bluefish? Disease? Didn't catch anything else, but pods moving down the coast every 30 minutes or so. Saw others reel fish in, about four others, but nothing bigger than the one I had. Stuffed dead

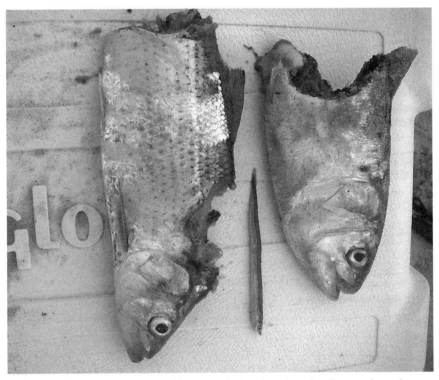

Fall bluefish spit up a variety of baits, including herring, bunker, and sand eels—all in one cough!

peanut bunker in my wader pocket, until it morphed with the Johnny Walker Bottle, tasted great. Two tips to note. Take a small leadhead, about ½ ounce, and thread a freshly dead peanut onto the end; if peanuts are not available, you can jig it across the bottom and the hook on the jighead will hold it fast. An egg sinker needs a plastic insert to avoid abrasion on the line, and when no fish are prevalent, use the 1/0 treble, hook a peanut on each barb through the lips and cast out for a three-way dead-bait fishfinder rig that is explosive. AHHHHH-HAAAAAA!!! Loving life, loving fish!

October 24

Got out of work again and headed to Osborne Ave to check the scene. Then went down to Johnson Ave and walked up to see some anglers following a school of peanuts. I dove in in my waders and proceeded to snag a bunker and liveline it back. The guy next to me said he had been picking from the school for the last hour and had a small striper out of it. We walked that school all the way down to Lyman Avenue and beyond, a good two miles, and got bit off a few times by what I assume were small blues under the school. The winds were west 10 knots, still flat ocean, and there were sporadic schools of peanuts, but no luck.

It's truly amazing how one day can be so explosive and the next a ghost town. I suppose to do it right, you should just not sleep, and follow the schools wherever they may roam through the night hours.

October 24

Peanut bunker schools plit-platting all over, tried snagging them, no waders, too many holes, they are on order, saw bass moving through them outside the bar, hit it at 3 p.m. West winds, clear water, couldn't connect but saw fish. A guy cast a small plug by me and had a 30-incher on the sandbar, so cold that my hands went blue, and couldn't feel my legs so walked back to the house.

October 25

Hit my beach 6:30 a.m. high tide 10:30 in morn in front of T-bird, when *bam!* Bunker schools got worked by bass torpedoing thru the schools in the undertow, cashing and splashing, boiling and rolling, but only in 3-minute bursts, then they sounded. I snagged a peanut and left it behind the school, pulled out a 33-inch bass. Followed school down to Jimmer's Hole, moved slowly. West winds, clear air, temp 42 degrees, water temp 62. Proceeded to hook into two fish that busted off my treble, one had to be a 25-pound-plus bass, then landed two more bass of 33 and 35 inches. A guy had a big blue of about 18 pounds on a Kroc spoon, I lost another two fish, pulled hooks, then followed school to 2nd Avenue and pulled out a 37-inch bass from it! On the inside on the edge of the school. Bunker continued to plit-plat, I actually may have snagged a bass ripping thru the bunker schools. One bass I had I was reeling in the bunker along the bottom to change up when it hit. Mullet school passed by moving fast, big 6- to 8-inch mullet chunky corncobs, rainfish beached themselves last night, mostly peanuts around as bait though.

___
October 27

Hit Philly Ave in Lavallette. Water gin-clear at 2:30 p.m. Two big peanut schools sitting within casting range. The circus was all there, casting and snagging, though only saw three bluefish jumping on the school. Made a move to my beach where peanuts were getting crashed on the inner bar. Guys were hooked up with bluefish. Worked that school for nothing. Shell E. was around, though only saw blues come out of it, then at T-bird hole, Jeff, Dave, and I sat with two other guys on a p-nut school that was pinned on the north side of a cut. The two guys were throwing 10-inch metal-lipped swimmers and pulled out 5 bass to about 31 inches on the outside of the school. Cool thing is on Philly Ave I saw what looked like a Labrador swimming, turned out to be a seal just outside the bar feeding around, and a whale was found off the north jetty feeding in 10 feet of water, too.

On the 28th and 29th, 40-knot to 50-knot winds chocolated up the 5- to 8-foot surf, and pushed all the sand out, making a barrier bar again. I did see the crashing surf wash up an 80-pound cownose ray right onto the beach and it flopped back into the water on the next wave!

CLAMMING AND CHUNKING

Fall is mostly an exercise in casting with artificials, mimicking the forage, as bait schools of rainfish, mullet, peanut bunker, and sand eels inundate the waters. Many particular lures are fit to mimic them perfectly, though there is always a time and a place to kick back with sand spikes once again and toss out bunker chunks or fresh clams to wait out a tide and see what moves through. Hurricane season is still upon us then, but mostly one- or two-day nor'east blows pop through that really churn up the waters, once again cracking and crushing clams, and that makes for some good deadsticking. Bunker chunks invariably target the larger bass around, though, and a good day or night casting chunks can have you going toe-to-toe with a lunker linesider on any given night.

___
October 5

Hit Bway from 5 p.m. to 7 p.m. then Mickey came down around 10 we went to Claw till closing, came back here, then decided it was a good idea to go to IBSP. Drove on IBSP, only ones on the entire island, straight to the pocket. I tried drifting chunks first while Mickey was doing donuts in the sand, then started back to A10 when we came upon the mother lode of clams that washed up from the last blow. Loaded Mickey's front passenger section with a bushel, then James called at about 3 to 4 a.m. We were going to sleep, but decided to set up, fished till 7:45 a.m. Had one striper at daybreak, a bunch of skates and smooth dogfish, small ones, and a spotted hake. Mickey's truck stank like dead clams as we passed out before we unloaded them from the front seat.

October 7

New moon, beaches are cut up good with the past nor'easter, west winds, water a little tinged, high at 8 p.m., took Jeep out again to ride the stretch, at about 4:30 p.m. casted at Ocean Beach to mullet schools flipping and thick everywhere, along with sand eels, too. Matty Monogas was set up on 2nd Avenue. At dark I met him and Wade Brackman there to clam with them, reeled in two skates in about an hour, left at about 8:30 p.m., then drove down to Ortley Ave and Philly Ave clamming from my car while I sat in the driver's seat with the top down, heat on, radio blaring, and the rod locked into the gear shift and clamming! No hits but pretty funny though. Fished till 9:45 p.m.

Loading up Mickey's front seat with dozens of free surf clams that washed up at IBSP. The truck didn't smell so good the next day.

October 7

Mickey came down, hit my beach at sunset. Two bass hooked up, one about a 32-incher on clams, but he broke off on the surface. Also, had bass crash some peanut bunker in the suds at low tide.

October 10

Jeep's first day out with Beach Buggy permits! High tide at 12:30 p.m., headed out at noon, 3- to 5-foot northwest, glassy, looks good. Casting metals for bass and blues, heard big blitz at OB III this morning, dead-low daybreak, but only saw some super snappers jumping around. Fun to cruise the beach to Ortley. Water temp 64, air temp 65 or so.

October 10

Hard east wind about 15 to 20 knots. Surf 3- to 4-foot. High tide 11:30, low 5:30. Fished from 4:30 a.m. to 6:45 a.m. with fresh clams. Had two dogfish, but no bass. The water temps have just begun to lower to about 67 degrees now, down from 71 earlier in the week. Used hi-lo rigs and 5 ounces to hold. Apparently they are starting to see some

The ol' red Jeep beach buggy, primed and ready for some surfcasting adventures on Ocean Beach.

bass from the surf, especially Brick Beach and Island Beach. Supposed to go to Montauk tonight, but gale force freakin' winds expected, 35 knots through the weekend. Bass season is coming up fast. Oh, last weekend, during the northeast blow, a huge freakin' shark was hunting right outside the breakers. He was about 7 to 8 feet long, and got him on video. Right outside the breakers about 25 yards out!!! He looked like a thresher possibly, dorsal fin out of water, and a bit of his tail kind of slashing and swaying back and forth quickly. He was definitely screwing around and hunting, straight south down the coast. Uh-huh.

October 12

Jeep out on beach at 1 p.m. High tide 2:30 p.m., light northeast, 2- to 3-foot, blue-green water, looks real bassy, air temps mid 50s. Saw guy clam up a 34-incher in Normandy, had Deadly Dick ready to go, hit orange fence at OB2 north side, cast around. Cliff showed up; he had a 2-pound blue on after first cast and 15 others in morning. He left, and I immediately got whacked reeling in a Deadly Dick fast at 2:40 p.m., two bass on at once! A 28- and 30-inch pair and they hit right in the undertow, 5-second fight, big one got off. Then had more taps, another one on in the undertow. Pretty wild, they hit reeling fast for bluefish, aggressive for sure, and they are light-colored right now, possibly migrating fish. Terns diving here and there, some blitzes off about a half mile. Off beach at 5 p.m. Fun!

October 12

Bioluminsecence around last week, now hard northeast 25 to 40 knots, 8- to 12-foot surf, HUGE! The nor'easter lasted until the 15th and ate up all our beaches, but now as I write this on the 17th, what a deal of fantastic structure with literally islands out there now, and cuts and sloughs like I haven't seen in 5 or so years.

October 14

East winds at 20 knots strong, lots of heavy water on the inside at low tide 5:30 p.m. Keith was in the first hole to the left and had caught two bass of 27 and 29 inches, then grabbed a 32-incher, all on clams. He also hooked a croaker. Couldn't cast against the east wind, so after I casted off a nice Yo-Zuri Arc Minnow, I tied on a Kastmaster 1-ounce to beat the wind a little bit, immediately got whacked by a blue that took the Arkansas shiner tip on the hook. Cast again and hooked into a 3-pound blue, feisty one at that. Cast again, got hit about 20 yards out by another blue. No bass, but heard weakies were in the surf two days ago. Small ones of 14 to 17 inches.

October 14

High tide at 3:27 p.m. or roughly there. The surf has been large, 3- to 5-foot every day and the winds out of the northwest about 15 knots. It looked perfect, but the north wind blew in some warmer water again, so it is about at 68 degrees still. Had one skate on fresh clams, that's it. Nobody was doing anything else, stayed out till 5 p.m. The beach is a bit eroded from the pounding surf and currents as of late, offshore, well, nobody has been able to get out in like three weeks, 6- to 16-foot seas every day, and I still haven't been to the Hudson this year yet. Another storm forecasted for Wed., maybe some cooler water will come in and we will see bass soon.

October 15

Fished with clams again, the storm winds are picking up out of the east. Hit it from 3:45 p.m. to about 6:45 p.m. darkness. Had a dogfish, one skate, and two of the smallest bass I've had on clams, one of about 13 inches, one about 15 inches. Jimmer and Bo each put a nice slot and one of about 29 inches in the box. Darden caught a croaker, which we thought moved out by now since the water temps have begun to drop, they normally like 69 and higher. Fresh surf clams washed up on the beach so it wasn't hard to get bait. We got a 40-knot forecast for tomorrow, we'll see what it does to our beach, since the last blow of three days ago ate up most of the beach.

WADERS ON

It's usually about this time, the second week of October, that waders truly need to be donned on a daily basis. I wrote this piece after fishing one cold night in October:

One of the most trying times in a surfcasters life, in the cold months, is to deal with the process of slipping on waders time and time again, dawn after dawn and then dusk after dusk when it's cold and unforgiving out. That insulating neoprene skin keeps us in the game. Yes, it can be trying to find the motivation, not just to get up at ungodly hours during near-wintertime, but more than anything, to simply put one foot in, then another, stumbling and bumbling in the porch light's glow, pulling them up over the extra padding gained over summertime partying, to strap on over the shoulders and hear a *click-click* locking in the suit of armor so you're ready to battle the surf. And that's when you vaguely remember the leaks you forgot to patch in the springtime, thinking about how you put it off during the summer months to fix and seal 'em up. The fixing and patching never happens. There's always bluefish blitzing in October first, before the bass, and you never have the time to fix waders. The bluefish and bass are already here, and you've got leaky waders through December, and it's nobody's fault but yours. Your drive and motivation to fish, plus your laziness and penchant for looking the other way from discomfort, makes you enjoy this time of year, because when bass roll on peanut bunker schools, the northwest winds put a chill on the nape of your neck, and the ice forms on your snot, there is no better time to think about just where you are and what you are doing. You're here to surf-fish and that's it. Waders with leaks be damned.

What I'm getting at is: fix your waders before you go out.

RIGHT OF RESPECT

Surfsters know who's in and who's out when it comes to going to sleep after some sport-drinking and waking up three hours before sunrise at 5:30 a.m. When last call comes at the bar, you can see it in your buddies' faces who is serious and who isn't intent on getting up in three hours' time to chase down bass. A simple respect exists for surf fishermen, and their creed requires stamina—if you get to the beach spot first, you have the right to say you are the one that runs the show, bar none. You are there before someone else, and you've earned the right to work the waters. Now, conversely, you can get there ten minutes past the guy who was there before you and you fall into the category of "second-fiddle." The worst feeling is getting to a spot thinking you are going to be the first one there, and by the light of the full moon, you see a silhouette already casting, saying you missed the boat at claiming the rights to this beach.

There's a quick feeling of superiority for a surfcaster, not from catching bigger, more, or better fish than the others, but from getting to the spot first. While the rest of humanity sleeps in warm, cozy houses, you beat down the primal urge to get rest and give in to the more prominent urge to hunt, getting down to the business of catching fish before any other human being is awake or around. 5:00 to 5:30 a.m. is the cutoff point for most; get there within that 30-minute time frame and that's fine and respectable. But when you stand surfcasting a plug on a beach at 4 a.m., you have earned the right to claim any spot along that stretch of surf, whether or not you tie into any fish. When Orion fades, and the stars are bright and vibrant in the night sky, living their last sparkles before predawn begins to slowly fade them out to give way to an autumn daybreak, that is the time when serious surfcasters are truly forged.

October 20

Hit IBSP A10 with Mickey. The five-day nor'easter tore up the beaches: 10-foot drops at the dunes, really thin beach at IBSP. Be careful of driving—high tide comes right up to dunes. Calm waters, 1- to 2-foot, high tide at 9:30 a.m. Me and Mick hit it from 6:30 a.m. to 10:30 a.m. Had one 26-inch striper on a clam.

Looking back at these logs, it's a point to note that it always seems the second to early third week of October has a nor'easter and large surf rolling through. That stormfront gets things mixed up, but also seems to spark the bite big time on the other side of the cleanup.

October 21

Hit my beach, 4:39 high tide, WSW blow 10 to 15 knots, making the waves 3-foot, a beauty to surf. I fished instead. Cast out at 3:30 p.m. with Ernie's surf turkeys, and didn't even get a hit. I was reeling in empty hooks, though, maybe little stuff I couldn't feel on 6 ounces. Need baitholder hooks for sure. All the old guys came out to fish the eve, and I stayed till 5:30 p.m., some blues breaking outside, and Amos said he saw some fish jumping out in the lineup on his surfboard. By the way, Amos had the longest ride I have ever seen at our break, he literally went 100 yards on a backside right that delivered him to the Thunderbird's doorstep, it was insane! Some sporadic blitzes are happening now, you have to be at the right place, right time apparently. And a lot of action is on clams—not typical for this time of year. Some albies still being taken, just past the breakers too. Air temp still from 53 to 68.

October 22

After drinking at B'way, fished with Mark and Glenn on 2nd Ave from 11:00 p.m. to 1 a.m., 1-foot waves, no winds, reeled in a spotted hake and had a bluefish runoff.

October 23

Nor'east 4- to 6-foot, a clean nor'east with blues and whitewater, east winds 25 knots, rough surf, high tide at noon. Cast bunker chunks off my beach from 1:30 p.m. to 3:30 p.m. and walked them down, had a monster 14-pound bluefish. Mickey down in Beach

Haven had four bass 32 to 38 inches on chunks, IBSP guys getting 15- to 30-pound bass on metals and mullet and clams. Water at 60 degrees.

To clarify, "walking it down" is when the alongshore current is ripping and you cannot hold with any increment of lead, you cast out the bait, and walk it with the current's gripping pull, keeping the bait in front of you so it doesn't wash up on the beach in a minute's time. Keep it in the strike zone, and many times the bass are there waiting. It's a technique that makes a seemingly unfishable day fishable.

October 26

IT'S ON! Quarter moon. Water 58 degrees. Light 10 knots east/NE winds, ocean blue-green, 2- to 3-foot, lots and lots of water in the sloughs, great cuts, deep water even at low tide over the sandbars, so, the bass were here! High tide at 2 p.m. Hit my beach at 11 a.m. casting clams and bunker chunks, got whomped by a 35-incher, 33-incher, 30-inch, and four other shorts, 7 beached total. One monster 15-pound-plus bluefish that hit chunk and I had over 25 hits that were quick to drop the clam bait. I had three monster hits and fish on using big bunker chunks, but my braid kept snapping on the shock of the hit, it sucked! I pulled off about 40 yards after missing what were probably big 20-pound-plus bass or equal size blue dogs. Unreal bite from 1 p.m. to 2:30 p.m. or so, but had fish and hits through to 6 p.m., when I cast out plugs and Vision sand eels, had three fish on the eels and a 27-incher on a silver-and-black Bomber at dusk. I also saw over 50 other bass being pulled up at Brick III. Dave had a few to the right, Jimmer had some, Ristori came and landed a mess on metals, and Gary beached a 20-pound fat bass on clams. So many bass around, water temps about 60 today with mostly sunny skies, wore shorts in surf, but got cold after sundown.

October 27

Some bass reported around, south swell 5- to 8-foot last two days, water brown, but chunked bunker for two hours high tide to no avail.

October 27

Me, Singles, and Bugsy hit T-Bird with fresh clams washed up from the nor'easter. I got there late, around 2 p.m. Cali already had 5 bass from 18 to 23 inches. Light west winds, and low tide around 12 p.m. I then proceeded to catch 8 bass to 23 inches, Bugsy had one and Cali had one more, total 15 on the day. The bites were all small taps, and you had to kind of hold the rod in hand. Water temps now 63 and lower, and unusual amount of schoolie bass in the water.

October 27

Day Two: Unfortunately I wasn't able to get to the beach until 4:30 p.m. and fished for hour and a half to 6 p.m. High at 3 p.m. Northeast, 4- to 6-foot, drizzly and fog. I apparently missed "the bite" but managed to hook 17 stripers to 31 inches on metals, beaching 10 from 23 to 30 inches. Jimmer, Dave, and two other guys landed over 75 fish in front of me on clams, and Dave said he had another 15 or 20 from 2 p.m. onward. I'm tellin' you, I haven't had this rush of actually feeling a "Fall Run" in about 6 years. It's supposed to be northeast 4 to 6 through Thursday. The bass were hitting on the inside of the sandbar, dragging it over the top, first cast had a 30-incher on the AVA 17 green tail, darker colors working better in rougher surf. Same spot produced most of my hits, was basically the beginning of the outgoing, but the incoming end has been hot too. Used a red sand eel teaser to score big on the bottom for better visibility. This really feels like a Fall Run!

October 28

Fished with Mick and his charter at IBSP, water very tinged brown, air temp was 50 today, fished 9 a.m. to 2 p.m., high at noon, caught one spiny dogfish and one big leopard skate, only saw one short bass caught, super slow day. Waves 4- to 5-foot, south, still, 15-knot winds. Surf here has been real slow, but big cows coming from Holgate; a 57 was taken a few days back, a few 40s and 50s too.

October 28

Uncle Greg, Sophie, and Nite came down to fish at 1 p.m. to 6 p.m. Seas rough, northeast, 5- to 7-foot, brown and whitewater, heavy high tides, snotty and drizzly. Landed a 28-inch keeper in 10 minutes on clam in front of T-Bird and Nite had a 24-incher on

This particular bass was released back into a butter and garlic paste and thrown on the grill.

clam. Had 3 other hits but hard to hold with 6 to 8 ounces. Cooked up the bass on the grill: teriyaki and butter, garlic, red pepper, mmmm!

October 29

Uncle Greg fished 7:30 to 9:30 in morn, seas rougher at 6- to 8-foot, couldn't hold with any amount of lead, but he did have 5 hits and landed one short bass.

October 29

Me and Cali hit the beach with clams at 1 p.m. Dead-low around 2 p.m., north 10 knots. We managed a total of 5 bass on the day, me with 3, Cali with 2, and missed about same amount of hits. Bite once again on dead-low beginning of incoming tide and all small fish to 23 inches. Jeff had a short on a yellow Bomber near 3:30 p.m. or so. Bottom line: small bass, lots of them. Drank a Sierra Nevada and watched as some Jeep guy was hotdogging in front of the soft sand at the T-Bird, trying to impress his girl and got stuck with the tide coming in on him, up to the wheels, took him about 2 hours to get out, right before tide was splashing and moving up on him. And the dog with big balls was on the beach again, his name is Bear.

October 29

Norm stopped by my house coming back from the beach around 8:30 a.m. He had a 36-inch bass in his hands. The wind was 20- to 25-kt northeast and the sea was fishy. This looks like the beginning of the Fall Run. Went down to make a few casts, and saw birds working from Bay Head to Seaside. Big blues in the surf to 17 pounds and bass were being taken on clams and cut mullet. It was too stiff to cast plugs, even though I tried for a half hour. Norm said he caught five bass in an hour or so like that one. Big bunker are in the wash. Water temp is now 58 degrees and it looks like this is something electric. I had to go down to fish the new Ocean City Pier for a story today, and Bernie, Sean, and I got lambasted by sleeting rain and 20-knot winds. We managed about 10 small blackies, and finished a fifth of Bushmill's.

October 31

Nite and his friend came down fished from 1:30 p.m. to 6 p.m., howling 30-knot-plus south winds, sandblasted, at Jimmer's Hole, water brown and ugly, hard to hold with 8 ounces but they had 9 bass altogether, 3 keepers to 31 inches. I even reeled one in, saw gannets diving outside breakers, a chopped-in-half bunker washed up and so did a hickory shad chopped in half and a big bite out of its head too. Bass coughing up sand eels. Nite used a fishfinder rig.

BLACKFISH FROM THE BEACH

Everybody's got their surf secrets, and here's one of mine. As a fishing journalist, I am supposed to report on anything and everything when I hear it, save for maybe a day or two delay if the bass are blitzing at a certain spot; then the information must be delayed in its dissemination to protect the locals. But there's one thing I've never touched upon, because, well, it's too damn cool to write about and have people doing it on a daily basis to crowd it up. Blackfishing from the beach.

I've done my research. Hundreds of shipwrecks line the Jersey coast, and many of them are close enough to reach with a long cast on a dead-low tide. These wrecks hold tautog, porgies, sea bass, flounder. Pick up an old wreck book, study it hard, and try to hunt down these nearshore shipwrecks. Do the research and find the identity of the wreck if you can, learn the story behind the wreck so you can get a full sense of respect for the spot you are fishing. Ghosts of shipwrecked pirates may be around, but you have them on your side.

I didn't learn this on my own, though I had thought about its potential previously. One day walking the beach, I saw this guy with a huge chunking rod set up, whipping out cast after cast, using small bits of clam as baits. I thought it was odd to be bass fishing with such small baits, so I walked up to check what was in his cooler. Five fat blackfish, all between 3 and 5 pounds, were in it. I let my humility slide for a second and asked all the questions I could without looking too needy. I learned some pretty damn cool things and put them to use. Now, blackfishing from the beach consumes me in October and November.

October 1

Fished canal at slack at 12:30 p.m. with Mickey. Used princess crabs, they look like greenies, but are not, according to the drunk guy who catches them, as he drove up to the fence and gave his two cents' worth. I landed two nice 3- to 3.5-pound tog and had about 25 throwbacks, Mickey had plenty of little tog too. Spearing in canal, and needlefish too. Sunny, hot, 82 degrees or so.

October 2

Hit C—— wreck to blackfish but didn't have enough line on the reel! Spliced some 40 pounds tuff I had laying in the car, but still not enough to get out completely, only had a sea robin and two skates. Did have a toggish type of hit though.

October 8

Low tide 2:30 p.m. Sunny bluebird day, about 70 degrees, water temps warm at 68 still, waded out onto the bar at C—— wreck, deep sloughs even at low tide up to my armpits, but got on thin bar, and casted for none other than blackfish at the C—— wreck. Got there at 1:10 p.m., waves 1 to 2, water now clean and clear with 10-knot west winds. Immediately got a monster takedown and lost the tog in the structure, busted off! Then cast clams again, 3/0 Gamakatsu baitholder hooks, tie down clams, and reeled in a 3-pounder, then another 3-pounder, then lost a whopper hit in the structure once again, had another one on that got me tangled; I let him swim it out, but he had already spit the hook. I know that wreck now stretches to both corners of the marker house, with the south side holding a real sharp part of the structure, cut rigs aplenty, left side had more like rubble tangles. Total in just over an hour was 2 for 5 on tog, and I know there are big ones there! Some bass offshore a bit, boats working bunker schools, porpoises around too. Also had a lowly skate.

October 14

West winds again for beach toggin', 8 a.m. Checked the C—— wreck and had two speardivers on it already! Then C—— wreck had a guy anchored on it too!! Damn! Waited it out till 3 p.m. and went to a different wreck. Met Deg, Nicky, and Max there but only had sea robins on the take. Three speardivers hit it after I left too.

October 15

Hit C—— wreck again in 8 a.m., incoming tide. Clear and west again, 10 knots. Couldn't reach the good spot today, so only had skates and sea robins, but know those tog are there.

October 18

Fished the canal at high tide slack 12:30 p.m. to 2 p.m. with Bugsy and we absolutely hammered the blackies! Used the Belmar rig double-hooker, and between us both had 30 blackies with about 5 keepers to 16 inches. They hit greenies and clam bits, didn't matter, the bite was on from the end of the incoming but went hot on the slack in the middle of the canal. Saw schools of spearing all over hugging the bulkheads and snapper blues were schooling with them, but not eating them, unusual. Great time.

October 20

Blackfish from the beach! Went to try my spot, new moon two days ago, low tide 3:30 p.m., west winds 15 knots. Clear water. C—— wreck already had a spearfisherman on it, pissed off! So I went up to another wreck and lined up between the house and the flagpole. A speardiver was there. He guided me in the right direction where the wreck was laid out. I cast out and had a 9-inch porgy, a skate, small fluke. Then, I bagged with 2/0 hooks 60-pound Fluoro leader short, a 6-pound tautog!!! It fought like mad! You got to get out to the deep part on a dead-low tide and cast far. Then bagged another 16-inch blackfish. Awesome! The speardiver brought back 4 massive queen triggerfish and two 5-pound class tog and said they were all over the structure. Water temp still 68 degrees, air temp about low 60s.

October 20

Hit the canal for blackfish at the access on marine police side. Low slack around 3 p.m., I believe, and I hit it with green crabs. I pulled in four tog to 15 inches, and missed a

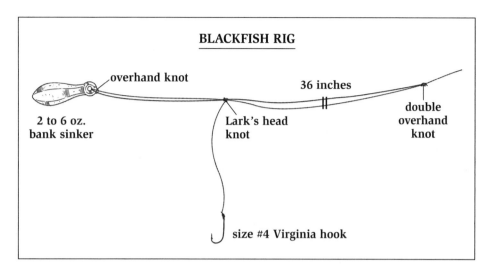

BLACKFISH RIG

overhand knot

36 inches

2 to 6 oz.
bank sinker

Lark's head
knot

double
overhand
knot

size #4 Virginia hook

bunch more in about an hour's time, before tide started screaming in. Northeast blow 20 to 30 knots started today.

October 22

Hit the canal with Cali at high slack around 3 p.m., and we put a whompin on the tog again. Had over 35 fish in an hour or two and they hit clams and greenies again. Most fish are 10 to 14 inches, but Cali had a 17-incher. Big time toggin'!

October 25

Hit canal for high slack at 9:30 a.m. with greenies again. Size #6 Virginia hooks and 3-ounce banks. Hit access area and missed about 12 hits. Very swollen high tide from NE wind and full moon coming in three days. Went back to fish the low slack with Bugsy and we went down a bit farther to the hidden access. I bailed four blackies to 15 inches and Bugsy caught his first about 12 inches. Green crabs took the bigger fish, the guy next to us absolutely hammered smaller fish on fiddlers about midway out on a piece. I found a nice piece of structure where hits were abundant, but found out too late—the tide started pouring in. The northeast blow has lasted the last 8 days, shutting down any outside fishing, 7- to 10-foot on shore and to 20 feet in the canyons. Only steady bite has been stripers in Barnegat Inlet. Point to note: word has it that the bass bite in Montauk in the last two weeks has been the best they've seen in 10 years. They are late coming down, water still at 62 degrees, but hopefully when they get here, they will pillage through!

October 26

Fished the high slack in canal at 10:30 a.m. with Cali, got there too late, think the NE winds let up and tides are back on schedule with 2.5-hour slack times. Anyway, got there just at the beginning of the outgoing, dropped down with one nice piece of green crab, and pulled in a 16.5-inch tog. Nice fish! Cali maybe got to cast twice with both times getting snagged! Couldn't fish the current after I reeled in that donkeytooth. Seas down to 4- to 6-foot, cleaning up a tiny bit.

October 29

Hit C—— wreck new moon dead-low tide 8:30 a.m. high, hit it at 1 p.m. to 4 p.m. West winds at 25 to 30 knots last three days, water temp 59 degrees. I cast out with usual stuff and had two blackfish of 14 and 15 inches. Water has been dirty all week long from steady winds, should clear up soon.

ASSORTED HAPPENINGS

With all sorts of life running in and out with the tides, there's always something interesting, odd, or cool going down. Weakfish and hickory shad seem to show up out of nowhere, providing some sought-after light-tackle fun from the suds. Add in sundials, croakers, bass, blues, and sturgeon—yes, sturgeon—and you've got a pretty wild time going on in October. It's the month when everything is on the move, and nothing should surprise you. Keep your eyes and ears open.

October 2

Took the Jeep out on Kittiwake, then went south to Seaside, people littered the beach like the summer, but went out at 4:30 p.m. to 7:30 p.m., drivable after 5:15 p.m. or so with less people. Seas 2- to 3-foot, westerly winds, with north in them, high tide at 3:30 p.m. Caught the outgoing, was fun to try to bucktail up fluke and cast Bombers and such. Matty Monogas was out, so was Joe O. Funny to see all the locals driving around on a 72-degree sunny day. Good day to be out buggying. Did find a nice hole around New Brunswick Ave, but both Joe and I had nothing for our efforts, save for a few fluke snaps. Did see some bait guys getting fluke too, and heard about small bluefish in Lavallette before we got up there.

October 3

Woke up at 4:30 a.m. and couldn't get back to bed so hit Princeton at 5 a.m., dead-high tide. Orion fades. Got to hit the beach Before Orion Fades, new title! Cast a black Bomber in the suds until 7:15 a.m. without even a sniff, but you cannot believe the amount of tincan bunker in the wash outside the bars, it was one mile long and thick, and they were flipping everywhere but nothing seemed to be underneath. No wind, 1- to 2-foot glassy seas, beautiful sunrise, pink and yellow more than red, and two shooting stars. And then found a little hermit crab on the beach in a snail shell, released him back into the big pool. Swordfishing should be hot on the full moon on the 6th, it was super hot on September's full moon, we'll wait to see, tuna fishing red hot.

October 5

Fished Point Pleasant Pocket, first hit Bay Head jetties at 5:30 a.m. to 6 a.m. to see if any bass. One hickory shad, then went to pocket. High tide at 9, full moon, west 15 knots, glassy and flat, with 2- to 3-foot rollers. Cast out AVA 007 with green tail and a yellow-white teaser; I kid you not, every single cast was a hit or a doubleheader of hickory shad! I fished 6:30 a.m. to 8:30 a.m. Literally caught over 100 shad, one keeper fluke, and four 3- to 4-pound bluefish. Weakies were there yesterday but I didn't have any today. These shad are Jersey Tarpon! They fight like a 25-inch striper! Out of the water aerial antics. Then packed up—oh, also caught a seagull, which I had to shirt over and release, went to Harris Ave in Bay Head to see what's up and saw some monster crashes in the undertow, then saw a guy hook up with a 16-pound class bluefish, thought they might have been bonito? Bunker and/or shad about ¾ mile off, paving the coast and flipping, crashing around. Saw Ronny at Supply at 7-Eleven; he said he had 35 or so weakies fishing a Ron-Z with black leadhead off Martell's Tiki Bar.

Evening

Hit Pocket again in hopes of hickory or weakfish, but not much going on. Did catch three short fluke and a sundial while dragging super slow on the teaser, could've probably had a dozen or so if I changed to a bucktail, but wanted a weakie to hit the Vision sand eel that the fluke could only mouth up. Nintendo CastleVania–like moon tonight, big rising orb with the split clouds set against its glow! One guy fishing next to the north jetty had a whopper hit on a clam float that took him into the rocks and snapped him off, probably a 20-pound class bass, almost took his rod in the water! Small 1-inch peanut bunker being sprayed around a little bit, and heard that big 15-pound blues hit my area this evening. Water temp about 64 degrees.

October 6

Hit Tiki Bar today 5:30 a.m. Glass calm, 1- to 2-foot rollers, everything went ghost, no weakies, but did catch two fluke, one 18-incher and others dragging a Vision sand eel. Nothing around. Heard of big blues popped in at Ortley, no wind.

Evening

Hit my beach at night 9 p.m. high tide, with winds now 25 to 30 knots, very tough conditions, even with 2- to 3-foot waves, south current strong, nothing doing, fished only half hour.

October 10

Hit Bay Head Harris Ave with Guy and his bud Steve and his son to throw plugs and stuff at 6 p.m., dark at 7. Some birds picking the surface, high tide, 3- to 4-foot waves, overcast, cloudy, looked perfect bass weather if surf wasn't 68 degrees. North wind 20 knots, decided to chuck a bucktail with squid strip on it at Osborne jetty, and had a croaker, fat guy, who whacked it in the wash. Croakers all over our beaches still, which means warm water still around. Tomorrow go to canyon with Bobby Bogan, but looks like 8- to 18-foot seas.

October 11

Hit my beach 5:30 a.m. high tide, evening, cast Gibbs 3-ounce popper and had a 25-pound-plus bass swipe at it in a 2-foot NE sea, 10 knots, clean and that blue-green-blue song that northeast brings in, then caught a 5-pound bluefish on the popper, water temp 64 degrees. Looks like this may be an October like the old days for the surf.

October 12

Fished evening tide, high at 6 p.m., hit 5:15 p.m. to 6:15 p.m., water brown on the east blow. Did have one sweet crash on the popper again, looked like another big bass.

October 13

Fished with Jackson on my beach, high tide nice at 7 a.m. Got to beach at around 6:30 a.m. Nothing really to show for our efforts, more people and buggies on the beach now. Worked south to the new house and got hit once but that's about it. Canyon fishing is going off, everything's on the bite in the Hudson and Toms, yellowfin, swordies, and whatnot, and bluefin showed up at the Bacardi last week, very tight.

October 14

Red tide in town, weird, dark red-brown color in surf, fire in the surf, phosphorescence lit up like wild in the dark.

October 14

Had my Cattus Park surf-fishing seminar last night, woke up at 5:45 a.m., sunrise at 7 or so. Fished my beach, the cuts and sloughs are awesome right now, deep waters inside, sandbars, cuts runs, holes. Water clear today, no wind when I got up, then easterly winds, 10 knots around 6:45 a.m., but no taker on anything thrown out! Water still 67 or 68 degrees, waves 1-foot-high, tide around 3:45 a.m. SO much bait in the water, but barely any fish in the surf. I don't know how long it's been since I had a decent surf fish, been holding the skunk big time, I'm due!

October 15

Lin came down, staying a few days. We got bombed at B'way, I picked up a black Bomber and hit the beach at 2:30 a.m., casting away, water 1-foot, west winds, did have one fish on the yellow teaser, fought for two seconds then he came unbuttoned, but the teaser feathers were all gone, maybe weakfish or short bass? Blue?

October 18

Fished my beach 6:30 to 7:30 this morn, water absolutely gin-clear, flat as a lake. But get this, I did see a seal in the water, paddling along, which was cool, but you have to help me figure out this one—I saw this thing jump out of the water, only 25 yards off the beach, what I believe was a small thresher shark or a sturgeon? It was about 5.5 feet long and it jumped about 3 feet high, clearly saw a head and tail, and it was bent like a U shape when it jumped!!! What the heck was that?!!! Rainfish all over the joint, cold this morn, but still fished in shorts, when I got out my feet felt like ice blocks in the 49-degree air.

NOTE: That wild thing I saw jump was most likely a sturgeon as a boater fluke-fishing right off my beach that day landed 5-foot sturgeon. That would've been a wild catch from the beach!

October 18

Hit my beach at around 6 a.m., 10 to 15 southwest blow, high tide at 9 a.m. Worked my way past T-Bird, with new cuts and sloughs had two bumps in front of it, but no connection. Black Bomber. Saw a pod of something get pushed in over the bar and it looked like it was getting worked from below but disappeared within a minute or two. Jeff had a bump on a popper too. Found a mantis shrimp on the beach and dead calico crabs still washing up from the heavy nor'easter.

October 21

Hit my beach at high tide noon. Cast out Storm shads and teasers, had a 24-inch striper. Northeast, 3- to 4-foot.

October 22

Drank at Crab's Claw till 11 p.m., then put on the waders and hit my beach. At about midnight, had a 25-inch striper inhale a Storm shad all the way down its throat! Released effectively. Rough surf, 3- to 5-foot north 15 to 20 knots.

October 23

Fished my beach at 3:30 p.m. high tide, rough northeast, 3- to 6-foot, semiclean, 15-knot winds. Cast out an AVA 17 red tail with teaser, had a 27-inch bass hit the white teaser around 4 p.m.

October 28

Lunar eclipse, full moon. Fished the surf, some bass being taken, nothing to nuts just yet, peanut bunker beginning to show in droves.

October 30

Fished morning hours my beach and hit T-bird hole casting Bombers and Vision sand eels. Got whacked right away in the dark hours at 6:45 a.m. Ended up catching about 6 bass and two blues to 5 pounds at the T-Bird then about 8:30 a.m. I moved over to Jimmer's Hole, where I beached another 6 bass to 29 inches that were boiling on sand eels. Altogether I went 12 for 23 on bass all morning long and they hit in the sunup to 9:30 a.m., when I left to get something to eat.

Evening

Went to IBSP with Mickey and Mike Carr at A10. I brought the blackberry and got there at about 5:30 p.m., right before sundown. Began casting Vision eels and landed three stripers of 24- to 26-inches, one had an American Littoral Society tag in its tail, the 24-incher, sending it out to see what its story is. West winds 10 knots, Mickey and Mike landed another three bass on Bomber plugs and one on a clam. They all hit right in the undertow at evening. Had 5 other taps too, one of my bass hit in the pitch darkness at about 7:30 p.m. We all went to Crab's Claw later, then UB's, then me and Mickey fished my beach till 3 a.m. to catch 4 skates.

October 30

Seas back to 3- to 5-foot, little more blue-green, cast around AVA 17 green tail and red teaser. Landed one keeper bass in front of my walkway, went over to Jimmer's Hole and landed another there. Also had three sundials attack the AVA jig, fished from 3:30 p.m. to 5 p.m.

October 30

Daylight savings passed, low tide 7:30 a.m., sunrise now about 6:10 a.m., hit my beach at 5:45 a.m., the big barrier bar is there, gotta to wait for a few tides to cut it all up now. I did wade out to it and almost got dunked on the low tide, as 5½ foot cuts laid right before the bar. Ristori and I been trading messages every day for last two weeks trying to find fish. Blackfished the canal around 10 a.m. low slack with Heckel, stayed for about 30 minutes, water too chocolatey. Interesting thing was there was a low water advisory for the bay, the lowest the bay has been in decades, you could see the land exposed in the bay like a tsunami was coming! Explanation was due to all the water that went down bay with the heavy west winds for last five days, and the wild blowout tides.

October's inherent beauty simply cannot be beat. But when it comes to getting down to the real business of Jersey Shore surf activity, where the lifeblood of a surfster is worn on his sleeve, look no further than November.

9 November

PAYDIRT

I f there's one month to pick above all others for bass fishing, it's November. Striped bass dictate the economy in November along the Jersey coast. Tackle shops, food stores, bars—the entire range of businesses that remain open after the summertime mayhem thrives in November. The beach economy is based on the fact that every single trip from a tourist or day-tripper is laden with the promise of tangling with linesiders, morning, noon, and night.

The winter chill is real now. All the merganser and mallard sea ducks have begun to move south for the warmth of a southern winter, but a few seagulls still remain to pick up the scraps of bait piles left by anglers. The culmination of the Fall Run holds a truth—bait schools root down hoping for salvation and a safe journey to southern climes, but ultimately end up getting pummeled and eaten by hordes of bass and bluefish. Orange sunglows spark the morning horizon and on certain frigid predawn mornings of 20-degree air mixing with 50-degree water, a ghostly, wispy, cloudy mist rises from the chemical reaction.

Don't let the cool fool you. Everything is red hot. This is go time. When the stripers run off, Jersey is at its pinnacle, and there's no better place on the entire planet Earth to find bass than right here, right now. It's a calming game of sorts, when you can put your time in enough to get accustomed to the daily rhythms of the surf's soul. In a two- to three-day affair, you get used to the big payoff bounty, catching bass after bass. For day-trippers reading of scores of reports, it's a run-and-gun affair, casting and blasting to get their fish as they come down before work and have to leave at 8 a.m., change of clothes in car, to be at work a little bit late—or, if the bite's hot, a lot late—but it's all worth it. Locals have the advantage to be on the blitzes when they happen, to put the wood to the fish when they pop in and out, but it's all good either way.

The clam and chunk rods take a backseat, and it's all about artificial baits: metals, plugs, poppers, and plastics reign supreme here and now. It's an active approach. There simply is no time to sit and wait it out; you go chase the action now, while the bass are aggressive and hungry as they bask and flourish in 53- to 60-degree water temperatures. It's survival of the fittest, as bass look to fatten up and winter over off Virginia and North Carolina.

Now is the time when talk among the bar rooms revolves not around the fools of summertime that invade the area, but of war stories of waking up or staying up into the wee hours of night to tighten up a line with a striped bass. The visuals are astounding: sand eels, peanut bunker, and spearing schools spraying like buckshot to the left and right of you. You can barely hold yourself together tightly enough to make a cast as the anticipation of the hookup shakes you down to your soul. Yes, you always remember November as being the best bassing days, and for sure, it's the time when stories, legends, and tall tales are born.

FIRST WEEK

It always happens. The first week of November, could be a Sunday, Wednesday, Saturday, doesn't matter, at least one day during the first week of November will hold precious amounts of boiling bass to ignite the fire within and keep us going. It's a fueled-up, adrenaline-infused week; there is always some sort of action from the 1st to the 7th, every year, no exceptions. If you are going to take a vacation week off, this is the time of year to use up sick days, because you will be into bass on some level. Pay attention to the dates in this next barrage of entries, it always seems like November 1, November 10, and November 22 end up being good days; note the weather and tide specifications.

METAL MILITIA—START OF SAND EEL SEASON

With sand eels and spearing the predominant baits in the November surf, it's time to get your metal on, as many metal and tin lures are perfect doppelgangers for the slim baitfish profile. Deadly Dicks, AVA jigs, and Crippled Herrings reign supreme in the fall surf, as you can cast them a country mile and there is basically no hard technique to master; simply reel them in at varying speeds. One thing is for sure, always use a 3/0 bucktail or 3-inch Felmlee eel teaser in front of the metal. It's a simple trick, but that teaser ignites a primal instinct in a feeding bass or blue, as they see it as a fish chasing another fish and want to get in on the game. Teasers account for more hits than the lure on many days. When sand eels choke the surf in the last three months of the year, it's a slam bang affair with a metal and teaser combo.

November 1

Hit my beach 3:30 p.m. to 4:30 p.m. with AVA jigs. Had one short bass with one whitish, ghost-like eye from some early damage somewhere. Also had two 4-pound bluefish. Winds back to north 10 to 15 knots, water cleaning up slowly, awesome sandbars, sloughs, troughs, holes, and cuts.

November 1

On beach at 4 p.m., gets dark at around 5:20 now. Low tide at 3. Waded out on the sandbars to cast out farther, nice cuts and sloughs again, developed from the pounding nor'easter of a week and half ago. Jeff caught a bass on a plug to my left, I fished down from the path. Saw spearing get chased a few yards from me with a few boils behind them, no luck though with a yellow Bomber.

November 1

Just like last year. Mayhem! Southeast wind 15, water blue-green clear. Bunker schools getting worked and pushed against the sandbars, which are large and in charge since the big blow. They were pinned up with the southeast push, peanuts to 4 to 5 inches. Also, big spearing in the wash. Low tide around 1 p.m. got there at 3 p.m. because of a call from Cali. We snagged and immediately hooked up. First thing I got was a 27-inch bass. Then it was blue after blue after blue, had about 18 on the day to 14 pounds, mostly 4- to 7-pounders. Cali had about the same amount and landed a bruiser 14-pounder. It was nonstop till dark at 5:30 p.m. and then we didn't have any flash-lights. Lost about 5 rigs on blues. Cali also had two bass and some blues in the predawn hours on my beach. The bass bite is getting hot on plugs now, and peanuts all over the place. The blues were spitting up five or six peanuts at a time, gorging themselves like mad, you could feel them tapping the bunker and see them breaking through the schools.

November 1

Hit Jimmer's Hole, blowout low tides at evening, deep sloughs inside sandbars makes incoming tides dangerous when on the sandbar, don't want to get caught. West winds, 1-foot clear water. Cast out Bombers from 5 p.m. to 6:30 p.m., caught four 3-pound bluefish on teaser and Bomber combo, no bass today. Jimmer also had 3 blues.

November 1

Took Jeep out 1 p.m. to 5 p.m. High tide 3 p.m., northwest winds 10 to 15 knots, seas 2 to 3, water clean. Casting Vision surf eels at OB, I landed a 14-pound bluefish, Joe O had one on a swimmer, then had another just south of Ortley Ave that bit off the surf eel. Pods of huge corncob 8- to 10-inch mullets running in wash, thousands in each pod, big mullet, snagged one with a bunker snag and kept casting it out, thought I felt a tap and

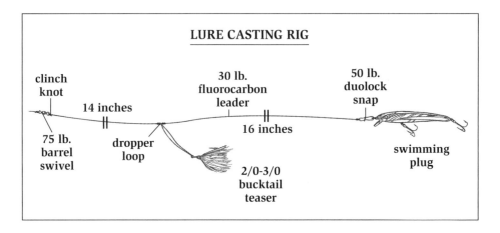

LURE CASTING RIG

it was gone. Bass and bluefish on IBSP today, blitzing rainfish schools. Hit my beach from 5:30 p.m. to 6:30 p.m. casting around, did have one bump, and saw a 25-pound class bass being clammed or chunked up at Deauville. Just a thought, that thresher I may have seen a few weeks back may have actually been as sturgeon, as one 5-footer was caught on a boat near my beach that very next day. Profile was very similar with short nose and rounded snout.

November 2

THE GAME IS ON! I walked up to check my beach at 11 a.m. and witnessed all-out mayhem! High tide 10 a.m. 5 to 10 knots light southeast, water fairly clean, peanut bunker schools were blackening the waters, and bluefish were vaulting out of the water to get on them! I ran back to my house and called Jackson on the way, out of breath, to meet me on my beach. Grabbed my gear, bolted out of the house and began to cast poppers, which were broken off by the teeth of blues, then tied on some metal. Had four bluefish immediately, they were crashing at my feet, slamming into the peanuts! Jackson came down and had one bass and three blues fast. We proceeded to take ten more blues in the 4- to 8-pound class out of there. Worked Storm shads underneath and had three more bass to about 28 inches.

Bite got sporadic, low tide coming up, so we hit Ortley Ave in Lavallette. Immediately went down to the south side of the jetty and cast out Storm shads, Guy and I grabbed a bass each right away, about 25 inches each, and then had more bluefish. Worked the north side of the jetty when a flyrodder abandoned his post and had three bluefish from there trying to get a bass, then walked up the beach to a sandbar break and pulled blues and two bass from there. The one bluefish I had slammed by bait at my feet and, as he had my whole 6-inch shad and weight in his mouth, I opened his maw up to extract the shad when two live peanut bunker jumped out of his mouth and swam back in the water! Who says I don't practice catch-and-release?! I got my shad back.

Low tide means Seaside with the deeper water there. Hit 20th St. in Seaside Park, then Seaside Pier, then just north of pier, all looked quiet. Then made a move to Lavallette, hit up Kittiwake Avenue on a jetty and parked at about 1:30 or 2 p.m. Soon as we hit the beach, a pod of peanuts was working with four anglers on it. We went down and began to snag them. Those guys pulled out five or six bass from it before we got there. Guy and I began to get in on it, pulling bluefish after bluefish out of the sides of the pod and livelining peanuts. Bluefish now all from 6 to 13 pounds! Then some bass came up to bat, Guy had one and I had another. It started getting hot, and everyone started to move in, it was absolute chaos, but we all worked a stretch of about 25 yards with 20 people literally all cooperating for the most part, to go snag a bunker between some guys, then move to the outside of the school. The pod was only about 15 yards long.

As darkness began to settle on the end of the outgoing tide at around 4, east winds pushed heavy water inside even on the low, things went ballistic! The bait was pushed onto the beach and against the jetty on the north side and was getting pummeled, by vaulting bass and bluefish. The blues were punishing my drag and we lost about 15 each on the day, snapping them off, and these bluefish were tarponing out of the water! Like nothing I've seen, two to three feet in the air shaking their heads and teeth! We must've totaled 60 bluefish and 12 bass between Guy and I on the day. Guy's rig with a Dipsey Swivel duolocked on the barrel swivel and then the leader was working better than a regular fishfinder frig, he would cast out and slowly drag across the bottom.

Then met Jim Bramble and his buddy Bud, who worked for PowerPro and Megabait, and shot the breeze with the old guys for an hour and a half just BSing about fun stuff, showing us old Nantucket fishing pics and other lures, rods, reels, etc. All the stuff to make a memorable evening and to make new friends, these guys were hilarious! What a day!

November 2

All during the day, sporadic blue schools from Bay Head to Lavallette. Cali had four bass this morn. About 1 p.m. I went up to my beach with Hutch and waded out with no waders to the sandbar, which was about 60 yards out, setting up with a Storm shad and some snag rigs. Blues started to come by, and when they passed over, the peanut schools were in thick right in front, in the shallows of the bar. I snagged a few and caught about 8 blues from 5 to 12 pounds out of it, with p-nuts and Storm shads, but when the blues passed, I threw the snag p-nut out on the outside of the school and let it sit. About 7 minutes later, it got picked up by a 29-inch striper; I know they have been hanging behind the blues on the outside of the p-nuts swooping in and picking them off leisurely. Left the beach at about 3, but heard the bass bite went ballistic at nightfall. Low tide around 1:30. West winds about 10 knots, glassy.

November 2

3 for 6 on bass. Nor'easter from Hurricane Noel, 6-foot, 25 to 30 knots, going to 8- to 13-foot. 60-knot winds tonight. Cast clams in the undertow, all shorts to 27 inches, walked the clams down. T-Bird high tide 3 p.m., hit it at 12:30 p.m. to 2 p.m. Sloppy whitewater. Fun!

OK, so I lied. There's still time for some clamming in some years when the surf just doesn't have the bait around.

November 3

Tried the morning hours from 5:45 on, sunrise about 6 now, high tide 11 a.m. West winds hawking at about 20 to 25 knots. Cast a black Bomber until 6:45 then came back due to technical difficulties with my line. Birds antsy but not diving, water whipped up a bit. Try later.

Stopped by Downer Ave to check the scene at noon and saw a line of birds from Downer to Lyman, called Guy and we met at Downer 20 minutes later. Went to the right and made a few casts, hooked up with three bluefish 4- to 8-pound class on Crippled Herring. Guy had three as well, decided to follow the birds since they went south. Stopped in to head them off at Brick 1 and walked up to them, waded out on a bar and intercepted them on the outside where others couldn't cast to. Had four or five blues on shads and poppers, some guys had bluefish on and I saw them swimming by my legs with poppers in their mouths! Ran and chased them southward again to my beach. Waded out on a bar and cast, had about 6 more, broke off two poppers and countless shads. Guy did the same.

November 3

Fished with Mickey in Beach Haven with guys from *VICE* magazine, set up at 6:30 a.m. with bunker chunks and clams, got two hits, finally third one reeled in a 32-incher on clams, full moon high water, no beach, heavy inside water 4- to 5-foot, light east winds. Left at 10.

November 4

Evening tide, everybody on the beach, 2-foot, west, high tide 7 p.m. Fished till 5:30 p.m., pitch black with full moon on November 6th, some small blues went thru, and guys had a few, got bumped real small, probably blues. Sporadic bass activity last few days, occasional blitzes.

November 4

Fished Jimmer's Hole from 9:30 a.m. to 10:30 a.m. West winds 5 knots, clean water 2- to 3-foot, high at 9 a.m. or so. Casted Vision surf eels and landed two stripers, lost a teen-sizer in the undertow, then had 5 bluefish, biggest about 10 pounds, and busted a monster off. Cast and reeled in reel slow on the bottom, lots of taps too.

November 4

Hit the beach at 5:45 a.m., 20- to 25-knot northeast winds, low tide about 6:30 a.m. The winds pushed heavier water on the inside once again, sunrise around 6:20, had a hookup and a missed surface strike on a black Bomber. Tried to cast a Hopkins, it got through the wind, but the plugs were working magic. Cali joined me. We worked a little bowl just a bit to the right and I had my first bluedog that tarponed out of the water again, released him, then had another hit, a nice 23-inch striper! Then, as Cali was working out a snag, since he lost his last lure to a runaway seagull, I cast out along the edge of a cut where the plug was taken by the north push, and ended up drifting along the cut and WHAM! Right in the undertow, a 32-inch striper! The air temps dropped to 37 last night, which might have triggered a better bass bite. Cali's out there now, I gotta go paint my house now.

November 4

Hardcore northeast 15- to 20-knot wind and fog rolled in thick as molasses. Fished my beach at 4:00 p.m. Cast out a Kastmaster with a Fin-S on the back and it got whacked quickly, sent it out again, got whacked again, but no hookset. Put on an AVA with a Fin-S and bailed 5 bluefish between 4 and 6 pounds, nice fat scrappers whose bellies were full of peanut bunker. They vaulted out of the water, shaking their heads free like little tarpon! They were thick in the water, and the steely gray surf hid them well, but they were definitely on the bite.

November 5

Fished my beach again, looked promising, bluefish surfacing here and there, saw bluefish actually jumping out of the water on the high tide inside at like 4 p.m. Casted to get two hits but no solid connection with metal, then realized my rod guide broke and I had to go home and leave a potential bluefish extravaganza. Water getting cooler, around 58 now.

November 5

Walked up at 4:15 p.m., saw Dave, Jimmer, and Chev all hooked up. Got my gear cast out, Vision sand eel and olive-green teaser, reeled in slow on the bottom and was into action until 5:30 p.m. Beached 6 bass, had to keep one that was bleeding bad, almost a keeper! Oh well. Not going to let it die for nothing, so it came home with me. Dave also had a small 3-pound bluefish. They bit right up into the night, and we were at dead-low tide and the incoming beginning, seas 2- to 4-foot, west winds 15 knots, glassy and clean. You can see sand eels schooling up. Fish-N-Fiesta tomorrow!

November 6

Hard nor'easter coming through, 8- to 12-foot seas, 30-knot winds, Mickey is slamming 'em in Holgate, had a 36-incher and 14-pound blues. I didn't get any hits casting plugs in the slop. Oh, cool thing was all the little jellies that washed up that looked like little Metroids!

For those who don't know what a "Metroid" is, it's from the old-school Nintendo game Metroid, and it was a nasty, jellyfish-looking big boss you had to beat in the game. Still sends shivers down my spine.

November 7

Nor'east, 4- to 7-foot, clean though, no wind. Hit evening tide high at 2:30 p.m., not a tap in hour and a half on plugs, looked very fishy though. Water temperature 57 degrees, air 59 degrees.

November 7

Hit the surf with Cali at evening. No dice still. Though cool thing was that I got to see the shipwreck that is just north of the T-Bird, as two stakes about 20 feet apart were exposed from the strength of the last nor'easter. Wonder what wreck it is?

Those magical seven days to start November are always a rush. The first week is really when all the boys begin to take the notion seriously about making the hour and a half drive to come down before work, to fish and fight the traffic back north to slide back into their desks by 9 a.m. You can hear their voices shaking with unbridled anticipation on the phone: "How many bass per day are you getting? Is it an all day thing? On bait or metals?" Then when you see the look in their eyes as they pull up to my driveway, open the driver's door, leaving it open, and stuff themselves into their neoprene waders before they even get into the front door of my house, you can tell they're seriously addicted and there's no turning back. All that raw passion and excitement! Oh, then comes the second week of November.

SECOND WEEK

On one particular alcohol-infused 48-hour surf-fishing trip, me and a few of the boys got together to fish. As tends to happen when fishing is slow, our activities devolved into the basics of wrestling and fighting to pass the time away. Lido and I were wrestling, and as we threw each other off a ledge at the undertow, he landed with all his weight on me, literally snapping my shoulders together as they touched in an instantaneous, pain-addled blow. He proceeded to keep the fight going, but I couldn't move, and had to go to the hospital at 3 in the morning. I broke all the cartilage in my chest, my sternum, fractured my collarbone, and could not do a thing about it—no brace, no cast, nothing but a few pain-killers. Couldn't put my shirt on for 2 months without help. The worst part of it all was that I couldn't fish without mind-numbing pain. But I tried anyway. Oh well, all in a night's surfcasting.

November 8

Haven't been able to fish because of my jackass sternum affliction, but bass and blues seem to be everywhere since the winds switched to the west. On poppers, swimmers, and snagging live bunker. This sucks. I can't cast yet, but I suspect by early next week, I will be able to be back in the game. Let's go, collarbone, sternum, get it back!

November 8

Hit the beach, drove around from Ortley to Bay Head looking for a fight. From noon on, peanut bunker schools moving down the coast still. 20-knot west winds still, now air temps getting down to low 30s at night, 50s during daytime. Finally stopped in Bay Head at Harris Ave to cast around. Walked up to just below Osborne and stopped on a peanut bunker school. Switched to a snag rig and dipsey rig and then started to catch blues around 3:45 p.m. Missed two hits that maybe were bass since guys to the left and right had brought bass onto the beach. Followed the school north to Osborne, then it went back down south past Bridge and then, Karge. Ran into Dan Ottmer and talked it up a bit, then he got slammed on his popper with a 5-pound blue and I immediately got hammered by a 4-pound blue on a dead peanut. You can feel the weight on the end of the line just take off when a fish inhales a peanut. Walked down until nightfall and followed the peanuts, took about 5 bluefish out of it, but no bass. Cast and lost a black Bomber on the Bridge Ave rocks, have to get that in the afternoon low tide when I can walk out to it! Supposed to go down to 26 degrees tonight, could spark up the bass bite. High tide at 4:30 p.m.

November 8

Of course you know it went off after the Fiesta. Mantoloking. High at 9:30 a.m., gray skies, sunrise at 6 a.m. now with clocks turned back. Casting AVA jigs and white teasers, hooking bass. They are boiling all over, right in undertow, outside the breakers, flipping and rolling on 3- to 4-inch sand eels. Was using Loomis and Spheros setup 'cause it was set up for heavy surf, but today at high tide it was relatively flat, broke off two large fish that snapped the teaser dropper, lost AVAs and teasers on both. Then tied on Vision surf eel and lost that to a snap-off. Before that landed 4 bass of 26 to 30 inches. And a sun-dial and an 18-inch fluke! So pissed no teasers, leader all sucky, drag on reel sucks. So ran home and changed out for my huckleberry rod, came back, first cast landed 27-inch bass on green neon tail AVA, then hickory shad moved through and land a dozen or so of them, then another nice bass of 33 inches. Must have had 26 or so hits, landing about a dozen bass altogether, they were nipping at lures, not committing, hooked up with at least a dozen that shook the hook on me. Bass are around. Northwest winds 25 to 40 knots now.

That's one of the strangest things about November bassing. Some days, all they will want to do is short tap the lures. Whether it's because there is so much bait around and they make a last second judgment that the offering isn't real enough, or simply that they just lose interest, I don't know. But it is frustrating to get those days when all they seem to do is barely nip at the lures. That's when you switch up to live baits if you can snag some.

November 8

Fished my beach from 10 a.m. till noon with fresh clams, waters south and a bit dirty, but heavy water inside, overcast misty fog, no hits.

November 9

Hit my suds at 5:30 a.m., west winds. Had one blue dog about 5 pounds, nothing more, bay anchovies and peanuts all over. Went back home. Cali stopped by at 7 a.m. to give me some business about not being awake, but I was, and we decided to put the waders back on and hit Lyman where we saw some birds working. Got to Lyman, they were way far up about a mile, hoofed it to the school, gin-clear water, p-nuts moving thru in the undertow, and that's when I saw a 15- to 18-pound bass with gills flared, open-mouthed, vacuuming the peanuts into the absolute undertow sand like some sparkling painted picture, and then moved back out into the school! I then threw a Storm shad out and proceeded to hook up with a 23-inch bass at the front of the school. Air temps dipped to 26 degrees last night and they were at 35 degrees in the a.m., water about 57 degrees, and bait was moving south to north, which is unusual???? All day. Went to Chadwick Ave in Bay Head and me and Cali worked schools till 10:30 a.m., livelined peanuts for an hour in the school, nothing doing. Cali left and I went to look for my black Bomber on the Bridge Ave jetty when I saw birds working again at Chadwick jetty. Hopped in car to chase again and had a bluefish of 10 pounds whack a Kroc spoon. Bluefish pulled out a few left and right, then birds working like mad ¼ mile off, too far to cast. Hit the suds later that night with Bugsy and Jackson, who just got off the plane at 3:30 from NC, hit it at 3:45 p.m., nothing doing, but bait everywhere. One guy had a bass on live p-nuts on a clam stick rig.

November 9

Air 65 degrees or so. Hit my beach low tide at 6 p.m., south winds 2- to 3-foot. Had 3 blues to 6 pounds on Vision eels, bite slowed up last day due to south winds, had half dozen bassy taps too but no hookups.

Truly, November 10th looks like it hits blackjack every year. The lucky number. Is it possible that stripers have this particular date on the lunar and earth orbital cycle hard-wired into their brains to make them bite on this particular day? Who the heck knows? All I know is that it has produced every year for the last 10 years.

November 10

Hit Mantoloking at 5:30 a.m. and Princeton was packed! So was Albertson! Couldn't believe it. People are spot burning like mad now and old secrets are common knowledge now, I guess. Low tide at 6 a.m., seas 2-foot, glassy and a bit foggy. Unreal how many bass were jumping out of the water and spraying sand eel schools. Saw at least 80 pouncing on sand eels, but they wouldn't hit a thing! Managed a sundial and a 5-pound bluefish, saw only 7 or so fish landed out of 70 guys. Then out of the shadows, an angler creeps up on my spot in the darkness, I was about to MF him for mugging me when I saw it was Johnny Singles! We BS'ed and then met up again at noon to drive the beach, hitting all the holes but not catching anything, left at 4 p.m. Found a Bomber plug and a Super Strike needlefish in the surf, fun times, especially when Singles was pissing and a guy walked up with his golden retriever mid-piss!

Which brings me to the topic of mugging. Before the days of the World Wide Web and instantaneous spot burning, you actually had to have a little knowledge and put in time to find where the fish are. The instant reporting now on fishing websites has led to an overwhelming amount of anglers on the beaches, especially during peak season in November. Thus, many people are finding themselves mugged. Here's an article I penned for the *Fisherman Magazine* that delineates the basics of how to avoid mugging, and protocol for dealing with it. No exceptions!

BEACH MUGGING

Mug. (verb) To hold up, knock-off, loot, plunder, hijack, swindle.

If you've fished the beach long enough, you know what "mugging" is. Loosely defined, it's the direct, uncomfortable encroachment of the area you are fishing by another angler, usually occurring after the said angler sees you hook up, or after said angler thinks there is enough room to fish the same exact spot as you. However you look at it, you know what it feels like when it happens to you and it can lead to expletive laden verbal exchanges, fistfights, and even missed fishing time, all of which destroy a fishing outing. So how do you know if you've been mugged or if you're doing the mugging? Here's a few quick guidelines to follow to keep you on the straight and narrow.

First Come, First Served

The Golden Rule. If you are the first one to get to a spot, then that spot is yours to fish. No other angler has the right to mug you. Get up earlier if you want to put claim on a spot.

Deadstickers/Bait Fishers

An angler is the first to the beach and sets up two sand spiked clamming rods in a hole. Other anglers should not fish anywhere between the deadstick rods but should stay and fish on the outermost sides of the rods. I live in Normandy Beach year round and some mornings I walk up to my beach to what I consider "my hole" to start plugging, only to see a deadsticker there. I feel trespassed, but he was there first, and it's his hole to fish, plain and simple. I move on. Which leads me to the 20/50 yard rule.

20/50 Yard Rule

If a deadsticker is set up in a hole, and I want to plug, it is not considered mugging to walk 20 yards down either direction from his outermost rods and start making casts. However, if you are also deadsticking/bait fishing, it's best to go down to the next hole to set up camp and stay at least 50 yards away. When anglers are plugging or snagging bunker, a comfortable distance between anglers actively fishing is usually around 30 to 50 yards.

Bunker School Protocol

When adult bunker schools come in close enough to snag from the suds in the springtime, it can get competitive from the beach. Always stay on the outskirts of the snagging crew. Say there are five guys all snagging bunker, but the school has begun to move south fast. You are on the tail end of the snagging crew. You don't have the right to pick up and muscle your way in between anglers 2 and 3, or 3 and 4, but should frog hop the entire bunch of anglers and intercept the school ahead to start snagging again. This rule applies only if the pack of anglers is fairly tight, if not, see 20/50 yard rule above in respect to reentering the snagging crew in the middle.

Boat vs. Surf

The concrete rule. No boat has the right to fish so close in the surfcaster's average casting distance without expecting repercussions. Surf fisherman should get first dibs on surf fish, as it's only right, if a boat fishes a bunker schools or boiling bass close enough to read the writing on a surfcasters hat, the boater must expect the possibility of being pelted by errant plugs, heavy metal jigs, or weighted bunker snags. A surfcaster need not give way to a boater.

Blitz Conditions

This one can get really hairy in the heat of the moment, so it's best to keep it ultrasimple. Don't "cut in." An angler walks up to the beach to see bass and blues busting the surface all over. If the pack of anglers is tight, don't walk down and begin casting between two anglers already spaced evenly apart. You'll encroach their already established personal space and screw up the whole dynamic. Walk to either end of the pack anticipating the school's movement and begin casting. The school moves, then the other anglers pick up and frog hop to the forward motion to the forward progressing end of the line to begin casting again. It's bad karma to "cut in" between anglers.

Beach Buggies vs. Walk-Ons

Out of all my surf-fishing, 80 percent is walking on, and 20 percent is by beach buggy. Beach buggies have the decided advantage to chasing blitzes and scoping out spots, but this is how it goes. Most mugging will happen via beach buggies to walk-ons. Too many beach buggy anglers sit in the comfortable heat of the truck with binoculars without making casts. Once a walk-on has a bent rod, many times the buggy will scream on over, run out of the truck, and start casting 20 yards away. Bad move. It's not bad to want to fish where the fish seem to be, but buggy anglers shouldn't do drive-by muggings and a nice gesture would be to ask the walk-on if he minds you casting there for a few. Common courtesy goes a long way.

Put the Muzzle on Mugging!

When surf-fishing in Jersey, all that really matters is common sense and a little respect. We've got a lot of anglers in this state and 128 miles of coastline to hit hard. Sure, there will be days where it's a ghost town and you have the beach all to yourself, but there will be days when it will be jam-packed. React accordingly. The saying goes, "Do unto others that which you would like done unto you," or something like that. If it feels like you are mugging somebody, chances are you are. Whether you're a "Local" living year round in a beachside community, a "Part-Timer" who owns a house or rents to enjoy a few months out of the year, or a "Day-tripper" driving from inland towns to enjoy the beaches, we are all "Fishermen" and all have the same rights, respect, and responsibilities to share the beach equally. Respect the Angler—don't mug!

November 10

Hit my suds at 5:30 a.m. with Cali, nothing showing, except for a bird that took Cali's plug. Fished till 7 a.m., 6 a.m. high tide. At 12 went to Bridge Ave to reclaim a black Bomber I lost a few nights before on the jetty, west winds, low tide pushed water way out, walked all on the rocks of the submerged jetty, didn't find my Bomber but came up with a Storm shad and teaser. P-nuts locked in the south side of the jetty, dead-low. Birds working offshore but overall quiet today all around, few blues here and there. Made a few casts at Lyman on the way home, where some bluefish were visibly breaking just outside the far sandbars, but they were very fickle on the take today. At 3 p.m., I went to Princeton to check it out, saw a few birds just in casting range. Threw out at them for nothing. Then they reconvened and I saw tiny baitfish jumping, cast out and had a 3-pound bluefish. The blues got smaller during the last day and half, winds now south at 10 to 15 and I think that shut it down a bit.

November 10

Last two days Cali had 4 bass each morning on black Bombers and teasers at Princeton. Hit Princeton evening time with a 15- to 20-knot east blow, seas 3 to 5, solid and churny and roily beach break, thick water inside but that greenish-clear water. Hard to make any casts with a silver-and-black Bomber and teaser but finally punched one decent one through and right in the undertow. It got impaled by a 28-inch striper that came tumbling in on the waves. He had the teaser and head of the plug in his mouth, he pulled some nice drag and gave up quite a fight. Cali was dragging an AVA jig and claimed he had a hit as well, though he's been known to fib.

November 10

Surf N/NE, gray, 4- to 5-foot, high around 11:30 a.m. Hit Albertson again from 7 a.m. to 9:30 a.m. First bass 27 inches on a Vision surf eel, tide started coming in hard around 8:45 a.m., guy next to me casting orange-tailed AVA and whacking them along this one cut you could barely see. I jumped in the spot when he left and went 6 for 8 on bass there from 24 to 28 inches, on the Able 2 metal orange-tail. Gannets outside the breakers diving on what looked like mullet corncobs; when they were in front of me was when I had that first bass. The key to hooking up with the other bass was to cast at 10 o'clock, and keep the line tight to 2 o'clock reeling slow, got all hits around 1 to 2 o'clock in the hole dropping off the ledge. Played the swift current right and I scored.

It was all about orange that day. Any other color never got a sniff. The orange color must've been highlighted nicely in the gray churning surf and the bass were dialed into it. There's something about those rough and tumble, stormy, rain-filled days that are a little higher up on the ladder than beautiful postcard sunrise mornings. I dunno, it's the true blood of the salt water drenching me, taking waves "over the bow" of my waders, getting the salt spray in my face and hair and lungs and breathing all of it in, with deep inhalations, charging hard with fortitude and conviction to punch casts through ever harder, raging and elevating winds, to beat the odds with every cast, all the while looking and feeling like a sad, wet dog left out in the cold. Any other normal or sane person observing while sipping on a cup of hot coffee from their front porch must think I'm nuts and pathetic. But to me, it's those days, those times and moments of dedication and conviction, that I feel the most alive in life, and I walk off the beach, smiling ear to ear, with nothing to say.

November 10

Waters cleaned up nice now, west winds, high tide 4:30 a.m. Hit Princeton Avenue, started with black Bomber, then Vision eel, saw some sand eel schools jumping out of the water with boils on them, then switched to an AVA 007 flo-green tail and immediately hooked up with a 21-incher. Waded out on the bar south of Albertson pyramid house, and saw boils, cast to them and whacked with a 24-incher, started walking back, in front of Cannon's house, cast again, had a 25-incher that hit the teaser with rainfish plastic imitation. And saw one boil beside it when reeling him in. Slow pick today, 3 bass fished 5:45 a.m. to 7:45 a.m. Man, seems like everybody knows about Princeton now, doesn't anybody work??!

Evening

Blitz! Hit my beach at 4 p.m., immediately get whacked by bluefish 4 to 6 pounds and fat! One after another, hit after hit, Jimmer and Bo doing the same. Had doubleheaders, snapped off a few, missed bumps, then scored a 24-inch bass around 4:20 p.m. Then double header bass and blue, bass hit the AVA jig. Another 26-incher. You could see blues chasing sand eels in the wash, saw a bass in the undertow that almost bumped me, then cast out black Bomber once it got near dark twilight, had a 29-inch bass on the teaser that rolled me and unhooked itself, then the big whack. On the Bomber, a solid strike and it had shoulders, then beached a 32-inch striper! Total 4 bass and 13 blues in hour and 20 minutes!

Blitzing bluefish make for happy anglers. AL RISTORI.

November 10

Peck boys came down, we fished from 3 p.m. to 5 p.m., high tide, 5-foot, glassy and clear, still. Nite had a 26-inch bass and 3-pound blue earlier, at 4:45 p.m. to 5:15 p.m. I landed a 23-inch bass, kind of cloudy and light brown in color, Fancypants had a nice 7-pound blue on an AVA reeled fast, and Dave had two bass and a blue on a Crippled Herring into the dark. Mine hit a black Bomber.

November 10

All-out mayhem! Got frigid cold, dipped into the high teens, normally 40 and 50s, now for two days straight, with a northwest blow. Got to Osborne Ave at around 1 p.m. The road was lined with trucks and rod racks. Ran up the deck and saw shoulder-to-shoulder anglers, birds working from Point to Mantoloking, and saw a few with rods bent. Mostly bluefish, but saw hordes of peanuts in the suds. Got home, ran north of the T-Bird saw some birds working, ran out on the low tide bars, and cast out a snag rig, immediately hooked into a bunch of fresh peanuts. Saw some peanuts getting crashed, little spurts of silvery explosions, but nothing too crazy. Then saw some serious bluefish crashing them, missed my shot. I sat in the spot for over an hour and a half livelining peanuts, and a steady stream of the suckers kept running through, an immense amount of nuts in the surf right now. Occasionally some birds got active on a spot but it would disappear quickly. No fish biting today. But finally blitzing.

When the economic crash jolted the nation in 2008, it was no doubt a crazy time of sudden unemployment and definite economic uncertainty, and to date, it still is. The one thing I noticed on a daily basis while surf-fishing is the amount of people that really started populating the beaches after the economic downturn. Spots that you would rarely ever see one other angler were being choked by 4, 5, even 12 anglers. Not only were some people out of jobs, it seemed like friends and their friends' friends were all out of work, and everybody went to the beach to fish.

It was a double-edged sword. As a sportsman, I loved the fact that so many people were waking up at the crack of dawn to enjoy the sport of surf fishing, but on the other side, the beaches were packed, and that sacred time of soulful solitude spent in the surf alone was no more. That part sucked. I definitely amended my schedule to fish more wee hours of midnight to 6 a.m., and walked private beaches farther than a mile to get away from crowds since then. It may seem foolish, but some days, I'm not there to catch fish, but to be alone with my mind and the ocean's soul, just casting.

November 11

West winds 5 knots, clean and clear, 1-foot. Hit Albertson since Princeton is like a parking lot with unemployed people I guess, 14 people on Princeton! Anyway got there 5:45

a.m. cast out Bomber, got a nibble then switched to AVAs, in the false dawn saw some boils, then got hit by a 23-inch bass, another 10 or so casts and had a 26-incher on the flo green-tailed AVA. Had about another 10 bumps that didn't connect, guy near me had 7-pound bluefish. Fished till 7:30 a.m. Water gin-clear now, west winds 5 to 10 knots, high tide 5 a.m. Water getting colder to 55 degrees.

November 11

We're bracing for a monster nor'easter with 12- to 16-foot seas for the next 3 days. Singles texted me he hit Mantoloking 6:15 a.m. to 8:30 a.m. and landed 8 bass from 28 to 32 inches so I put on the waders and hit my beach. Howling 30 knots northeast, 5- to 7-foot, dead-low tide and I landed 6 bass out of 8 that hit AVA 17 green tail and teaser too. Bass hit in ankle deep whitewater on the sandbar as well as on the edges south of the hole at Jimmer's, a guy from Virginia hooked into 8 that I saw with keepers thrown in. Unreal fishing till 9:40 a.m. when I got off the beach to write my columns. Those bass that didn't hit yesterday sure hit this morning! Probably going to be unfishable the next four days, but we'll see how bad we get hit from remnants of Hurricane Ida.

That year was strange, to have a push from a nor'easter come that early and have a hurricane come so late in the hurricane season. But the fish certainly didn't mind!

November 11

Hit Albertson again, early sunrise, water really rough now, winds 25 to 30 knots northeast, tough fishing, couldn't even hold ground with an AVA 27, fished about an hour to no avail. Storm moved in, will sit on us for a few days.

November 12

Was going to go fish with Jackson on his new boat with Cali but the boat shit the bed in the canal at 6:30 a.m., wouldn't start, so I hit my beach, where bluefish and bass were being taken. I tossed a Gibbs popper and teaser out on the 60-yard sandbar into the horizon at around 7:45 a.m. and got wailed by a 14-pound bluefish that really tested my reel, he hit the white teaser and depth-charged the surface! I also had a bass of about 28 inches on, that I lost in the wave where he shook the hook. Also had two more blues or bass follow my popper and take a few swipes at it on the way in. Water flat, calm, sunny as all heck and clear, that's why poppers work now, to confuse the fish so they don't get a clear eye on what is going thru the water. Cali and I then went to hit the dead-low tide at 10:30 a.m. at a beach spot to hit the wreck for tog. Waded out far on the bar and cast with clams, got banged after second clam, solid blackfish hit. Re-baited and threw out again, had another solid bang and then it got tight, he bulldogged me into a snag, it was hung up, then the line chafed and snapped! He beat me! Cast out again and had a nice tap, set the hook hard and reeled him out of the structure and beached a beautifully dark-colored 27-inch striper. Cali had some whacks too. There are definitely tog there. Cast 3 ounces on west wind, blowout tide, full moon coming up in four days, maybe hit it then again.

November 12

Fished Princeton, less people now, dead water, clean and clear, north winds 5 knots, 5:30 a.m. to 7:00 a.m., one bass 24 inches on AVA jig, only one that had a bent rod, sand eels all over the undertow. Air temp about 40, water 54, slow day all around apparently.

November 13

Crazy 40-knot winds ravaging through for no reason, gust to 58 MPH. Straight west. Blow-out low tide, walked out 200 yards and was up to my knees. The farthest I've ever been out there on legs. I stopped in at Kupper to check the scene at 4:30 p.m. and saw a massive 150-yard bluefish blitz, birds and all, right off Jimmer's Hole. Could reach them with a popper no doubt, ran home, ran up to beach, and they moved off about 300 yards, too far, but stayed and cast in the chocolate milky, glassy-waved water. Jimmer had a hit on a white plug and I chucked a white popper to no avail, though I launched it as far as about 100 yards, seriously. Jimmer has taken bass every morning, still on clams, and had them to 40 inches yesterday.

November 14

Southeast winds 20 knots, waters weird with clean water but southeast choppy to it. High tide at 10 a.m. Fished 9:30 a.m. to 10:30 a.m., birds picking away at surface, possibly blues around cast an A17 into the wind, no hits.

THIRD WEEK

A chill permeates your outer shell, seeping into the cracks of your inner warmth during the predawn sessions of the third week of November. Its "puttin' the wood" to the bass time and the weather begins to weed out the sissies and less dedicated surf anglers. It's a good time to see old friends as the beaches thin out, while it's also a good excuse to hit the Crab's Claw or Broadway for a few warm up shots of blackberry brandy to keep you warm for casting. Whatever the case, the third week is ripe with activity.

November 15

Cali had 11 bass on clams from Princeton, mostly shorts, two slots, one 30 inches. Hard south 15 to 25 wind, believe it or not, fished 5:30 a.m. to 7:30 a.m. Hottest bite, high tide around 5 a.m. I took pics for *Shallow Water Angler* and made a few casts.

The last entry, I said "believe it or not" because that was one of the first times ever, EVER, in surf-fishing with a stiff south wind, that the bite was on. If you learn one thing fishing the surf in NJ, it is that nothing ever bites on the south wind. It is the death knell for all fishing. If it's got a little east in it, or west, fine and dandy, you'll catch fish, but a straight south wind? No way. Theory says it's the conditions of upwelling that occur, bringing in colder water and pushing the warmer water offshore, but it is truly uncanny how fast the bite dies when the wind goes south. You can have a great day fishing east winds and pulling one bass or blue after another all day long, and at 2 p.m., the wind switches over to south? Pack it in. It's no joke. That day above was one weird anomaly that happens as much as a fisherman tells the whole truth and nothing but the truth about a fishing trip.

November 16

Cast out at Risden's and Bradshaw's beach at 4 p.m. with Gordo, where the water is deep even on the low tide. Schoolie and slot bass being caught throughout the day, but no real blitzing yet. Where are the big bass? Maybe bunker staying offshore with big bass following offshore. No dice there with Gordo, but did have a bump on a yellow Bomber, maybe a small bass, and did see baitfish in the wash. West winds, 3- to 4-foot surf.

November 17

Hit Top of the Mast again with Jackson at 4 p.m., on a good tip from Jim Bramble. Light west, 3- to 4-foot. We went right down to the beach, dead-low about 5:30 a.m., heavy water on the inside even though almost dead-low. Guy worked a 3-inch white shad and had two bass immediately, the guy next to me had two bass on a Danny's yellow-and-white swimmer. Both fellas were having action on the north sides of the sandbars with a north current, probably pushing food into the cut and churning it up there. I tried shads, yellow and black Bombers, and had one stop me for a second, but its mouth was probably too small to get a hook in it. Jackson pulled another two out, 24 to 28 inches. I walked north to try a north side of a hole when around nightfall I hooked into something that bent my rod at the first guide! My rod was bowing, and I thought I hooked into the 50-pounder. I waited for five seconds for it to make its move but it stayed in one spot, then I walked back to put a tiny bit more pressure and realized I had hooked into a shipwreck of some sort. It was solid, whatever it was, and did not move one inch. I ended up breaking it off with my hands. Still, maybe it was an 80-pounder!

November 18

Hit morning about 5:30 a.m. with Cali to 20th Street in Seaside again. Worked the same area where Jackson had his luck the night before, casting 3-inch Storms, got whacked once then put a slot on the beach. Then another. Cali kept trying. At around 7:30 a.m. I saw some activity right in the undertow, rainfish were being chased and bass were boiling behind them. I cast out a small metal popper and tied into a short bass. Regular shads and Bombers didn't work because the bait was too small, so I threw on a 1-ounce

Crippled Herring, and that opened the door. I had a bluefish about 3 pounds on immediately, then as I reeled in the metal, I saw a bass whack it in the glassy wave! Was a slot fish, and then witnessed bass actually chasing the peanuts in the undertow wave, where the bait fell out of the wave with the bass falling out onto the beach! After Cali didn't get anything for his efforts, we decided to run up to Princeton, then Lyman, where we saw bluefish blitzing. I threw out a popper, then a metal and had a 5-pound blue, Cali nothing. We went back to 20th Street, around noon now, and as I walked on the beach, at about where I lost my Bomber yesterday, I looked down and saw my black Bomber with my leader and knots and tangled line! It must've dislodged over the night in whatever it was snagged onto. Found more bass right where we left them, and Cali finally tied into a short bass on a metal.

November 18

Hard NE blow yesterday put a bunch of sand back onto the beach, and with it tons and tons of surf clams. I went out to check out the Leonid Meteor shower and instead ended up scavenging about 4 dozen clams in a 30-yard radius! I'll shuck 'em up tomorrow, It's supposed to get down to 28 or so tonight, which might ignite a bass bite, since we now have west winds with a churned surf, and there is talk of intense bass action still up in Montauk, which means we should be seeing those bass sooner or later.

Stoking the beach campfire, the lifeblood of the November overnight shift.

November 18

Fished IBSP at A10 with Mickey, got out around 2:30 p.m., set up clams and bunker, I had two fish on clams to 26 inches, Mick had a nice one shake off on a bunker chunk, all hits from 3 to 4, supposed gale but only about 20 to 25 knots west/NW. High tide at noon, seas 3-foot.

November 19

Hit the beach around 2 p.m. High tide 6:30 p.m., held with 5 ounces. The west winds went southeast at about 15 knots. I casted out those clams I found yesterday into the hard in-your-face wind. I got one hit. I was talking to Norm when I looked over at my rod and saw the whole operation—rod, sand spike, and all—freakin' launch out of the sand and fly like two feet in the air before it hit ground and started going for the surf. I hightailed it as fast as my adrenaline could over to it, picked up the rod, reeled the slack and set back on the biggest seagull of my life. What a freakin' deflation. A seagull, no 70-pound linesider, a seagull. Norm laughed. That was the only action I had except for a quick tappity-tap nibble at dusk. Kenny and Paul showed up on their ATC, drunk as skunks and classically idiotic.

RELEASING SEAGULLS

Kenny and Paul are two of the local-yokel beach boys. Sock hats with the little puff balls on the top, snow suits on, like *Strange Brew* guys. You know, drinking, riding three-wheelers on the beach, good times. But the preceding story is most important for another point—that of releasing seagulls. Without a doubt, if you surf-fish long enough, you will have a seagull fly into your line and tangle you up, and there is an actual method to the madness of getting them untangled. First, reel him in slowly so as not to startle him into flapping furiously away. Keep your drag tight. Once you get within an arm's distance, he's going to be snapping and trying to pierce you with his bill, so to combat that tactic, simply take off your shirt and throw it over the head of the seagull. Next, get the least smart guy of your crew to hold the seagull down gingerly with the shirt over its head. Cut the line out of the seagull's wings, pull the shirt off its head and scoot backwards as fast as you can. Voila! Seagull released.

November 19

Northeast, 3- to 5-foot, 10 knots, overcast, high at 8:30 a.m. Hit my beach at 10:45 a.m. with five clams I found washed up, nice big ones, two rods out and hit a cut, lots of whitewater, but fairly clean, went 2 for 3 on bass, 28, 27 inches, both fat, and missed a hit. Tagged both of them for the American Littoral Society. Fished till 12:45 p.m. Wayne had a small bass on an AVA jig. Big sandbars since the blow, that's where our beach is at now, but cuts starting to form, air temp almost 60 degrees, water 55 degrees, this weather pattern has been the same for a long time, may be why bass sticking around in good numbers, boats are crushing them, but it's always been rough out.

November 19

Surf-fished with Bugsy on my beach Jimmer's Hole for bass, clamming at 3:30 p.m., we had 8 bass on the clams and I pulled another two in on a Bomber plug in the roiling wash of 3- to 4-foot, northeast.

November 20

Me and Cali went to IBSP at Area 20, winds west at 5 to 10, high tide around 10 a.m. Got there at 6 a.m., and right before false dawn I had a 22-inch bass on a black Bomber that really whacked the plug. Cali then had a hit that was a 20-pound class bass that ran off drag and hurt his rod, but he dropped it. Then he had a 23-inch bass on a Yo-Zuri Swing Mullet. Bass and blues kind of around for boaters, some bird play offshore, but water temps still up to 56 degrees, so cold front this week should turn the bass bite on. My waders are so leaky now, that it is re-go-dang-diculous how much water gets in 'em along with sand foot. Ate breakfast at the Bayside Café, Cali had a bunch of trouble getting toast.

Nothing is more inconvenient or annoying than a leaky pair of waders. That first seep on a cold mid-November morning sends chills up your spine for the entire day, not to mention that wet feet in sloshy socks suck.

November 21

Hit my beach from 1:30 p.m. to 4:30 p.m., high at 2, seas 1- to 2-foot with clams out, water clean, west winds 15 knots, sunny day. Set one rod out, put it in holder and it bent down with a 25-inch bass! Set it out again 15 minutes later, went down with a 22-incher. Set out another rod and continually got picked by smallies that didn't inhale the 8/0 circle hook, about 12 taps that didn't set, then had another set around 3:30 p.m. with a 22-incher again. Three bass total, bunch of hits. Oh, also had a massive sundial inhale a whole clam!

FOURTH WEEK

Dominant northwest winds start to lay the foundation for the approaching winter, as glassy clean waters begin to be the norm, while the remnants of peanut bunker schools still file on through. The mullet are long gone, and sand eels are the predominant bait now, flitting by the zillions in the surfline as bass corral them in a daily smorgasbord. Unmotivated days in the frigid cold mean it's still clamming time, while you set one rod in the holder and cast lures around with another to prospect the area for visual bites. Days are short now, but the bite remains long into the night if you can convince yourself to bundle up and brave the elements. It's also Thanksgiving time, and there's no better way to show the family you care than slapping freshly caught striper fillets between the turkey and cranberry on the dinner table.

November 22

Got let out of work and home by 2:30 p.m. Set up some lines at Jimmer's Hole, we got a south wind driving at 15 to 20 kts, high tide around 10:30 a.m., so fished the end of the outgoing. Banged out three short bass between I guess 17 and 20 inches. They tap the clams ever so lightly and then they're gone. You almost have to hold the rod in your hand like springtime fishing. Jimmer had two more and said they were taking plugs earlier in the day. Found another 18 clams on the beach when I walked up. Could this be from the draggers that are unearthing them just outside?

Night

Went out in front of the path a bit to the left. Winds shifted to west about 15 knots. Two rods with lite brites on them. Caught three skates, one of which was the biggest I have ever caught, the sucker went about 34 inches nose to tail. You can tell a skate hit as it gives a steady pull then nothing, then a steady pull then nothing, check your rod if you see that happening. In all the pandemonium, I did manage two short bass of 17 and about 13 inches, which I of course kissed for good luck when they are that small. Used those clams again, and I believe I missed about 4 bites only because I could not get to the rod within the split millisecond you need to set back on these tiny bass. But they sure are fun late at night, where I went out at 10:30 p.m. and came in at 1:30 a.m. Let's go, ol' pajamas, where are the big boys?

Sometimes, a little voodoo is what's needed to bring in the bass . . .

November 22

Me and Cali hit Princeton to see what was up. Got there at 5:30 a.m. to cast around, nothing doing, then set up on clams around 6:30 a.m. West wind 10 knots, almost dead-low tide. At around 7:30 a.m. I started to wander around looking for things, and found an old Rat-L-Trap washed up. Brought it back to Singles and shook its BBs at the rod to make some fish-calling noise and put some voodoo on my rod. Within 5 seconds my rod went down and I reeled in a 20-inch bass! Then sent it out again, rattled it up and in another 10 minutes had another 22-inch class bass. Cali was dumbfounded. Crazy thing of the morning was looking in the slough close by and see what looked like a giant great white fin breach the surface, lazily wobbling back and forth and then going under three seconds later. Did not look like plywood, the way it moved. It had to be a shark or even a sunfish!??

November 22

Hit my beach 11 a.m. to 1:30 p.m., high at 3 p.m., out on the low tide bar, clean water, northwest 15 to 20 knots, seas 1- to 2-foot, out on the bar, saw sand eel schools waving around, cast out 007 AVA flo green tail and ended up snagging a few, inadvertently sent them back out on the 2/0 white bucktail teaser hooked through bottom jaw and out top of hard part of head, first cast I dragged it so slow, then BAM! A solid heavy hit! Reeled in, and was excited because wanted to tag this one with my first tags from the ALS, walked back through the slough and beached him—he already had an ALS tag in him! #734140. I took number down and released him at 22 inches long. Made a few more snags and casts and about 5 minutes later WHAM! Outside the bar a walloping hit, this was heavier, fought him back over the bar and over slough again, beached at 31 inches and about 11.5 pounds! Tagged him and sent him on his way—first ALS bass #763160! Awesome fish. Then had another one on that I dropped. Tide too high this time to fish safely on the bar with deep slough, so set big rod up with AVA 27 and teaser with a 4-inch Gotcha plastic on it. Cast out and reeled ultra slow on bottom when I feel dead weight, then it starts taking off, slow but heavy, fluke? Fight it to the beach and it was a massive 16-pound fat ass bluefish! Released it, held it up to show Brezo on the beach, then went home to eat breakfast! Need a snag rig to get those sand eels then drag them for bass.

Tagging fish is truly like hunting; it's a rewarding experience that can come back to give you rewards by paying it forward some years down the road, when someone returns a tag from one of your previously tagged fish. It's cool to see where a fish has been, and it adds a sincerely personal element to catching and releasing fish. Check with the American Littoral Society at www.littoralsociety .org to get involved with fish tagging in New Jersey.

November 22

Hit my beach 11:20 a.m. to 12:30 afternoon, northeast 15 to 20 knots, 4- to 6-foot but clean, blue, and clear and sunny, looked island-like, summertime rough surf I see in the Caribbean! Cast an AVA 17, high tide at 11, had two bumps on an edge, then got whacked big time, battled a monster fish until my gears in Shimano Sustain started slipping! Eventually muscled in an estimated 17- to 18-pound bluefish monster gorilla! I couldn't even get hook out, it snapped when bluefish rolled on it! One of top 3 blues I've ever caught in surf . . . then recast immediately with 007 and got banged by a 26-inch bass, but couldn't reel him in as my gears were almost completely shot and slipping from years of use, so I had to walk it back a few dozen yards and hand-over-hand tug the line in to bring bass up on beach. Just then Joe O came cruising by and lent me a rod to cast. What a gorilla bluefish! Water temp 54, air still in 50s, lukewarm and steadily comfortable, no gloves yet! Sand eels thick all over.

November action is fast and furious, with doubleheader bass hookups the norm.

November 24

Fished IBSP with Mickey and his charter Dana, got there at 6 a.m. Northeast 25 knots hard, seas 5- to 8-foot, brown, dead-low at 6, high at noonish. Barely held with 8 to 10 ounces, checking baits often, landed 3 bass shorts on clams. Rain, miserable conditions, barely any beach to drive at high tide.

November 24—Thanksgiving

Didn't fish but Cali said he had about 20 bass to 34 inches long. Surf was a little rough, 3- to 4-foot. Said sand eels around now.

November 24

Hit my surf to no avail. Dark at 5 p.m. now, 1- to 2-foot, southwest winds, full moon blowout tides, lots of cuts and sloughs now, Jimmer had a few fish last evening.

November 26

Hit Princeton with Cali and Herb Segars to shoot for offshore. 1- to 2-foot, northwest, glassy. High tide around 3:30 p.m. now. Got to parking at 5:15 a.m. and cracked open a Celebration Ale, Singles arrived and he cracked one too. First cast around 5:45 a.m. right at the first hole and in about 10 minutes had a bass wallop black Bomber right in the undertow, almost on the sand, too dark to see what it was, it got off on the wave, literally hit with about 15 feet of line out. Felt like a slot bass. No more hits for me, but Cali hit a hole way down to the right for a total of five bass, so he says, on a Yo-Zuri plug Swing Mullet. Left beach around 8:15 a.m., and then had last Celebration Ale.

And one year, early in my log journals at 2001, I simply didn't have enough time to write it all down, so the last month and a half was a jumbled paragraph of entries that went like this.

Nov 14 to Dec 31
   HOOK IN HAND

First things first. Once again, if you surf-fish long enough, you are going to have a "hook in hand" experience eventually. Sometimes, it can be serious, requiring a hospital trip, sometimes a mere point puncture that requires a little whiskey and a strong gut. Either way, it's never pretty.

Fished about another 14 times before end of the season which fell on December 14th this year for me, ending in an all-out bass blitz which I fished from 4:30 p.m. on through the dark, managed to go 4 for 7 on bass, none under 26 inches, ending with a 31-incher that upon releasing it in the pitch black dark at around 5:15, it flopped over onto my hand, sinkin' the two size 2/0 treble hooks into my right hand. I bit off the line, then released the hooks from the fish. I walked over to Bo, who was catching bass, and he said, "Whoa! You gotta go to the hospital!" The one hook I pulled out it was only up to the barb, the other was sunk in past the bend in the hook, about ¾ inch in. I asked Jimmer if he had some cutting pliers, we went to walk to his house, got up to the light on the walkway, and with a thrust, pulled the hook out past the bend, up to the barb, which was still lodged in my hand. I then pushed down on the barb hard, and pulled it out, clean. It hit my nerve in my hand, sending electric shocks up and down my arm.

But back to those end-of-the-year reports.

Anyway, there were about three solid days since last writing of bass fishing. One day in late November I was so thick into bass, I caught 19 bass, mostly all shorts that day and walked from Bay Head down to Princeton Ave again. It was a full-on fall blitz for real. I saw two bass through the glassy waves chasing a sea snake, no bullshit, they were nipping at it in the water on the crests of the waves. I broke off a huge bass using an AVA jig, followed peanut schools all the way down the coast. Started fishing around 2 p.m. but didn't land my first fish until about 4 p.m., then all short bass, one or two over 26 inches, but mostly shorts that bit on through the entire night, I had to leave at about 6:30 p.m. to get ready to film for *The NJ Fishing Show* the next morn. I couldn't believe how hot the action was on Yo-Zuri plugs, Crippled Herrings, teasers. I landed about a 16- or 17-pound bluefish from the suds as well and saw bass coming right up my feet. The striper run didn't really happen, we had successive northeast maelstroms that pushed the fish offshore, and only when it was kinda light west and clean-up did we see some fish, about five solid days, maybe once a week for good fishing. For most of Nov and Dec I smelled like fresh peanut bunker, all over my clothes, and remember casting in the evenings, with peanuts crashing around my legs, bass chasing them around me, missing a few on topwater poppers, and hooking into some on late-evening black Bombers.

TROPHY TOGGIN'

OK, so I dabble in beach-togging in October, but when November hits, the tog go on a mad dog bite. It's nothing like I've ever experienced as far as straight, in-your-grill wreck-fishing from the beach. Snags, duck-ins, break-offs, and all. November has been the prime month to target tautog from the sands, and this little secret has taken a lot of my mental time to plan out a strategy effectively over the years. And it's all worth it. If you have a serious tog affliction like I do, you may want to really pay attention to the forthcoming information. Just sayin'.

November 2

Tog from beach, dead-low at 12 high noon, walked out on the bar to cast out between the marks, had about 8 or 9 really solid hits that took my baits, I had one on for a few seconds but dropped him. Full moon, blowout tides make it easier to cast to wreck now, used a three-way swivel rig, may have to go back to a fishfinder to make it really work. Headed in about 2:30 p.m. when the bar was covered with water again, I saw the slough was menacingly dark, took a step and it was like jumping into the deep end of the pool. I went under and didn't touch bottom, I swam with my waders filling up like an anchor and sucking to my legs, dropped my rod underwater, looked down and found it, and kicked and swam to where I could stand, completely almost drowned! Now I know how that feels to get stuck on the bar. Air 45 degrees, water 58.

CAUGHT AT THE BAR

No, not caught at the bar drinking, though that could be just as dangerous if your significant other thinks you are supposed to be somewhere else, but I'm talking about being caught on the sandbar on a rising tide. It's a tempting situation. It's a lower tide, you walk through a slough, out onto a sandbar to get your casts out to where the deep water is. The bite is fast and furious, and the tide starts moving in. What was ankle-deep water an hour ago on the bar is now up to your knees, but you keep on casting as this bite is too hot to let go. The water gets up to your thighs now and you decide it's time to head back to the beach, only 30 yards behind you. Problem is, all that incoming water has now filled the slough behind you, and it's deep, a lot deeper than the waist-high water it was when you came out. The other problem is now it's 35 degrees out, and you have thick neoprene waders on. Now what?

If you're smart, you line up the access point of shallow sand from which you entered and make a relatively safe exit, but if it's already too late in the incoming water, then it gets dicey. Case in point—on one particular day, I was too greedy on the tog, and when I tried to make my exit through the thinnest point of the slough, it was already 7 feet deep, way over my head. I tried to feel it out with the tip of my rod, but the unseen underwater ledge was too steep, and as I put my first foot down, I went ker-plunk! Straight under the water, over my head. I was sinking fast as the neoprene waders clung to my legs and waist, pulling me down. I panicked, clawing for the surface, but also kept it cool enough to find the rod I dropped sticking to my feet underwater and grabbed it as I tried to gain some kind of footing, which I eventually did in three or four paddled steps. I was able to crawl out on my hands and knees with about 50 pounds of water in my waders, soaked to the bone in freezing water and air temperatures, and I immediately began to shiver violently. I ran up to the Jeep and blasted the high heat though it didn't help, and it took an hour-long shower in piping hot water to stop the shivering.

Point is, when fishing the outer bar on a hot bite, always have a game plan for the incoming tide. Note an anchor point on the shore, a chimney, flagpole from a house, whatever, where you enter at the shallowest point. Try and fish the outer bar on a dropping tide so you know the low won't be for a few hours. Never fish more than two hours after the start of the incoming tide if you are out far, as the sloughs will fill up faster than you think; an easterly push of wind and water will fill the sloughs up faster than an offshore blow will. Never fish the outer bar on 3-foot-plus surf.

If you feel that you are screwed with high water, take off your waders on the bar before you attempt to navigate back through the slough or cut. Never exit where there is a cut of running water that may riptide and carry you farther out. Above all, be vigilant and smart about your surroundings. I hate to say it, but no fish is worth losing your life over. Just be smart and plan to hit the next tide around; the fish will still be there. Though it is always tempting on a torrid bite to stick it out, take off the waders on the sandbar, and swim back to shore if need be.

November 5

Hit up the Princeton Pipe for blackies and finally did it! Low tide 1:37 p.m., hit it at 12:45 p.m., light southeast, 2- to 3-foot. Used fishfinder rig, 3-ounce pyramid. Tie down clams, and wham! Got hit and brought in a 28-inch striper. Recast a few minutes later, wham again! Another 28-inch bass. Guy next to me on the bar also had a 24-inch class bass. Sunny day. Then, I started getting tapped at the dead-low. Tap-tap-whomp! Felt the vibration and set back and played in a 17-inch blackfish! Finally! Recast and immediately got whomped, then it took off, fought and battled a 3- to 4-pound blackie to the shore! 22 inches. Then, recast a fresh clam, took off the extra tie down and got walloped. I fought this thing in that was vibrating, and pulling drag, my freakin' Penn reel lost the drag top on it so couldn't loosen it up, it dogged me, pulled some drag, then about 25 feet away it made a run and pulled the hook, it had to be a 6- to 8-pound class tog. Absolutely unbelievable for 1 1/2 hours of beach fishing.

November 10
Went back to fish the C—— wreck. Dead-low tide, so far low, hit sandbar at 11 a.m. low tide 11:30 a.m. fished till 1:45 p.m. HOLY MOLEY! On south side of the house, almost off of it, I reached the real sticky part of the wreck. Lost two tog in it, one snapped hook off in wreck, other cut clean by sharp part of the wreck was snagged on. UNBELIEVABLE TOGGIN'! Finally used size 4 blackfish hooks, worked real well to hook fish. I was working the wreck from the middle of the house to the south side, seems to be in a few parts. Altogether landed 12 tog, now get this three were 3.5-, 4.5-, and 6.5-pound! WHOPPER TOG! Others were 13 to 16 inches long. I can't even describe how hard that 6.5 fought really rooted down and dirty and bulldogged me the whole way, pump-pump-pump. I must've had another 15 hooked and lost, too.

That was the best beach togging day yet!

November 12
Hit C—— wreck with clams from 12 noon to 1:30 p.m. Nibbles but no hits, way low tide with full moon tomorrow, actually hit C—— wreck and lost a rig snagged, right off the flagpole. Went to a different wreck to hit it, but a freaking spearfishing boat was there.

That's also a problem with beach-wrecking. The knowledgeable spearfishers and boat fishermen know where these shoreline wrecks are, and many times you have to be the first on the spot to battle for positioning.

November 23
Hit C—— wreck, dead-low, high noon, full moon tide tomorrow. Fished till 2:30 p.m., 2-foot, 10 to 15 knots NW. Water semiclear. Caught 12 stripers, one each of 34, 29, 28, and 9 shorts, all on tied down Ernie stink clams, saw a sand eel wash up too. Left 'em biting when I ran outta bait, took a snapshot with some kids and some other girls! No blackfish though canal still supposedly producing.

November 30
McD came down to fish for whatever, he just needed to fish. We hit the canal for low slack at 11:30 a.m. and it was a ghost town for blackfish, besides the current was already starting to flow out. We packed up and hit the Inlet with green crabs off of the jacks. It was a bit slippery, and overcast and cold, and we only managed to pull out five

bergalls, big ones at that, when we decided to pack it in for the day. We then proceeded to go home and play the blues on git-fiddle and harp about all the missed blackies during the day.

FISH-N-FIESTA

Ahhh, where to begin? I might as well just lay it out plain and simple. When I moved down to the beach in 1998, I devised an idea to get all the boys and family together every fall, to have a simple morning surf-fishing session where we could all hang out, swap good time stories, and catch a few fish. That ideology turned into a monster with its own mind over the years, morphing into what is now known as the Fish-N-Fiesta, a 72-hour-straight surf-fishing adventure that starts on a Friday morning and ends sometime late Sunday night, with someone always fishing—could be one rod out, or 28 rods out. Some years, there's more fishing, some, more fiesta, but there are always sick, wild times had by all.

For some, it's an excuse to get away from their wives, for others, it's all about seeing how drunk you can get, while others are there for the food, music, fire, and fun—shit, who am I kidding? Everybody's there for a good time, for all of that, plain and simple. The Fiesta has had an evolution from the time I was 23 to 37 years old. The older days were full of drinking bottles of booze, wrestling in the fire pits, night swimming, and eating sand-crusted hot dogs on dune fence

Sunrise brings a warm greeting to all the boys at the Fish-N-Fiesta.

sticks over the open flame, whereas it's now gravitated toward a sense of maturity, with 10' x 10' stand-up tents containing propane heaters and lanterns, two fully equipped grills splayed out with halibut steaks, venison sausage, fresh Alaskan salmon pate, and a more mellow ambiance of beer drinking, minus all the hell-raising—well, not minus *all* of the hell-raising. And as always, there is constant, around-the-clock fishing. For some Fish-N-Fiesta-goers, it used to be an excuse to get away from whatever social responsibilities they may have, if only for a few hours; now, some even bring the wife and kids down, as everybody is welcome to fish, fiesta, or both. What more could you ask for? Regardless, it always ends up burning some downright funny memories, and entertains as a shit show on some level every year. No matter how old we get, we become kids again, invoking the aura of camping out by the river in high school, doing things that you aren't supposed to be doing around adults.

Here are the yearly Fish-N-Fiesta excerpts:

2002

November 1–3

Lido, McD, and Peck came down, went to the Piper to about 1 a.m., came back and instead of sleeping, decided to hit the beach, high tide 3 a.m. Chucked clams out and had two bass of 33 and 28 inches, four dogfish and three skates, seas 1-foot, west winds 15 knots. Too much fun stuff to write, but in a nutshell, saw an incredible comet that burned in the sky for over 25 seconds, thought it was anything from a missile to an alien spaceship, to give you an idea of our state of minds. Fished till 7 a.m. then went to sleep with a fractured gristle, or sternum from wrestling with Lido. Apparently, from talking with a guy at the hospital who was waiting for his wife, there was a huge bluefish blitz on my beach around 8 to 9 a.m. but we were too zonked out to stay awake for any longer.

November 2

While I was at the white house, or hospital (for my broken collarbone wrestling with Lido), Peck and Lido managed to catch one, and only one, skate all day, but we fished to about 10:30 at night and had nothing. Decided to pack it in and fish early in the morn.

November 3

Woke up around 5:30 a.m. and set up four rods on the beach with clams. Nothing going on all morn. Went to Sunny Hunny at 11 for pancakes and came back, McD went to the hospital this time for his asthma, 2 out of 4 to the hospital isn't too bad for a weekend, but came back and set the rods out on dead-low new moon tide. Lido waded out to the sandbar and casted out as far as he could. We did that with all the rods and pulled in three bass of 33, 27, and 24 inches by 3 p.m.! Couldn't believe they hit on dead, real dead, low tide in the middle of the afternoon. Tide started coming in and we had a legitimate blitz of bass, they were rolling, and breaching the water, sucking down rainfish, everybody was casting but nobody was hooking up, until one guy dragged a crocodile spoon along the bottom and came up with a 33-inch bass. There was a bunch of them breaching here and there, with birds working, and bluefish were outside crashing and splashing. Looks like the beginning of some nice bassin', if we can stay out of the hospital. Apparently sporadic bass blitzes from Bay Head to IBSP, just have to be in the right place at the right time. Seas dead flat. Water temp 58 degrees.

2003

November 1

The Fish-N-Fiesta Four took place, Dad, McD, Lido, and the Peck brothers showed up late Friday night, when I was still bombed from the K-Kat fiasco. Woke up at 4:45 a.m., set up six rods on the beach covering all the holes from the T-Bird down. Fished till 10 at night straight through, venison burgers, Wiffle ball games, football games, Inferno, Heinekens, and scrappy fights, and NOT ONE FISH! OK, three skates! What a difference from last week! High tide at 1 p.m. and south blow all week, including today, shut down any bite. Casting Bomber plugs into the sunrise shared with Dad was the illuminating highlight of the event. Packed it in for the night, swashed around a bit, guitar, harmonica, then woke up at 7:30 a.m. to do it again. Set up with a northeast wind, good stuff, but still no fish. Fished till 1 p.m. and finally a rod went down, Lido picked it up and reeled in a 21-inch striper in the 21st hour of fishing! How about that! We didn't press our luck, packed it in and called it an event.

2004

November 6

Fish-N-Fiesta, and what a fiesta! Everyone showed up. Big Irish came down the night before, we hit Broadway and Reel Life to stock up, then at 11 p.m. we hit the hole in front of the T-Bird with black Bombers at a relatively low tide. Herlihy got whacked and pulled in a 26-inch striper! That was all for the night, but the Red Iceberg moon came out of the horizon like a bloody electric ghost ship with an ominously blood red sail. Turns out it was just the moon. Anyway, tied rigs till 2:30 in the morn then woke up at 4:30 a.m. to fish. We set up right at the end of the lane casting around, Dad showed, Austin, then Lido and Jerry. I had the first bluefish of the day at around 8 a.m. on a Hopkins, then birds started to work and Irish and Austin each had a blue. We picked at them until about 10 a.m., then it went off. Niles and Kelly and Austin went to Wawa to pick up some food, and right when Irish got back we saw birds hammering bait by 6th Street. Everyone ran down, and I stayed with the 4 deadsticks. As they were just out of range, I saw the water erupt in front of me, and it was a thousand depth charges going off at once! All four rods went down and I whistled loud when Knightlius turned and saw me. Just then Lido, Jerry, Knight, and Peck all hooked up and I was stuck fighting four bluefish on four rods! Cleared the rods, then started casting poppers, metals and we were all moved back into our area by then, all absolutely bailing bluefish in the 4- to 14-pound class. We amassed 67 bluefish in the 45-minute blitz and I think we kept them there with 10 of us casting poppers in a frenzy. We created our own blitz, 'cause the boats started moving in toward us! West winds were at 15 to 20 knots and high was at 2:30 p.m. It was so hot and heavy, everyone complained how sore they were! The blues were spitting up bay anchovies, peanuts, and even round herring, that look like anchovies or cigar minnows. A 5-pound weakfish even beached itself by another angler with a tail chunk missing! The blues we cleaned had weakfish parts in them. There was so much action, it was insane!

2005

November 4–5

Fish-N-Fiesta! As history now dictates, Irish came down early on Friday night and we scoped the beaches for some action. At about 3 p.m., we set up at the T-bird with clams to find some bass. It was a south blow of 15 to 20 knots crappy con-

Sledgehammer grabs onto a chopper bluefish that slammed a topwater popper.

ditions, but we managed a 17-inch striper on a clam! Alright, at least we didn't get blanked, got one on the board. We didn't get anything else when Cali came to join us, so we packed up and went out to Frankie's and Reel Life to meet Sledgehammer and stock up. Came home, the Pecks and McD were in the house, and we went up about 10 to set up on the T-Bird. Beers were flowing, dips were pushed in, and we blanketed the hole with 6 rods rigged with light sticks. We got banged about 18 times, had six spiny dogfish, three skates, and an as-yet-unidentified type of hake, with a black spot on the dorsal sail, and white spots running horizontally along the body, whiskers and all linged out, about 10 inches long?? Packed it in around 1:30 a.m., got to bed at 2:30 a.m. Woke up at 4:30 a.m. Set up at the T-Bird hole again with a total of 23 rods on the beach! Everybody was down, we plugged the predawn hours, south winds still blew at 10 to 15. Threw out bunker chunks marinated in bunker oil, and at around 7 a.m. had our first blue of about 5 pounds, then a doubleheader on my rod with blues. And then one more on my rod about 14 pounds, nice fish. The day got slow from there, a few skates, Lido

Chewin' the fat around the campfire during a lull in fishing at the Fish-N-Fiesta.

dropped a bass, and Knightlius had one more blue of 5 pounds or so. No bird play, all slowed up. Packed it in at nightfall, got debunkered and went to UB's for some food and pool. Got back and went to Crab's Claw, Peck passed out on couch, Cali up to beach. Cali called us at about midnight saying he had eight skates and a 20-inch bass. He was plastered! He sat on a bucket, hunched over, reeling in his Calcutta, said he actually passed out on the beach and got run over by a Bronco! There were tire tracks that seemed to run on each side of him, proving his point! He woke up and reeled in more skates. It was hilarious! One of the highlights was the hot-ass girl with nothing but a towel who came down to the surf at 8 a.m. and disrobed butt naked in front of Lido and jumped in the ocean. About six guys went over to talk to Lido and she was flat out hot and naked and swimming in the undertow! Where she came from, we don't know, maybe a mermaid?!! Cali brought Lefty down to the beach as well to get stuff. Herlihy hit McD in the nuts with a bunker head, clams were slapped on faces, bottles tied to sleeping rods, couple of rasslin' matches, falling into the undertows, and debauchery of world-class caliber.

2006

November 10–11

All night long! For first time the Friday night lights were on all night, as I came back from Maine and Peck was waiting in my parking spot with a beer and guitar at 6:30 p.m. We hit up UB's and then Heckel came down at 9 p.m. We packed the gear and hit the beach south of Jimmer's Hole and set up shop. Limo came by with a truckload of wood to burn and Dave came up with fireworks (thousands of them at home!), and we lit off Bass Bombs to call in the stripers. First hit about 11 p.m. and then pulled on bass thru the night, had about 8 decked by 3 a.m., then guys got tired. Knightlius showed up around 11 p.m. Heckel brought up some pulled pork and we ate like champs, it got cold and people began to pass out around 4 a.m. I was left with Heckel on the beach watching the rods, and it was shivering cold, winds out of the north about 15 knots. At sunrise, Singles was the first to show, with a smile, then Irish and Sledge showed around 6:30 a.m., then Lido and Pete trickled in. We all set up clam rods and everybody began to pull bass from 6:30 a.m. onward, with a total of 17 bass on the Fish-N-Fiesta. Winds picked up out of the south at 20 knots, seas got to 3- to 5-foot and predicted worse, so guys stayed thru about 3 p.m. on Saturday and fished continually, picked away at bass of 18 to 25 inches. We were all spent. Lido hit up the canal afterward and pulled on two dozen blackfish, nary a keeper though.

2007

November 16–18

Fish-N-Fiesta! Heckel, Mike Drew, Teuthis, Sledge, and Irish made the night shift. We set up at 8 p.m. in a 15- to 20-knot west wind, seas 1-foot. From 9 p.m. till 11 p.m. had three short stripers. The Far Out Fishin guys were there with the tent and tons of good eats: venison sausage, fried chicken, pierogies, and blasting baits out! Thru night we

Clowning around with the legendary skate helmet, a mark of distinction among surf anglers!

totaled about 40-plus spiny dogfish, then from 2 to 4 a.m. had four more stripers on clams on Friday night. Sat morn me and Irish set out on a sandbar low tide at 7:30 p.m. and saw bass rolling on peanut bunker schools that were thick. Couldn't get a hit then blues came just out of casting range, Irish hooked up with an 8-pounder. Tommy came down and at 11 a.m. had to go home and sleep—sleepless for 26 hours! Woke up at 4 p.m. and Deg came down, missed him, Knightlius also in town now, slow fishing thru Sat day and night, Uncle Greg came down and brought tons of conch salad, smoked steelhead (which I'd caught), and lox and peppers and onions, ate well Sat night. Wind dropped out, Rosie running around chasing birds, then Niles came down, slept from 1 a.m. till 8:30 a.m., up to beach. UG had a 28-inch bass on beach and bass busting all over. Casted out plugs, had no hits, though other guys scoring 10 fish. Northeast blow 15 knots now kicked in and getting nasty on Sunday, I cast around later in day to catch one bluefish and had a few bass taps. UG cooked that striper up at my house, me and Knight ate it up with bananas, garlic and pepper concoction on it. Was awesome! Fish-N-Fiesta in the books and Heckel is now Mr. N-Fiesta! Total: 10 bass, 1 bluefish, millions of spiny dogs.

2008

October 24

Fish-N-Fiesta! Well, 35-knot winds were predicted for Saturday, so we started fishing at noon on Friday, everybody came down by 3:30 p.m. and we had ten rods set up in front of yellow house. Immediately Lido had a 26-incher on an AVA jig at about 4, and then reeled in the first clam bass about 15 minutes later. Then, guys to the right were hitting bass on plugs, I cast out a black Bomber and got whacked at nightfall by a 25-incher. Then darkness fell and the bite was absolutely dead. Was northwest then southwest winds by evening, 15 knots, didn't get any real hits till 4 a.m., which left us with a lot of drinking to do. We drank, built a big bonfire, ate hot dogs, venison burgers. Fancypants crapped out for most of it! But we put a skate on his head and kept lighting black cats underneath his chair! Shooting roman candles at each other, Saturn missile down my pants, bottle rockets, then at 4 a.m. the bombs went off, Mickey had first three bass, then me with 5, Lido, Knight, and Heckel all had fish, we ended up with 9 bass in 40 minutes, totaled 16 bass to 28 inches. Saw Rich Swisstack and he said at about 8 he had 20 bass in Lavallette on plugs. Right near sunrise, the winds picked up to 35 knots southeast and raining, so we pretty much called it quits, but great times up for about 20 hours drinking straight and eating and fireworks!

2009

November 6–7

Fish-N-Fiesta! Well, 2- to 3-foot northwest winds, 15 to 20 knots to start, dropping out to 5 to 10 knots overnight. Water temp 57, air cold at 40, overnight 32. McD came down at 10:30 in the morn and away we went, set up on Jimmer's Hole, starting casting Vision eels and got whacked by a 10-pound blue that busted me off, then got bit off again, McD then landed a 10-pounder on a Kroc spoon, bluefish busting up the water, came in with hundreds of birds diving, in and out, all day long. Started clamming, wading out on the bar and casting as far as I could, got banged back to back, bass after bass, landed 6 in a row within 45 minutes, largest was 13 pounds on the Boga Grip! Then everybody else came down around nightfall: Nite, McD, Pecks, Austin, Bugsy, Mike Drew, Uncle Greg, Big Irish. We cast out on the sandbar at evening time and Irish had two bass, I had 3 more blues and a bass I think? Marc and Mickey were reeling in blues to 12 pounds, Glenn and Mark there, everybody sufficiently drunk on brandy and whisky and beers, Glenn reeled in a few bass around 10 p.m. high tide, then it was all spiny dogfish through the night with skates too, over 36 spiny dogs and skates. Fished the a.m. with Irish on the bar, no hits, extremely tired. Greg reeled in a blue or two hits, I went to sleep. The guys stayed till 2 picking 4 more blues. All said and done: 17 bass from 24 to 33 inches and 19 bluefish to 12 pounds. Good times!

2010

November 5–6

Fish-N-Fiesta! Or Fishless fiesta. Well, solid 5- to 7-foot seas, hard northwest winds 15 knots, large booming bomb waves, new moon tide made for difficult fishing conditions, as 8 to 10 ounces wouldn't even hold during the day or nighttime in the sloughs, casting metals was almost as futile. Greg came down at 12:30 p.m. and we went up. I set out a clam rod at the dead-low and got a big whackdown in first 10 minutes that came off the hook, the only hit for 34 hours! Anyway, this fiesta was defined by the food, as the spread consisted of halibut ceviche, andouille sausage, venison steaks, chili, Jersey Mike's subs, salmon and halibut smoked dip, so much good food. Lin made it for his first fiesta. Had Irish's car and his buddy's car on the beach after high tide receded, his bud Russ got stuck in front of T-Bird to the chassis, took 15 guys to push him out with me driving! Built bonfire, I stayed up till 3:30 a.m. then crashed. Woke back up at 8 a.m. and fished again, stayed on beach till 5 p.m. then ordered Lenny's pizza for dinner. They delivered pizza right to the beach, made this poor kid walk two blocks on the sand to serve a bunch of drunk guys! Lido did eat a sand eel and moon jellyfish. Two guys came at 1:30 a.m. dragging live eels, said they had a 22-incher. Russ had a 24-inch bass on Brick 1 right before he came to Fish-N-Fiesta. Tough conditions, but insane food and drinking of course. Huge bonfire.

2011

October 21–22

Well, living in Florida for now at *Salt Water Sportsman*, but flew home to host the Fish-N-Fiesta, and I got sick to start! We started off again with fire permit now and everybody showed up after 4 p.m. Friday, first landed fish I got was a tiny smooth dogfish at about dusk, 7 p.m. or so, then it was all skates during the night. Cemented sandbar made it impossible to cast over during mid tides, could wade out on low tide, but had no line left by the time you got back! Final tally was something like 6 smooth dogs, 10 skates, and one lonely, pitiful spotted hake that Bugsy reeled in a 5 a.m. when we were packing it in for the night. High tide was at 3 a.m., westerly winds, but ripping south current. Uncle Greg was missed this year as we only had rolled hot dogs and burnt kielbasa on a grill! Big fire, Dad and Billy showed up and metal detected, total of 26 people came this year, lots of fun, huge bonfire, and insane drinking, but everybody packed it in at 5 a.m. with the rough surf.

Nothing like a good Fiesta.

10 December

SWAN SONG

Maybe it's a fact that December has a way of weeding out the day-trippers or the not-totally-committed-to-the-sport-of-surfcasting, as a noticeable lack of angler participation evinces itself in the twelfth month of the calendar year. People have blown the whistle and called it quits; after all, it's too cold to be waking up at 4:30 in the morning, ice on the windshield, thick furry gloves donned, where not even piping hot coffee can warm the insides. Ice on the rod guides, hands that go numb the instant the glove gets wet from a splashing wave or a bass's slime from a release, and the sweat inside your neoprene gloves hardens to concrete, makes casting a difficult job.

It's not as fun; in fact, it's a downright chore to fish in single digit conditions. Some mornings, the air is so cold that a glacial vapor rises off the sea water as the sun breaks the horizon, almost like the Atlantic is a big bowl of dry ice, the sea protesting and heeding its warning of deathly cold temperatures. All the factors add up to a desolate beachfront and plenty of striped bass on the prowl. These are the times when surf men are made: when the deck is stacked against you, and you keep plugging away, because you know, well, bass are in them there waters.

December bass are not the cows you write home about; conversely, they are the young gun rats that barely break the 22-inch mark. What they lack in size, they make up for in quantity and spirited, youngblood fight. Doubleheader catches on each December cast are commonplace when the schools move through, and if you could rig up with four hooks, you'd probably have four fish on each cast. December surf bassing is a test of your willpower and creed, and for those who take the challenge, well, you are rewarded beyond belief.

Nuts or not, December surfcasting in a blizzard can put up serious numbers of schoolie stripers.

SAND EEL CIRCUS

Scrappy stripers are aggressive, as they are committed to feeding during the morning hours, especially when the sand eel schools extract themselves from the sandy bottom and move into the feeding zone. This game is mostly about casting slim-profiled metal lures and slender plastics to mimic the sand eel profile, and no well-stocked surf bag is without an array in its quiver. Dominant northwest and westerly winds produce super-clean and clear surf, and on low full and new moon tides, you get blowout conditions that allow for a walk out to the outer bar to cast a country mile. If you can bear Ol' Man winter's wrath, especially during the predawn conditions before the giant red ball of fire heats things up, you will be rewarded with more than a simple fish tale.

December 1

Hit my beach, high tide at 5:30 p.m., full moon blowout low tides, sandbars and bowls everywhere, west winds, seas 1- to 2-foot mostly clean, up there at 3:30 p.m. to 4:45 p.m., dark. Had one bass on that shook the hook then had a sundial chase down my AVA 17 jig and hit it fast and hard! Pretty wild to see how aggressive these flatfish are!

Another guy had 2 of them. Dave had a doubleheader bass at dusk. Bass seemed to be bumping the lures as I felt a few taps. Some adult bunker schools being splashy out of casting range and sand eel schools rippling the waters near us. Water temp still warm at 54 degrees, last night was first night of cold weather at 32 degrees, but today about 50. Full moon evening session beautiful with blues and pinks on the horizon as the moon rose, a reverse sunrise!

December 2

All out bananas! Day after new moon. Me and Cali hit up Princeton in the morn. 2- to 3-foot, glassy, west 10 knots, water temp 48, air 28 or so, and we started casting southward. First bite happened at around 6:15 a.m. or so, false dawn, had a 23-inch bass on teaser and AVA jig, while Cali pulled in a bass on a Crystal Minnow. Then it all went berserk. Sand eels began to unearth out of the sand once the sun was in the sky, about 7 a.m., and the bass were on the feed. AVA jigs, Bombers, teasers, Storm shads, everything was hit. I managed 23 stripers from 7 to 8:30 a.m. and then had to leave, Cali had probably 27 or so. Bass were semiblitzing on the surface, ravaging the sand eels, and we had stripers to 31 inches. Cali had a double header of a 30- and 26-inch bass! It was every other cast to every cast a bass and it was on fire! Had to leave for paying job which was very, very hard to do.

December 3

Called Lido, Irish, Sledgehammer, Singles, and team AA Pete and Chris, to fish the morn. Irish and Sledge got to Princeton at 5:30 a.m., good boys, and we hit the beach. First cast, Kelly had a 25-inch striper on a black Bomber, freakin' cold, about 22 degrees out, then Jerry had a bass within two casts in the dark hours, another slottie. I moved down to the right and Cali found a piece that was super hot, I saw him reel in about 12 bass while I got blanked, another guy fished Pyramids and pulled out 7 bass, one after another, from 6:30 a.m. on. I then got lucky and began to hit the bass, all on Storm shads, lost a yellow Bomber to a bluefish, but managed to still reel in a 24-inch bass on the teaser. Saw Lido make his way to me and we stood shoulder to shoulder slamming bass for the next hour and a half till 8:30 a.m., when I had to leave for Kovo's wedding. Sand eels predominant bait still. And total on the two and a half hour time: over 100 bass between us all. I had 27 or so, Cali had about 34, lido about 18, Irish 16, Jerry 12, Pete and Chris about 20 total, it was incredible. All the fish were from 16 inches to 30 inches, mostly smaller slot fish, and they were all over the outside of the shallow sandbars. High tide around 8:30 a.m. Seas 1-foot. West blow 15 knots.

That was some red-hot fishing for sure, but even more remarkable in that passage was the fact that Big Irish and Sledgehammer got to the beach at 5:30 a.m.—right when I told them to! Most guys like playing that, "Oh, 5:30? Okay. See you at 6 or 6:30" type of game where they dilly-dally grabbing coffee, donuts and bagels, or whatnot, and it doesn't cut it. If you don't get to the spot when you're supposed to, you're either gonna miss the bite, or miss setting up on a prime cut or slough and thus, lose out on the action. Sometimes the hardest part of fishing is showing up when you are supposed to, a decidedly much harder chore to do in the middle of a December night. To Big Irish and Sledge: nice work, boys! Though that only happened once.

December 4

Woke up at 6:10 a.m. to hit the beach for bass with black Bomber. Can you say frigid? The temps were at a balmy 16 degrees in the morning and I decided to hit the high tide at 6:30 a.m. Winds 5 to 10 W. I cast and my retrieve was super slow due to the fact that I believed the bass were moving slow with the water hovering around 45 degrees now. I saw some peanut bunker in the undertow when I walked the beach, and did see a huge swirl from a 20-pound-plus-size fish in front of the T-Bird. I also saw some swirls right in the undertow when I would be at the finale of my retrieve. I eventually hooked into a short of about 18 inches in the undertow, and then whacked another of about the same size who jumped out of the water with the flavor of a tarpon. My rod had ice in the guides and my line became sprung coil off the spool, so it became hard to fish. I managed an hour and a half of casting, enough time to see the sun rise and make the frigid salt water smolder with an eerie smoke as the heat burned off the beastly cold. Anyway, reports that they are slaying bass in Raritan Bay still with mostly slots and shorts on plastics, but some reaching the 25-pound mark. Snow predicted for tomorrow with 25-knot NE winds.

December 4

At 1 p.m. looked at my beach and thousands of gulls picking at the water, diving and bird play. Anglers with bent rods showing bluefish in 3 to 8 pounds and bass. I worked till 3 p.m. then hit up 2nd Ave in Normandy, immediately caught three bass on teasers and shads, only two other guys there, then went south to Ortley Avenue to intercept the school moving southward. Set up and a small blitz occurred around Bryn Mawr Ave, pulled out about 11 bass there on shads and Bomber plugs and teasers, blueback herring of 9 to 10 inches in the undertow getting worked. I snagged one and livelined it on my teaser where a bass inhaled the Storm shad underneath and I fought both to the beach! Other anglers had just as many bass, lots of 16- to 24-inchers. Mate from *The Dauntless* on Sundays was there; he worked a big Danny plug and had a big swirl behind it, another guy had about a 28-incher. Good bait around, big herring, some smaller spearing, seems like the December rats began to show up today. Went back to my beach around 4:15 p.m. for the dusk bite and pulled one rat out of the surf, though saw some herring moving northward. Total 14 bass in two hours. Water clear, west winds at 15 knots, 1-foot.

December 7

Me and Cali got a tip from Frank at Betty and Nick's that Surf Club was going off. I was at Broadway from 1 p.m. on, so I was pretty well oiled, and got a fifth of Dewars to stick in the front waders pocket. Got to the beach around 4 p.m., nothing showing, birds up by Ortley Ave, went there and cast out on the low tide bar, f-in cold! Like 20 degrees out, and didn't get a sniff. Moved to Deauville and Cali cast into a rip and pulled a 25-inch striper out at about 5 p.m., nightfall. Word had it that Jimmer, One Spot Jeff, Bo, and another guy had about 4 to 7 bass that evening standing out on the bar.

December 8

Hit my surf from 4 to 5 p.m., nightfall at 4:45 p.m. Black Bombered it up, had first hit at 4:30 p.m. or so at Jimmer's Hole, an 18-inch brute! Then Jimmer left, it was about 5 p.m., and I got whacked good on the outer bar, reeled in a 25-inch bass on the plug, then made three more casts, on third cast saw something whack my teaser, hooked in undertow, I flipcasted back, same thing, hickory shad? Then flipped again, it hit the plug hard, saw it was a bass right in front of me. Flipped again and it followed the plug to my feet, I varied slow then fast then twitch, then it finally hooked itself on the teaser, a 26-inch bass! Awesome to see it fight and keep coming back to it, there had to be hickory shad and other bass there too. Air temp was cold, 25 degrees, water at 46 now. Seas flat to 1-foot, no wind. High tide 3 p.m.

December 9

Cali and I fished Elizabeth Avenue jetty and jetties south today, high tide 2:20 p.m., west winds 15 to 20 knots, gusts to 25, 2- to 3-foot. Got there around 1 p.m. and cast around with an Emperor Minnow and yellow Swing Mullet. Cali had three bass and I had three bass, all between 16.5 and 24 inches, small fish. All caught around jetties and in the holes between. Definitely fishy looking water, bass were fickle on the bite, with most strikes getting bumped once or twice first, then they hit about 10 yards off the beach. Fun! Done at 2:30 p.m. Good to see bass during the middle of the day on the bite.

December 11

Sean came by after his captain's class and we hit the beach at 4 p.m., high tide 3:30 p.m. Light west winds, and cast Bombers and shads. I pulled out one bass of 24 inches around dusk, and Sean had two hits, but didn't see the hook! As a school of bass came by, swirling in the undertow.

December 11

Today was warm, about 56 degrees, low tide at 5:30 a.m., light west 5 knots, 1-foot, water temp 54 degrees. Fished evening with the whole crew and had two pops; that was about it on Bomber plugs, but Jimmer pulled one in at nightfall around 5 p.m.

Apparently, One Spot Jeff had 15 bass in the cut in the morning hours. Yesterday was apparently very good with larger bass moving in of 28 to 34 inches, along with the rats.

It's worth noting that One Spot Jeff got his name because any time of day, any tide during the day, whether a cut, hole, or sandbar was evident, he fishes the same exact spot right up the Shell Avenue pathway, and never moves an inch to either side. Not even during a blitz.

December 12

Hit the cut past Jimmer's Hole at 6 a.m., sunup around 6:40 a.m., got there in 15- to 20-knot northeast winds, hard to cast into. One Spot Jeff was there, and Jimmer came 5 minutes later; we all cast out and I saw Jeff and Jimmer hook up. Then I started whacking away at the rats. Had four bass of 16 to 23 inches long on black Bombers, and a teaser. The key was to reel in fast so that the plug could bite in the turbulent water. 6:30 low tide, but enough water on the inside with the NE push. Jimmer had about 5 fish, same with Jeff, I had missed three other bumps and they all seemed to hit right in the undertow. I had one fish that hit the plug as I was pulling it up to recast, only 5 feet of line out!

December 12

For word's sake, Cali lambasted the bass from 3 p.m. to 5 p.m., high tide 4:30. He said it was the best bass fishing he's ever had, stopped counting around 60, and had probably over 100 in two hours' time, hitting swing mullet and shads. Every cast was a hit or a bump, and he had tripleheaders, two on the Bomber and one on the teaser! See ya tomorrow!

December 14

Hit the suds at 6:30 a.m. with Singles and Jackson, casting storms. It was f-in' cold out at 12 degrees, mist rising with the sunrise on the ocean surface. The bass were bumping the lures so lightly, it was uncanny, but eventually we began to hang a few around 7:45 a.m. I ended up with four from 12 to 16 inches—rats! Singles had 3 and Guy had 1. All the same size. Evening time, north winds 10 to 15 knots, I picked up Al Ristori at the Johnson Bros boat launch; since his stroke, he's not allowed to drive, told me he's been goin' nuts not fishing the beach each day. We ended up on Princeton at 4:15 p.m. and casted Storms and black Bombers. I managed a 21-inch bass and had another that shook the hook in the undertow, along with about 5 more solid bumps. Al had a few bumps but no connections, but we stayed until 6 p.m., total darkness in the 20-degree weather, shows you his determination! It was awesome fishing with a childhood idol, and he kept walking farther and farther away from the Jeep, way past nightfall. It was cool seeing him walk toward the sunset, casting away in the frigid temps with no intentions of leaving, ever. True passion. Reading him when I was young and then fishing with him. I brought him back to his house after some good-natured conversation and dropped him off, letting him know I can always come get him. The stroke can't keep him from fishing, ever! Passion of a surfcaster.

Al Ristori is awesome. And if you don't know who Al Ristori is, go get yourself an education in saltwater fishing. Enough said!

I will never forget in 1986 when Al was called upon to take over the deceased Bob Duffy's historic saltwater fishing column in the *Star-Ledger*, because every day at breakfast before 6th grade class, I would spread out the outdoor section of the *Star-Ledger* and read Duffy to see what was going on in the ocean, and now I saw Ristori writing it. It was a tough pill to swallow, but eventually my immaturity warmed up enough to let him in to my soul to feel comfortable that he alone could tell me what saltwater happenings were going on. Then, quite a few years later, when I got my first real post-collegiate job at the *Fisherman Magazine* at 23 years old, and got the opportunity to meet and work with Al one-on-one, I told him that story of how I felt about him replacing Duffy. Ristori gave me a wholehearted laugh and said he would do his best. I am forever grateful to and humbled by that man for teaching me so much with just a smile. I continue to fish with Al to this day. We are great friends now, but I still think of myself as his student, and I thank him for everything, not just as a fisherman, but as a man who wears his passion on his sleeve.

December 14

Bass all over the place! Feeding on sand eels, mackerel, sea herring, and round herring. Morning from 8 a.m. to 10:30 a.m., red hot on the beach with bass to 38 inches taken on plugs and shads. Boaters lighting them up silly 300 yards off the beach. Mantoloking to Seaside hot. Guy had a few bass this morn to 35 inches. I hit my beach at 3:30, dead-low at 4 p.m. Waded out on sandbar with a silver-and-black Bomber to mimic the round herring, teaser in front. Northwest winds 15 to 20 knots. Then dropped out at sunset, water temp 47, air 30. Cast out and about 4:15 p.m., got first bass of 26 inches, then went a total of 9 for 11 on stripers, all from 20, 24, to 33 inches! They whacked the plugs and put up a solid surface battle, splashing and crashing like mad dogs! Helluva fight. One Spot Jeff was next to me, pulled in a 35-incher on a 4-inch Bomber, and had about 4 more bass. Past two weeks, all but rats in the surf, looks like the bigger boys have come in to play ball. Last hit around 5:30 p.m., almost pitch black, that was the 33-incher.

December 14

High tide 9:30 a.m. two days after full moon, seas 2- to 3-foot, light west, water temp 42, air 25. Couldn't sleep. Woke up 5 and hit Princeton at 5:20 a.m., dark, full moon, nice light. Black Bomber immediately got whacked, reeled in a 22-incher! Saw two streaking bright shooting stars! Then, walked to cannons area in front of spooky window and bailed bass. Can't even tell you how many taps, maybe 35? But hooked into 19 bass, landed 10 of them, all shorts and rats, but tons of spirit and fight in them! They all hit a black Bomber right in the undertow, chasing it all the way in, literally 15 feet out, all hits. December sunrise was spectacular—pinks, red, and yellow-orange, with butter clouds in the sky. Said confession and my Sunday prayers, crossing myself with the salt water, and got whacked immediately afterward!

December 15

Fished my beach at 10:30 a.m. to 11:30 a.m., west winds 5 knots, seas 2- to 3-foot, glassy, gray skies and waters, lots of short and schoolie bass in the wash, new moon tonight, too. Had one bass of 20 inches, but loads of bumps, Storm shads working better than AVAs now, I think. Heard of some guys this morning had dozen or so fish. At 3 p.m., Mickey came down for togging tomorrow, hit B'way for beers and wings, then hit my beach around 8:30, high was around 6 a.m. or so. 2- to 3-foot west winds, balmy 45 or 50 degrees. Two guys already in my hole, went to Jimmer's and cast black Bombers, went 4 for 7 on schoolie bass that shook heads and hooks and actually pulled drag! Also had half dozen more bumps. Mick had two bumps. Fished till 10 p.m. or so, until water got too thin in the darkness. Good night bite.

December 16

Hit my beach with Sledgehammer and his bud Dave at 6 a.m., dark until 6:25 a.m., but cast Storm shads and Bombers and teasers still. Had one bass in front of T-bird, so did Jerry and Dave, all small, about 18 to 20 inches long, and they were all feeding in the undertow. Some peanut bunker flipping on the surface inside, some boils by bass as well. The real f-ed up thing this morning was at about 6:45 a.m., I looked in the direction of the walkway and saw what looked like an airplane vapor stream of cloud, but it came right from the ground, vertical into the air. It was erratic and looked all wrong. I followed it to its head and saw a huge flame from a rocket or missile that was launched, probably from one of the air force bases near Oyster Creek, and it was scary, like a nuke being launched. It gained control of itself then it took off far over the ocean and rocketed away. Still don't know what it was, but definitely strange.

December 18

Fished my beach, busted a guide off the ol' St. Croix. Some scattered peanuts in the surf, west NW winds, 10 knots, 2-foot glassy. High tide around 5 a.m., today, 65 degrees out, water at 53 degrees. Caught one bass in front of T-bird that tapped my Storm shad and came back for it in the undertow. 19 inches long. Got about 3 other taps and two solid hits too, saw one bass follow all the way to my feet fast before he turned away in the undertow, small li'l guy, but seemed feisty as he followed it in.

December 21

Cast my beach 6:30 a.m. 10 knot SW winds, hit that cut off the Tiki Bar, Jimmer came down. Got one bass there, so did Jimmer. Then one out of the end of the path hole, sea herring still around, couple of bumps too. Bigger bass up at Shrewsbury Rocks, 15 to 25 pounds. Water temp at 51 degrees still, air temps in the high 40s–low 50s. Bluefin tuna reported at Shrewsbury Rocks.

December 21

Hit the Lavallette jetties with Cali, casting Storm shads to no avail. No signs of bass, bait, or nuthin. Though it was an extremely placid and peaceful evening, with almost a summertime feel to it, with the sun setting below the house line and the water super-clear, west winds 5 knots, glassy, 1-foot. I did walk out on some of the jetties to see around them, looks like some excellent structure to cast around come regular fishing season.

December 28

Hit my beach, west winds 5 knots, seas 1 to 2, high tide 3:30 p.m., hit it at 4:45 p.m. till 5:15 p.m. Had three scrapper bass of 16 to 18 inches and had another 8 hits on Mambo and teaser, all bass hit the plug. They were actively feeding, splashing in the undertow chasing bait. Water still 50 degrees, air temp 54 degrees—warm.

December 29

Hit my beach, dusk patrol from 4:30 p.m. to 5:15 p.m. dark. Had a bang right in the undertow that didn't set, and then had a small bass follow the tail of the Mambo right to the end of the rod tip, where he bulleted out of the water and splashed, getting caught almost on the beach, it startled me like a live wire jolt! NE winds 10 knots, seas 2-foot. High tide around 4:30 p.m.

It seems weird that I never really surf-fished on December 31 of any year in the last 10 years, but that's probably due to some New Year's Eve commitments for debauchery, as well as lack of any real bite going down, because sure as I love my kielbasa and blackberry brandy, if there were bass around, I'd be fishing for them.

LAST CHANCE TOGGIN'

Sure, the water is painfully cold, even for resident stripers, but tog have yet to vacate the waters to deeper wrecks in early December, and some promising action remains to be had. Better yet, some straggler bass hang on the pieces of structure on the wrecks to boot, and a two-for-one deal of bass and blackfish rounded out the twelfth month beach wreckfish season!

December 2

Past three days, hard southeast, 4- to 8-foot surf, churned up clams, debris, and what not. Yesterday 40- to 50-knot west winds. So today went beachcombing, found sea glass and a part of a shipwreck with brass screws and hardware. Went to C—— wreck to scavenge when I saw a guy pull a tog out of the surf, dead-low tide at 5 p.m., was there about 4 p.m. He had caught 7 or 8 tog since one o' clock, along with slot and short bass. He cast out far, where I think a shipwreck or snag is located with the dead-low blowout tides, he said he catches blackfish on. One tog went 4 pounds! He used a fishfinder rig, with a 3-ounce pyramid sinker, and then an 8- to 12-inch, 90-pound stiff leader, crimped on both ends with a 4/0 baitholder hook with a tie down on a salted clam. The snag by top of the mast where I snagged my black Bomber on the C—— wreck I think it is, might be a good spot to angle for tog on the low tide. Found a large piece of red glass on the beach. That's good luck!

December 3

Hit the beach for tog. But got there too late, looked like Scott was anchored on the spot with his boat and four guys who were pulling tog over the side all afternoon. Though did talk to a guy on the beach and found out what it is out there. There are three 15-foot sections leftover from C—— wreck that make an H-formation with tog all inside and around them. The guy said he snorkels it during the summer and sees nothing but teeth coming out of there. Line up with the C—— wreck about 75 yards off the beach.

Yes, the locations are generic for a reason. Sorry, no spot burning.

December 3

Hit up C—— wreck for blackfish. Dead-low tide 12:39 p.m., west winds 15 knots, 2- to 3-foot, water a little dirty from blow last two days. Cast out and lined up the house, and immediately got whacked with clams. Totaled 16 stripers in two hours' time, all from 18 to 25 inches, and had one or two solid blackfish on for sure, dogging me and pulling the hook. The bulldogs are still there! Have to use a fishfinder slide to feel the bite and set the hook.

December 4

Did the beach tog thing again but only had slated clams, had four or five hits that were tog but I think Scott cleaned a bunch out of there. I did get one nice hit, and set back, and fought a 28-inch striper onto the beach, I thought it was the mother whitechin at first! Low tide mid afternoon, west winds, water super-clear.

And that's how you round out a final calendar month's surf fishing for the year. No matter how cold it gets, you plant your feet in the hard sands and make that cast.

11 January

NEW YEAR'S PROMISE

anuary. The promise for the start of something new. Resolutions to stop drinking beer and dipping tobacco are made and broken almost immediately. The only thing that remains true and absolute is that I will be surf-fishing again, and there is no better way to start the year off right than casting for a surf striper. It's a tradition. To end the old season and officially begin anew. More than anything, it sets the tone of motivation for the upcoming year, to prove to yourself you won't let anything get in the way of you and your surfcasting. Hangover be damned on New Year's Day! It's a pact to yourself that fishing doesn't start and stop when the calendar dictates; it's when you want it to, a drive and desire much more powerful than a simple number on a piece of paper. It starts when you make your first cast and never stops. It's the commitment you made with your inner soul to enter this line of love. Now, I'm not going to lie to you, catching a surf striper in January in the past decade, well, it ain't that easy. You have to get lucky and pick your places right. But above all, you have to stop thinking it's only a possibility and make it a reality.

2005

January 1

Hit my beach, 5- to 10-knot northwest wind, water clear, and about 45 degrees. Some rat bass still hanging around, 14- to 18-inchers, but fished the low tide around 4 p.m., waded out to the sandbar, 2- to 3-foot, caught nothing. Though it was 62 degrees out today, which was nice, casting around a teaser rig with a Mambo on it. Blessed myself with the ocean water for a promising year in 2005. Going ling fishing tomorrow, Reilly coming up tonight. Ling Fling!

2006

January 1

Hit my beach at 9:30 a.m., beautiful sunny day, light west winds. What a great day to begin the year. Walked right down from the path, and cast a Storm shad with Lido's homemade surf candy teaser, thinking how wonderful it was to be fishing. On the first reel in, about twenty yards out, I couldn't believe it, I got whacked! Pretty hard, too! After a short struggle, I beached a 21-inch bass—on the first cast of the first day of the new year! I then proceeded to walk down to Jimmer's Hole and catch two more bass and drop two more in only about 45 minutes' time. Yee-ha!

Local legend Ernie Wuesthoff, Bait 'N Tackle Shop, holds up Blackbeard the Pirate's flintlock pistol, found on a local beach after a hurricane.

2009

January 1

New Year's first casts on my beach, water brown and west winds 25 knots, no taps.

2010

January 1

Hit my beach to make first casts of year at 10:30 a.m., with Storm shads and teasers, seas 3- to 4-foot, northwest winds, nice-looking heavy water with full moon tides. Fished 45 minutes, no bumps. Did want to say that the last two days, the sucked out sands from the last few storms have uncovered a wreck in front of the 4th window in front of Thunderbird, big 35-foot beam exposed with joists sticking up; then the Nunnery Wreck is also exposed, 4 joists were sticking up about 2 feet each out of the water and sand, too. You can see the wreck probably lies north to south as the joists form a rectangle, thinner looking west to east, but all squared off and equidistant, pretty awesome! I wish I knew what wrecks these are. Did use metal detector to find an old metal butane WWII lighter at Nunnery Wreck.

January 3

Hit my beach for p.m. bite, high tide 8:30 p.m., fished 4:30 p.m. to 5:30 p.m. Southwest winds 10 knots, seas 2- to 3-foot. Had one tap on the Mambo plug, but no runs. Jeff had a small bass at dark. Saw Ernie today as he was doing inventory on the shop, which may not be open anymore, which would be sad. What an awesome shop, and Ernie let me hold Blackbeard's gun today!

Now I have to say, that was cool, the part about Blackbeard's gun. As Ernie told it, one summer morning in the 1940s, he was out wade-casting on the outer sandbar when he looked down at his feet and saw a clump of rust, that in his professional opinion as a gunsmith "looked a lot like a gun." He took it to his shop and after a year's worth of delicately chipping away at the brown rust, uncovered a Queen Anne's Flintlock eighteenth-century pistol, no joke. The wood was still on the handle, barrel hollowed out, and in pretty good shape for a 300-year-old gun that sat in salt water for probably over a century and a half. On the handle was a half of a silver heart; it seemed retrotacked onto the handle and not an original part.

Well, after decades of the word getting out and spreading about Ernie's old gun, a representative of the Museum of Natural History came down to check it out and said to Ernie, "You know what you have here?" Ernie said, "Yeah, a gun." The guy said, "See this retrotacked-on silver heart? Only one captain was known to have that on his guns—Edward Teach. Blackbeard." And so goes the

Spanish gold doubloon and piece of eight found on my local beach.

legend, another Barnegat pirate story along the Jersey Coast, and if you ever get a chance to stop in to Ernie's old shop, they might still have it there, lying among the mastodon jaws and tusks and T-Rex teeth that some commercial draggers have found over the years.

January 4

First bass of the year! Light southwest winds, fished 4 p.m. to 5:30 p.m., got hit around 5:10 p.m. on the white teaser—a big ol' 13-incher! Wished for a great 2007, baptized myself with a sign of the cross in the Atlantic and sent him back to the sea.

January 6

For the record, it's 71 freakin' degrees today!

January 10

Hit my beach, lazy style at 9:30 a.m., lower tide. West wind 5 knots, clean water. Fished with shads for bass, fished an hour, no hits, though they should still be around.

I haven't fished too much after the first or second week of January, because it's truly a crapshoot to land anything then, when water temperatures generally are in the high 30s to low 40s, but February, well, that's an even crazier story.

12 February

FOR REAL?

And so it goes, the final month of the surfcasting year. February. Really? Give me any month but February for fishing, especially when it comes to the surf, because any smart fish are certainly long gone to warmer climates to enjoy winter vacation. But you know what? It takes a true angler made of steel (or stupidity) to head out in subzero February conditions and actually attempt to land a bass from the surf. It rarely ever happens, but stranger things have happened in fishing. Smart anglers put their money on fishing warmwater outflows from nuclear power plants, as resident bass winter over in the 60-degree waters, but straight up from the surf to catch a striper? Nearly impossible, as water temps are in the low 40s by now. Surely there are none to hang around, right? Or are there?

February 6 (2008)

Walked down my path, on my beach, determined to catch a February bass and prove all doubters wrong. It was 1 p.m. Cast a 3-inch Storm shad over and over. West winds, 1-foot, clean and clear. A half hour into casting, I could not believe my hands. Boom! I was on! I played the fish in with the utmost care, as I knew I would not have another chance, and in 5 minutes I had a 20-inch beautiful striped bass lying on the sand next to my feet! February bass, it can be done!!!!!

There is always the challenge of landing that second-month striper, and the outflows from Oyster Creek Power Plant put a death stake in cabin fever, serving up hope when the snow is falling and the pipes are iced up. There's a certain kind of warmth that comes with trudging through 3-foot snowdrifts in waders to carve out, then pack down, a spot on the side of the river to cast from. Then

Barnegat Bay in February, locked up with 3 inches of ice. No crabbing today.

Sublime and silent, Barnegat Bay's frozen surface speaks of a particular chilly February.

break the ice off the guides and make that cast into the slow-moving river. Looking for a February bass.

February 11

Hit Oyster Creek with Mickey and Dante and his two buds, fished north side of outflow bridge, walked about 300 yards down through deep snow where creek inflows into the outflow river. Dante casting 7-inch Hogy plastics, slow, bouncing barely on the bottom, and picked up a 35-incher immediately, then had four more. I didn't have any bumps but switched to Vision surf eel casted off bulkhead wall, and had a 29-incher pick it up and fight hard! They hit soft but definitely fought fast and hard! Very clean and seemed to be well-fed bass. Mickey and Dante had like 21 bass last week. Water temps in low 50s there from outflow.

There are always resident bass that hang in that 60-degree warmwater outflow waters, and any surfcaster jonesin' enough to pull a bass from the banks can make it happen, so long as they have the drive to get it done. By this time of year, the blizzards are rolling in, ice fishing takes front seat for piscatorial pursuits, and there always seems to be something else to do, like vacuuming the house or something, instead of trudging through snowbanks in subzero conditions to catch a striped bass. But I still make a cast every February, because I'm amped up that March is right around the corner, the official start of surf striper season. Or is it February? Or August? Does it even matter? Exactly.

13 The 12-Month Program

There are 12 months in our fishing year, and every single month in Jersey offers up some serious action, whether you launch a bait or lure from a jetty, bridge piling, or the sands. There is no "off-season" for fishing. Times may be tough and personal and economic hardships weigh heavy on our mental capacities and fiscal budgets, but there is always time to give back into your soul, 365 days a year, in the saltwater realm. This logbook is a testament to fortitude and to inspiration. I encourage every serious surf angler to write down every single trip they embark on, not only for practical information that can be assimilated in order to see patterns year to year, month to month, and day to day, but also to have something tangible that allows you to relive each and every magical experience you have in the surf. Start your own log book about fishing. It is a history to tell your loved ones about, to show them that this world is a magical place, with real rewards.

Reading back through these entries, there is not one—not a single one—that I read now and can't vividly remember the feeling, the scenery, the emotions of the day when I wrote it, the fish I caught or lost, and the people I was with. Shoot, if anything, keeping a log makes you truly remember the days you have chosen to truly live life full, whether you caught fish or not. Besides, the most important aspect to remember when holding a stick in your hand at the edge of the Atlantic is that it truly isn't the fish we are after. It's the promise to open up the window into our souls, to peer into our deepest desires, hopes, and dreams, that keeps us coming back for more.

Surf fishing cleanses the soul, no matter what problems or issues burden your back. Sometimes we bring darkness to the beach, all the issues and problems that seem to control our lives. It's not right. But in the moment of one simple cast, all is forgotten.

There is an ultimate foundation built by surfcasting that brings a sense of meaningful existence no other man can comprehend unless he's been there. I've seen it firsthand on a smiling kid's face the first time he or she has tangled with a surf fish, or when a seasoned angler has finally caught a fish he's been targeting his whole life strong. That sense of meaning is real. For a silent second in time, all is one transcendent moment.

Before the black Bomber plug gets unhooked from the fourth guide, before the bail is flipped over, the cast made, there is the moment when I cross the dunes and look to the everglow of eternal predawn, that lets me sit in utter and eternal awe of the beauty of the universe. I take a minute or two to quash my adrenaline, forget about the fish, and remember everything that has meant anything to me, and to respect what has built me into the man I am. I say a silent prayer to whatever God is, take a deep inhalation of the salt air, hear the gulls screech their song, and I see the twinkle of Orion's constellation above me. Just for one blissful instant, that single, defining moment, everything and anything, good and bad, comes into total focus, and I know there could never, ever be a better place to have come from or to go to. It is all here, right here, and right now, in the surf. And it is truly, truly wonderful. As the sun barely cracks over the horizon, and I am tight to a fish, there is much more at stake than simply reeling in that challenger of the Jersey Surf. I find the direct line back to myself.

Epilogue

TO DAD: TIMELESS MORNINGS (1998)

Inspiration comes in many splendid forms. Perhaps there is nothing that inspires me so greatly as waking to the all-too-surreal sunrises that slowly inch over New Jersey's silent shoreline horizon during the blustery fall months. Somehow, they always crack open the darkness and warm up every isolated corner of a lonely soul, simply breeding happiness on a transcendental plane, from an unknown, forgotten, primeval level. Witnessing the sun's smooth and serene path from the surfline ignites the fuel of motivation in me, giving me reason to push on, especially on a blustery October morn. The sun is powerful. My father knew this about these sunrises.

My father and I spent a bucketload of our time outdoors—and as far as textbook father-and-son relationships go, we looked like the quintessential Norman Rockwell family-values type of painting you see in your doctor's office. We spent all our free and borrowed time in the fields and forests, pursuing whitetail deer and traipsing about wild trout streams in search of rainbows and browns, both of us relishing the fact that we weren't just participants in outdoor pursuits; we were a living, breathing part of an outdoor playground.

But stop there. No mention of saltwater fishing. My dad was never what you would consider an expert on the saltwater side of fishing, and thus neither was I. Sometimes he would come home from work and mention some tidbit of information he heard at the office about how the blues were in thick in the surf, or how the stripers were blitzing the beach, but he was never avid about the subject. It was just hearsay. But somehow, during the wee hours of the morning one late October, my brother and I found ourselves being woken up, sent to the kitchen to have an obnoxious helping of Quaker Oats shoved down our throats, and rustled out the front door through pitch blackness into the faded green

Dodge pickup with a full tank of gas. Trout season didn't open in late October and there were no 12-gauges in the back of the truck. What the heck was going on? I heard Dad mumble some conviction about getting there, just getting there before the sun rose up and unfolded its splendor. We were headed south, to the sands of Island Beach State Park.

It was to become a new ritual for my pop, to realize his calling and extend his horizon to the annual fall striped bass run—and we were all involved. Leaving my mother to conjure up more than her share of virtuous excuses as to why both of her sons missed school on these particular days, the truck was already 45 miles down the Garden State Parkway, on the way to chase the lurking shadows of cow stripers on their fall migration. For my father, we had to get there before the sun rose, to get there in time to see the entire world ignite with the promise of a day well-spent. As a kid of seven years old, I wondered why all that really mattered to my dad was to get there before the sun rose, but whatever the case, on this groundbreaking trip, I was not there to contemplate all the senseless hoopla about a sunrise that happens every day. I was hell-bent on catching striped bass. Period.

Despite the constant punching and clawing of my brother and me in the front bench seat, after the endless hours of driving, we arrived at Gilliken's Beach, section A21 at Island Beach, a so-called "hot spot." The engine shut off, and my brother Billy and I continued to slap at each other. "I'll turn this truck right around and send you both back to school right here, right now, if you keep it up—you hear me?" Whew—we heard him. Fishing or school—our choice.

With that understanding, we began lugging all our gear across the hilly, windswept dunes in the twilight of dawn, waiting for the promised morning to begin. The sand spikes were driven into place into the high tide line of the sloped beach, and the lines were cast out, fixed with hi-lo rigs and hunks of juicy clams hooked on them. All we had to do was sit back and relax, waiting for the sun to come up in a few short minutes, bestowing warmth onto the cold planet, extinguishing the dark loneliness that blankets the earth on a chilly October night.

Then my boredom would set in. I had no patience for lifeless rods. Instead of waiting uselessly by still rods, all I wanted to do was comb the beach on the high tide line with my nose inches away from the sand, searching for old tangled fishing line, weathered plugs and metals that washed up, bright pieces of plastic from shredded lures, or anything else that could easily be classified as useless junk to put in my daily collection that I always assembled on these trips. It was simple to a kid: no action, no interest. However, broken lures and colorful junk—now *that's* what I was interested in.

"Hey! Put that garbage down . . . throw it down! All of it!" my dad would bark. "You're gonna end up with a case of the squirts if you keep touchin' all that rusty, dirty junk . . . and don't put your hands in your mouth, for chrissake! Drop that crap and go wash your hands in the water. And I think you should start paying attention to the rods."

Yeah, yeah whatever. Look at that! A piece of fluorescent green tubing with rust stains on it! Definitely throw that in my pocket.

"Alright, don't come cryin' to me if the world-record bass runs off with your line," was vaguely what I heard in my wandering ear, from a voice all too commandingly familiar, as I continued accumulating pocketsfull of purposeless pieces of colorful debris along the beach—tenfold more interesting to me than developing the virtue of learned patience. There was no bite, no action for a good hour and a half in the twilight of pre-morn.

Every now and then on the surfline, I would look up and glance at the sun that finally edged over the horizon, but it was no big deal to me. I'd hear from 25 yards away, "Newt, look at the sun. That's beautiful, isn't it?" he'd ask me in sort of a telling-me kind of way.

"Yeah, dad, I guess so," is what I mumbled back, inaudible to him. I'd stop collecting junk for a second, turn around, and see him standing there, transfixed for a short time, taking in the sun. I wandered back in his direction.

"The bass will be in the wash soon. Empty that junk from your pockets, and clean your hands off again. You mother has written enough sick notes for you this month."

Whatever. I didn't know what all the hubbub and concern was all about, but unquestioningly, I found myself dragging my feet to the undertow, emptying my pockets of debris, dipping my hands in the salty water, and shaking them off nonchalantly, all the while grumbling some brand-new choice words that I had heard on the playground the other day. And then when I reached to pull out the last rust-stained green plastic tubing from my waders' front pocket, everything went bananas.

The big 10-foot Meat Stick that was set right by my dad's side bent over like a loaded catapult. I stood wide-eyed, mouth agape, my heart skipping a beat the instant I heard and listened to the grating sound of the drag screaming uncontrollably like it really hurt that old, salt-seasoned Ryobi reel. I was stupefied.

"Get him! Get the rod! Hit him!" my dad rattled off almost in perfect order, as if he was projecting his own action but had just enough willpower to hold back his own motive and voice it to his doofus son, who was standing dumbfounded in the surfline, fishing line and junk hanging out of his pockets.

Oh man! This was it. In all the frenzy, I trampled foolishly in my oversized waders, stumbling through the sand in the general direction to get to the rod fast. I swaggered back and forth drunkenly with full force, and overran the rod by two steps, had to regain composure, backtracked and finally gripped the rod out of the sand spike. I wielded the rod and set back on it as hard as if I was trying to stop a battleship. Dead stop. I swear I thought I hooked bottom when instantly my drag erupted into a scream that brought me bumbling toward the churning surf like a stumbling circus clown. I was not going to lose face to this fish, this justification of my being there, at this ungodly hour, in this outlandishly chilly weather.

With all my available concentration, I reeled and gave, reeled and gave. Seeing the look of abject confusion on my face, my dad offered some encouraging words to "play him out" and follow him down the beach into the wash. I staggered, cross-footed, down the beach, following his run as all sorts of rusty, plastic, multicolored junk fell out of my pockets.

"Don't stop, Nicky! Forget that junk! Fish on!" he ordered.

That fish ran three times straight east on me on hefty runs that truly made me question if this wobbly Ryobi reel could finish the job. On each run, he stretched my dreams and seven-year-old pride out thinner and thinner, but quivering moments of reflection kept me focused on the knowledge that my dad had brought us down to Island Beach this time for the virgin trip of the Striped Bass Round Up. I knew this wasn't a critical time; it was judgment day. This big thing on the end of my line was the only frail connection that existed between a notion that would decide whether Dad's grand idea to surrfcast was doomed to die in a dark closet or would justify a solid year coated with the heavenly anticipation of next year's visit. What I did with the rod in my hands would have to inspire another year's motivation to get out of that comfortable bed, pack the truck, take off from school, eat the Quaker Oats, and travel to Island Beach.

The reel started to sing a sad song of defeat, with line leaving at an incontrollable pace. Then it hit me. I had visions of sitting bored in school, being taught some outrageous algebra equations or something or other that would never come into play in my life. I had thoughts that all my livelong days would be spent *not* coming down to the surf with my dad to catch stripers, enjoying the freedom of fishing on the beach, of smelling the salt air, of seeing the sun rise. All of this could become a sick reality if I lost this fish. It was the last spark that kept the fire burning—and that's when it clicked.

I hit a peak of determination. I listened to my father as he shouted instructions for me to follow the bass because they tend to swim parallel to the beach, to be careful of my slack line because they tend to roll when they get close in, bring him close to shore and follow the final wave in to beach him properly, and so on. I understood and followed every order. All of that talk I thought he just picked up from the office was, in fact, truth from experience, and it was time I finally paid him the attention he was due. Forget the trout in the freshwater streams; this was "go time" on a striper.

When the brute on the end of my line finally reached the undertow, and the last remaining wave pushed with all its might, a clam-stuffed striped bass was laid onto the beach flopping in front of me. My father reached down and grabbed the bass with his two strong, hard-working hands and held it high into the sunlight, diamond sparkles of the morning sunlight gleaming off every scale.

"Fifteen, maybe twenty pounds, Newt."

The smiles on our faces shone as bright as the happiness of man can possibly allow. A silent acknowledgment of perfection in nature's purest form passed between us, and the striper was returned to the ocean. It was truly fantastic.

Yesterday I sat down and reflected. I thought of a time three years ago when I steeled my nerves, quit my first post-college job rather quickly—too abruptly for my mother's contentment—and relocated my life to that same stretch of shoreline on Island Beach, for reasons that only the deepest reaches of the sweetest solitude in my heart can tell you. I bought a satisfying, homey bungalow a half a block from the beach, close enough to hear and see the flocking birds screeching and swooping down into the wash when the bass are around, and to start my post-collegiate life off right.

This year, October came around again, like it always has a way of briskly sneaking up on you, and the striped bass run was underway once again. I got to thinking. Picking up the phone, I dialed and said, "Hey, Dad, stripers are here in the wash, thick right off my beach at the Thunderbird. Been here for a solid two days now. You comin' down?" Before I could wake up at our designated time of 5:00 a.m, I heard the noise of a new white Ford pickup purring outside of my house at 4:30, no doubt lined with striper rods, reels, and rigs on the inside. Not even attempting to entertain the frivolities of father-son talk, we piled into my Jeep and headed three miles straight north to Bay Head, where we could see from the beach the silhouettes of thousands of seagulls, terns, and cormorants flocking and diving to indulge in the masses of peanut bunker, mullet, and rainfish in the water.

We pulled up to Bridge Avenue, parked the Jeep and set out onto the beach lit with a predawn light that barely illuminated the other hardy figures standing alongside us, all holding Surf sticks in their hands. We heard incredible sounds ten yards away from us, sounds of large fish crashing, thrashing, and splashing, reels aching, drags whining. I glanced at my father, nodded in approval, and we both cast out our plugs with eager looks on our faces, our mouths tipped with the edges of full-blown smiles. I smelled bluefish, weakfish, and, oh, yeah, stripers.

"You going to pay attention to me today?" he questioned.

"You bet, Pop," I answered smugly.

As my third cast plunked into the roiling wash, I looked to my right. Before I had time to finish my retrieve, I saw my dad knee-deep in the undertow, pulling this huge striped thing out of the suds and onto the beach. The anglers behind him stopped their casting and turned his way to look in astonishment, as they saw my father bend down and grab something with his two hands. He lifted up and held a bass so high into an incredible burst of sunlight that just happened to split the horizon wide open—the most picture-perfect striped bass that pushed every ounce of the 20-pound class. As he raised that magnificent fish to the sky, I swear I saw some sort of fishing line, rusty broken plugs, and other assorted junk fall from his pockets.

"Nice one, Dad!" I blurted out, not knowing I gave away my pride.

"After all these years, I guess I still got to show you how it's done, eh, Newt?" he jabbed.

He released the bass into the churning surf to be free again. We both smiled ear-to-ear, and then somehow, in a silly, planned sort of way, time stopped. We stood side by side and glanced at the horizon, awestruck and silent as we watched the awesome sight of a burning crimson sun edge over the ocean, slowly and surely lighting up the world. Man, those surf sunrises sure are beautiful.

Resources

Shameless plug for my website
www.nickymagnummedia.com

American Littoral Society
littoralsociety.org

Betty and Nick's Bait and Tackle
bettyandnicks.com
732-793-2708

Charlie's Bait and Tackle
formerly Ernie's Bait and Tackle
732-793-1144

Fishermen's Supply
fishermenssupplyco.com
732-892-2058

Grumpy's Bait and Tackle
grumpystackle.com
732-830-1500

Jersey Coast Bait and Tackle
jerseytackle.com
732-451-1077

**New Jersey Beach Buggy
Association**
njbba.org

Pell's Bait and Sport
pellsonline.com
732-477-2121

Reel Life Bait and Tackle
732-899-3506

Index

Page numbers in italics indicates illustrations.